A PLUME BOOK

A FATHER'S LOVE

DAVID GOLDMAN is an author and advocate for the prevention and the return of abducted children. A graduate of Virginia Wesleyan College, he worked as a model in catalogs, magazines, and some television commercials. He also owns and operates a sport fishing boat along the New Jersey coast, where he resides today. He has appeared on *Dateline, Today, Good Morning America*, and NPR's *Diane Rehm Show*, and on Fox and CNN. Visit www.bringseanhome.org.

A Father's Love

One Man's
Unrelenting Battle
to Bring His
Abducted Son Home

David Goldman

with

KEN ABRAHAM

A PLUME BOOK

PLUME
Published by the Penguin Group
Penguin Group (USA) Inc., 375 Hudson Street, New York, New York 10014, U.S.A.
Penguin Group (Canada), 90 Eglinton Avenue East, Suite 700, Toronto, Ontario, Canada M4P 2Y3 (a division
of Pearson Penguin Canada Inc.)
Penguin Books Ltd, 80 Strand, London WC2R 0RL, England
Penguin Ireland, 25 St. Stephen's Green, Dublin 2, Ireland (a division of Penguin Books Ltd)
Penguin Books Australia Ltd, 250 Camberwell Road, Camberwell, Victoria 3124, Australia (a division of Pear-
son Australia Group Pty Ltd)
Penguin Books India Pvt Ltd, 11 Community Centre, Panchsheel Park, New Delhi – 110 017, India
Penguin Group (NZ), 67 Apollo Drive, Rosedale, Auckland 0632, New Zealand (a division of Pearson New
Zealand Ltd)
Penguin Books (South Africa) (Pty) Ltd, 24 Sturdee Avenue, Rosebank, Johannesburg 2196, South Africa

Penguin Books Ltd, Registered Offices:
80 Strand, London WC2R 0RL, England

Published by Plume, a member of Penguin Group (USA) Inc. Previously published in a Viking edition..

First Plume Printing, May 2012.
10 9 8 7 6 5 4 3 2 1

Photograph credits: Insert page 12 (top and bottom): Courtesy Office of Chris Smith, United States House
of Representatives; 13 (bottom): AP Photo / Eduardo Naddar; 14 (top): AP Photo / Silvia Izquierdo; 15 (top):
Courtesy Benita Noel, *Dateline NBC*; other photographs courtesy of the author

 REGISTERED TRADEMARK—MARCA REGISTRADA

The Library of Congress has catalogued the Viking edition as follows:
Goldman, David, 1966–
A father's love : one man's unrelenting battle to bring his abducted son home / David Goldman ; with Ken
Abraham.
    p. cm.
Includes bibliographical references and index.
ISBN 978-0-670-02262-5 (hc)
ISBN 978-0-452-29791-3 (pbk.)
1. Goldman, David, 1966– 2. Goldman, Sean, 2000– 3. Parental kidnapping—Brazil—Case studies. 4.
Custody of children—United States—Case studies. I. Abraham, Ken. II. Title.
HV6603.G65G65 2011
362.82'973092—dc22
[B]
                                                                                                2010053720

Printed in the United States of America
Original hardcover designs by Helene Berinsky

To all the children and families who suffer every moment of every day from the tragic separation caused by child abduction. May they stay strong, believe, and be brought back into each other's loving arms.

Contents

1

The Phone Call

A TWO-WEEK TRIP—THAT'S ALL IT WAS SUPPOSED TO BE. TWO weeks. I didn't relish the idea of being apart from my wife, Bruna, and our four-year-old son, Sean, not even for two weeks, but it was unavoidable. I had to work. *I can handle it*, I kept reminding myself. After all, I had clients scheduled aboard my charter fishing boat during the first week my wife and son would be gone. After that, I planned to join Bruna and Sean for the latter part of their vacation in Brazil, my wife's birthplace. In a few days we'd be back together as a family again.

I loaded the suitcases—there were more than the usual number of them—into my Jeep Cherokee SUV, along with Bruna's parents' luggage. Although citizens of Brazil, my in-laws, Raimundo and Silvana Ribeiro, owned a condominium in New Jersey, and visited often, sometimes for a month or two at a time. The night before, we had attended a local carnival sponsored by St. Leo's Church, and Bruna's parents had been at our home the day of the trip, after going out to lunch with my parents. Everyone got along as usual, two happy families united as one, with no tension among any of us and never a cross word between us. Now Sean's maternal grandfather, Raimundo—or

Ray, as he was known in the United States—and his grandmother, Silvana, were returning to Brazil with Bruna and Sean.

It wasn't the first time during our four-year marriage that Bruna had visited her homeland. She and I had traveled to Brazil before Sean was born. Bruna took great pleasure in spending time with her friends in her old stomping grounds. I enjoyed surfing off the beautiful beaches of Barra, a suburb of Rio de Janeiro. We both savored Brazil's barbecues and delicious mangoes. Bruna took Sean to visit our extended family a few months after his birth, and had made the trip by herself for her grandmother's funeral a few years earlier. More recently, in March 2004, she and a friend and fellow teacher at the school where Bruna taught went to Brazil during the school's spring break. So it didn't strike me as unusual for us to plan a trip during the summer, after Bruna completed her teaching responsibilities for the 2004 spring semester. We usually traveled as a family to Brazil twice a year, once during Bruna's winter break and once during the summer. Just as any couple whose family members live in different locations, we made special efforts to enjoy time together with all of our relatives, especially after Sean was born. Although Rio was a dangerous place, as Bruna and her parents often reminded me, it was still her hometown in her native land and it was beautiful. We wanted Sean to be familiar with both cultures, and to know that he was a part of something much bigger than himself.

On Wednesday, June 16, 2004, I drove the family to Newark's Liberty International Airport to begin their vacation. Under Brazilian law, when any one parent travels alone with a child to Brazil, the other parent or guardian is required to sign a letter of authorization. So before the trip, as part of normal procedures, I signed the release authorizing Bruna to take Sean out of the country for a limited period of time.

Since I was going to see the two of them in a week or so, I didn't think much of it at the time. Besides, I was busy planning Bruna's thirtieth birthday party. As a surprise present for her, I hoped to have our kitchen redone while she was out of the country. I was also working on an itinerary for another family trip to Turnberry Isle in Florida—one that would include Bruna's mom and dad—to celebrate her birthday in mid-August after we had all returned from Brazil. Ordinarily when we vacationed together, I made the arrangements. Having traveled as much as I had over the years, I found it easy to book all the family members' flights and hotels, and handle all the other details myself. But this time, Bruna's mom kept protesting, saying, "Oh, we can take care of that from Brazil." This struck me as odd, but I thought, *Okay, fine. We'll make the arrangements from Brazil.*

At the airport, after I got Sean comfortably situated in his stroller, I helped carry Bruna's, Sean's, and my in-laws' suitcases into the busy Newark terminal. I assisted in getting all the suitcases checked in, then walked Bruna and Sean to the security area in front of the Jetway leading to their flight. With passengers bustling all around us, I kissed Bruna and Sean good-bye and embraced Bruna's parents.

I watched as my family went through the initial identification checkpoint and started down the hallway toward their flight. Then, as we always did when one of us was traveling, Bruna and Sean stopped and turned toward me, and we used sign language for our final good-bye. I pointed to my eye, my heart, and then to Bruna and Sean, and mouthed the words "I love you." Bruna and Sean pointed to their eyes, their hearts, and then back at me: "I love you." Bruna turned and followed her parents down the Jetway, toward the security metal detector, pushing Sean in the stroller as she went. I watched them until I could no longer see them, and waited a few minutes longer in case they had forgotten anything or there was a last-minute flight cancellation. Then I returned to our vehicle and headed back to our home in Tinton Falls, New Jersey. It was going to be a long, lonely night.

IN MANY WAYS, ours had been a storybook romance. I met Bruna Bianchi Ribeiro in 1997 in Milan, Italy, where I was working as a fashion model and she was studying fashion. We moved back to New Jersey, where we married in 1999, and in May 2000, Bruna gave birth to Sean. We had a beautiful marriage, an ideal little family; it was perfect in every way, and we were head over heels in love.

At least so I thought.

THE DAY AFTER their flight, Bruna called from Brazil to let me know that she and the family had arrived safely. "Sean is so excited," she gushed. "He's eating mangoes and he just loves it here."

Bruna's unusual emphasis on how happy Sean was to be back in Brazil seemed a bit over the top, but I was glad my wife and son were safe and sound and already enjoying their vacation. We talked briefly, then said our "I love you's" and our good-byes.

On Sunday, June 20, Bruna called again. I could tell immediately from the tone of her voice that something was wrong, but I would not have guessed what she was about to say. "You're a great guy, David, and a wonderful father to Sean. I have no regrets about our relationship and having Sean together."

I didn't even have time to wonder where Bruna was going with this line of thought, as she continued without a pause, almost as though following a script.

"Our love affair is over. I've decided to stay in Brazil," she said. "I'm keeping Sean here with me."

Whooom! It was as though the earth had suddenly dropped out from under me, and I was hanging in midair. Bruna's brusque, curt words seared into my heart and mind. "What? *What!* What are you talking about, Bruna?" I could not believe what I was hearing. *Our love affair? What about our marriage?* The tone of voice with which she said those words to me was one I had never before heard from her. She sounded cold, calculating, and unemotional—not at all like the upbeat, vivacious, passionate woman to whom I was married.

I remember thinking, *What is this? Where is this coming from?*

The person I loved, and envisioned loving for the rest of my life, until death do us part, had suddenly become as cold as ice.

It got worse. Bruna had a list of demands. "You need to come here immediately," she said. I want you to sign over the full rights of Sean to me. If you ever want to see Sean again, you need to fly to Rio de Janeiro immediately. I have a document my lawyer has drawn up, and you need to sign it."

Lawyer? What lawyer? And how could she have secured such a document? She had been gone only a few days! It never occurred to me that this might have been a meticulously devised plan by Bruna and her parents in collusion with a Brazilian attorney.

According to Bruna, the document she wanted me to sign was ten pages in length and spelled out several demands, including that Sean remain with Bruna and her family in Brazil, and that I surrender my legal role as Sean's parent, in addition to giving full custody to Bruna. "And you need to agree never to press any criminal charges. Never to go to the police in the U.S. to file kidnapping charges, never file any custody papers in the U.S. courts, never file for separation or divorce in the United States, and you must do nothing that will interfere with my plans to obtain U.S. citizenship."

My brain was reeling, my body convulsing; I felt nauseated. *Bruna, what is going on here?* I was shocked and devastated at the same time.

"David, if you do any of those things and go against what I want—if you hire a lawyer—you will never see your son again, and you will spend all your money trying."

"Bruna, what is happening?"

Bruna was done and she wanted to get off the phone. "You must come here, David," she demanded.

"I can't believe this . . ."

"You need to come here now. Bye." Click. The phone line went dead.

I hung up the phone. My knees gave out, and I slumped to the floor, my face in my hands, my head still spinning, my heart pounding.

I thought it might explode into a thousand pieces. My mind refused to fathom what I had just heard, yet there had been no equivocation in Bruna's words. She had made herself quite clear. Our marriage was over, and she planned to keep our four-year-old son, Sean, in Brazil.

Our son, my buddy, my baby boy, Sean. I loved that little guy more than my own life. This couldn't be happening. I was crushed and confused, distraught and disoriented, by this ghastly turn of events. I had never felt so alone in all my life.

I called my parents. My mom answered the phone. "Mom . . ." I struggled to get sound out of my mouth.

"Oh, hi, David," she answered cheerfully. "Happy Father's Day."

Happy *Father's* Day? My wife has just run off with my son. It was not a happy Father's Day at all. It was the start of six years in a father's hell.

2

Jersey Boy

Nothing in life can prepare a person to deal with the abduction of a child by a spouse, let alone absconding with him or her across international borders. Nevertheless, my upbringing, in which I experienced the strong bonds of a loving family and good friends, gave me the foundation and fortitude to face the future with hope rather than despair.

My parents, Barry and Ellie (Poll) Goldman, were far removed from anything ostentatious. Just ordinary people, they possessed a deep, simple love for each other, unembellished contentment, and quiet human decency. They were the kind of folks many people never noticed, and Mom and Dad liked it that way. They didn't long for the limelight or want to be put on display in any way. They weren't perfect, but they were a model for what it meant to be good people. As an adult and a father myself, I am perhaps just now beginning to understand the depth of the sacrifices they made for me over the years, and I've been fortunate enough to be able to express my gratitude to them while they are still with me.

My sister, Leslie—twenty-six months my senior—and I were born in Philadelphia, at the old hospital downtown. Early on, I developed a strong belief in God. Mom was Catholic and Dad was Jewish, so Mom converted to Judaism before they married, and although we acknowledged God's existence and observed both Jewish and Christian religious holidays, including Christmas, Hanukkah, and Easter, we focused primarily on Judaism. My family celebrated my Bar Mitzvah, the traditional Jewish coming-of-age ceremony, when I turned thirteen. We were not a deeply religious family, but my exposure to both Judaism and Christianity from family and friends provided a basic sense of right and wrong, a moral compass on which I've come to depend. Faith would also prove to be one of my most essential survival tools in the years ahead.

Dad was the quintessential "man's man." In an age when many men were spending hours in therapy, or going out into the woods and beating on their chests, or jumping into their midlife-crisis sports cars and speeding off on a cross-country excursion to discover who they were, my dad always knew exactly who he was: Barry Goldman. Nothing more, nothing less.

Dad majored in geology at Cornell University, and after toiling for a number of years in the corporate world for Hess Oil Company, working in their Geology Department, he switched fields and became a stockbroker. He finally came to the point where he said, "I love the sea. I'm going to leave the corporate world, refinance the house, and open a charter fishing business." And he did.

When I was two months old, our family moved to Wayside, New Jersey, in Ocean Township, where I grew up thinking that all little boys get to go out to sea with their dads. My family wasn't wealthy, but if we needed something, my folks figured out a way to meet that need. As a family, we took a couple of vacations to Disney World, in Florida, although we packed up in a *Brady Bunch*–style station wagon and made the twenty-some-hour drive by car. We always dressed in relatively trendy clothes, and lived in a safe, comfortable middle-class neighborhood. My friends and I played outside all day long in the summertime, and our parents never feared that we might be abducted. For several weeks every summer, I attended Sea Shore Day

Camp, a supervised, structured program of activities similar to day camp programs today. We'd swim, play ball, do crafts, and generally have fun all day while we learned how to get along.

Mom was the emotional core of our family, generously and openly expressing love and affection to my sister and me. Although my dad was quite spirited when captaining his sixty-five-foot charter boat, and was a big jokester who enjoyed a good laugh, he was not as verbally expressive of his emotions. A trunk with deep roots, Dad embodied a strong sense of stoicism and integrity. He told me, "It is important to be honest. No matter how hard things get, always tell the truth."

My uncle Richard, who was actually Dad's uncle and therefore my great-uncle, was the grandfather I never had, since both of my grandfathers had passed away by the time I was three years old. Uncle Richard was much warmer than Dad, and was always quick to throw his arm around my shoulder to encourage me. Both men had a great sense of humor. So in many ways, when it came to male role models, I had the best of both worlds—Dad's strong personality combined with Uncle Richard's more effusive expressions of love—and I drew deeply from both wells.

NOBODY IN MY family ever said things like "I believe you can do it," but, then again, nobody ever told me "You can't do this," either. So I assumed that I could do anything if I worked hard and persevered long enough.

One of the best things my dad taught me was simply never to give up. As a boy growing up in New Jersey, I loved playing baseball, but when I was nine years old, I developed Perthes syndrome, a degenerative disease of the hip joint, similar to the problem that put an early end to the career of superstar athlete Bo Jackson. The physical problem with my left hip forced me to wear a brace, so I couldn't run well. Playing sandlot pickup games in the neighborhood, my friends allowed me to bat, but I needed a "pinch runner," someone who could run the bases for me after I hit the ball. My friends even argued about who would get to pinch-run for me, because they knew I would almost always get a hit, so they were fairly certain of getting on base.

I desperately wanted to play Little League baseball, but I could hardly make it around the bases, even if I could hit the ball a mile. Determined to compete, I tried out, wearing the hip brace. I did okay in fielding, but I really shone when it was my turn at bat. The pitcher throwing during batting practice must have thought he'd have an easy time with me, but I fooled him, and really smacked the leather off the ball. I was certain that I had made the team.

When the White Sox's assistant manager called that evening to speak with my dad, I handed Dad the telephone then quickly ran into another room and quietly picked up an extension. Imagine how disappointed I was when I heard the man say, "Your son did amazing. He hit the ball harder and farther than any of the other players. But, I'm sorry, I can't have him on my team. You have to be able to run to play in the majors."

Play in the majors?

This was Little League. That coach was more interested in winning than in encouraging a young boy to participate and to live life to the fullest. It would not be the last time in my life I would face such a twisted compulsion on the part of an adult who wanted to live vicariously through a child.

The manager of another team, the Indians, called shortly thereafter, and he had better news. "David can play on our team," he said. "We'll be glad to have him."

I was thrilled. I was finally going to be able to play.

For most of the season, the managers, coaches, and players alike regarded me as the crippled kid, almost feeling sorry for me. In our league, every player got to play in every game for at least two innings. But by the time I got into a game, it was usually to stand around in the outfield because the contest had already been decided. Nevertheless, some of the moms gushed over me. "Oh, you are such an inspiration!" I didn't really see myself as an inspiration; I simply wanted to be a kid like everybody else, a boy who wanted to play baseball.

Near the end of the second game of the season, the manager called my name and put me in to hit. I kept my eye on the ball as the pitcher wound up and hurled the baseball in my direction. *Wham!* I blasted that ball out of the infield, over the outfielders' heads, and hit the fence for a double! When I came off the field after a pinch runner replaced me at second, my cheering teammates and coaches in the dugout swarmed me.

Ironically, the managers who initially rejected me for their teams suddenly complained that my brace might be an injury risk to other players—especially after my first double, when they'd found out that I could hit the ball. It was crazy, but they refused to allow me to play.

Close to tears, and feeling sorry for myself, I was sure that Mom and Dad would join my pity party or try to console me somehow when I told them what had happened. But they didn't. Instead, they went to court and fought for me to be allowed to play baseball like a normal boy. And we won! I was not only reinstated on the team, but I was also permitted to have a pinch runner each time I went up to bat.

My new team, the Indians, won the division in our Little League and went on to the Tournament of Champions that year. We made it all the way to the last round of the State Tournament before we were finally eliminated. I felt especially good because I had contributed throughout the season to our team's success.

I was fortunate that the Perthes syndrome ran its course, and the next season, after having worn that awful orthopedic device for more than three years, I no longer needed the brace. I was able to run and play like a normal boy and enjoyed Little League ball for several more seasons. My parents' never-give-up attitude and their willingness to fight for what was right was a powerful memory that would stand me in good stead in the years to come.

I attended Ocean Township High School, where I was in the Key Club, played on the freshman basketball team, and participated in intramural sports. I enjoyed baseball in high school, too, but the season was in the spring, when the New Jersey surfing waves were at their best. I had to choose between baseball and the sea, and I loved to surf. Almost every day when I had free time, after school, often before school, and sometimes even *during* school, I could be found on the water. I enjoyed surfing much more than studying. I was an okay student but not highly motivated or ambitious academically.

When it came time to decide on college, I wanted to attend a school near the beach, but not so close that I'd be tempted never to study. I considered the University of North Carolina–Wilmington and several other schools but finally settled on Virginia Wesleyan College, which was tucked into a richly forested area on the border of Norfolk and Virginia Beach. It was close to Cape Hatteras, which has the best waves on the East Coast. I also liked Virginia Wesleyan's small-school environment, rich in Methodist history, ironically with 1 percent of the student body being Jewish.

My long-range goal was to become a lawyer. I hoped to practice maritime law, dealing with litigations over oil spills, international borders, and that sort of thing. I majored in sociology with an emphasis in political science to prepare myself for law school, and I graduated with a bachelor of arts degree in 1988.

My parents and grandmother contributed a great amount of money for me to attend college, and I also took out some student loans. Nevertheless, each summer while I was in college, I worked to help ease the financial burden, taking a job as a lifeguard on one of the nearby New Jersey beaches during the day and working at night as a busboy at Kelly's Irish Pub and Tavern in Neptune, the birthplace of actors Jack Nicholson and Danny DeVito. For the most part, lifeguarding was relatively easy work, a good way to stay in shape, to have some fun, and to meet some interesting people.

My first job as a Jersey Shore lifeguard was at Long Branch, a busy beach at Seven Presidents Oceanfront Park. Our boss at Long Branch came from a military background and ran the beach crew similar to a military platoon. "Squared away," he'd bark at us. "Everything has to be squared away." Within a couple of days on the job, we knew exactly what that meant; he wanted us to do our jobs with excellence. Each morning we swam a mile in the ocean and did a vigorous routine of beach calisthenics, so I was in great physical shape and enjoyed the camaraderie of my fellow lifeguards. But the job at Long Branch was hard work. As a college kid, I thought, *I love being a lifeguard, but I'd like to have some fun, too.* After two seasons at Seven Presidents, some friends told me that Belmar, a popular beach farther south, was hiring. I applied there, passed my swimming and rescuing tests, and was hired.

I was stationed on Eighteenth Avenue, where Jim Freda was in charge of the operation. Jim was known as "Pirate" because he pushed his lifeguard crew to prevail in the tournaments and contests between our fellow crews up and down the beach. I won nearly all of the rookie events, and Jim and I became close friends. By midsummer, I was able to move to Tenth Avenue, which was our version of the dream beach made famous by a line in the Bruce Springsteen song "Tenth Avenue Freeze-Out" on the Boss's breakthrough album, *Born to Run*. Rumor had it that Bruce's E Street Band actually got its start practicing in a garage nearby. Whether or not that was true I didn't know, but I did know there was always lots of action at Tenth Avenue Beach. College kids flocked there because there was also a McDonald's right off the beach.

As lifeguards, we tried to keep a loose rein on the beach, calling people in only when the seas were rough, or lightning showed up on the weather screens, or if some other emergency or potential danger loomed. We usually let people swim because we trusted our rescuing abilities. There was never a drowning on our beach, although we came close a few times.

One day when the seas were a bit rough, I was patrolling in the water when I saw a little boy get sucked away in a riptide. I responded instinctively, swimming in his direction as hard and fast as I could. Just as I got close to him, another wave hit him, dragging him under the water. I swam to where I'd seen him go down, and I dove deep, desperately reaching for him in the dark, swirling waters. Finally, I felt the hair on the top of the boy's head, so I grabbed onto it. We were taught to do whatever was necessary to get a drowning victim to air as quickly as possible, so I didn't worry about the minor pain he might experience from this. I pulled hard on his hair, yanking him straight upward and out of the undertow's strong clutches. The little boy's head popped up above the waves, his eyes wide open in fear. He gasped for air and choked on some water, clinging to me for dear life as I wrapped one arm around his upper body to do a cross-chest carry and started back-paddling toward the shore. By the time I pulled the little boy out of the water and got him stretched out on the sand, he was still sputtering and coughing up seawater, but he was breathing okay. Looking at him, I guessed his age at about eight years old.

"Thanks for rescuing me, mister," he managed to say.

"Anytime, son," I responded in my best "grown-up" voice. "I'm glad you're okay. Let's find your parents." We found the boy's dad, and the father shook my hand over and over as he expressed his thanks. A sense of quiet elation came over me. *Maybe someday, I'll have a son of my own,* I thought, *and if he ever has trouble, I want to be there for him.* I knew it was risky diving into the riptide, but it was my job and I had been well trained. The kid I saved was just a little boy fighting for his life against powerful, overwhelming forces. I had to do everything I could to help him. Had I allowed that child to be swept away by the tide, I would have been devastated forever.

On another day, again while working on the stretch of beach at the Tenth Avenue location, patrolling along the water carrying a "torpedo" life preserver, I noticed a camera crew on the sand. That in itself wasn't all that unusual. With our proximity to New York, photographers often found our beach to be a welcome location. But this crew was different; a photographer approached me. "We're going to be shooting some photographs here on the beach tomorrow with some girls in swimsuits," he said, "and we'd like you to be the prop: sort of the lifeguard with the girl in the photo shoot. Would you be willing to help us out?"

Before I could muster an answer, the photographer sweetened his pitch. "We'll pay you for your time, of course, and we're going to bring Kathy Ireland down, and we'd like you to do some shots with her. You know who Kathy Ireland is, don't you? She's a *Sports Illustrated* swimsuit model."

I was too nervous to say yes. I knew the magazine, and I was aware that *Sports Illustrated* did a swimsuit issue every year, but I really didn't know anything about Kathy Ireland, or any other model, for that matter. I was slow to agree to the photographer's proposal, and he must have recognized my ambivalence.

"Okay, I'll see you here tomorrow," he said, "and we'll see how it goes." And he was on his way.

When I got back to the lifeguard stand, I didn't mention the encounter with the photographer. Along with the guys on the stand, I had watched the photographer shooting catalogue photos of some beautiful women on the beach earlier that day, so I knew it wasn't a scam. That night, however, I called my college girlfriend at Virginia Wesleyan, as I usually did. When I told her about the photographer wanting to shoot some pictures of me with Kathy Ireland, she didn't believe me.

"Do you know who that is?" she asked.

"Yeah, sure I do," I answered nonchalantly. "She's been in *Sports Illustrated*."

I probably couldn't have identified more than two or three models by name, so my girlfriend filled me in about Kathy Ireland. She was, after all, hard to miss. She had appeared in eleven straight *Sports Illustrated* swimsuit issues between 1984 and 1994 and had been in a few movies and television shows. With her gorgeous green eyes, bright smile, and athletic-looking curves, she was the epitome of the wholesome "girl next door."

The next day, true to his word, the photographer showed up at my lifeguard stand, where I was watching the beach with a couple of other guards. "Kathy Ireland is here, David," he said. "Would you be able to come over and shoot some pictures?"

My buddies on the lifeguard stand roared their approval, and nearly threw me off the stand before I had a chance to say a word or to think through the ramifications of posing for pictures with a swimsuit model. I made my way over to Kathy, and the photographer introduced us. After some perfunctory directions, the photographer roped off a section of the beach, positioned Kathy and me in place, and started shooting.

Kathy Ireland was the consummate professional model, and so friendly, kind, and easy to work with—especially considering that I was a total novice. She was ravishingly beautiful, too, dressed in a pink one-piece suit, her skin lightly oiled for the beach, with her makeup perfect and every strand of hair in place. It was a strange, new feeling for me, being photographed, especially with all my buddies cheering me on and a crowd of onlookers gathered around the roped-off area. My fellow lifeguards were tremendously supportive. I was living out their fantasy. "Hey, that's one of our guys out there with that celebrity model."

Kathy did all the work, holding on to me or positioning her body into various poses around me. My job wasn't complicated, since all I had to do was sit still and act naturally. Kathy made my part fun and relatively easy. She was playful and spontaneous, totally comfortable with her craft.

At one point the photographer encouraged her to run her fingers through my hair, and of course my buddies went wild, hooting and hollering at the sight. I can't say that I was totally unaffected, either!

Before we finished the shoot I asked Kathy if she would be willing to take a couple of shots with my fellow lifeguards. "Can the rest of the guys get in the picture with us?" She graciously consented, and we did a shot with Kathy Ireland lying on a chair on the lifeguard stand surrounded by our entire lifeguard crew.

When we finished shooting, the photographer paid me a couple hundred dollars for my services, which seemed like a fortune to a struggling college student, but in actuality was a pittance compared to what they would have paid a professional model for such a shoot. I used the money to buy pizza and beers for my buddies, and we had a lot of laughs over my entrée into the world of modeling.

Over the next couple of summers, I worked with the same catalogue photography group, Popular Club Plan, a few more times and I enjoyed it immensely. On one occasion, during spring break my senior year, they flew me down to Florida and put me up at the historic Biltmore Hotel, a luxurious resort near the South Beach section of Miami. During the shoot, the producer provided a huge spread of delicious food from which we could freely partake, yet strangely enough, I was the only one of the models who ate anything! *Why aren't the other models eating?* I wondered naïvely.

I thought, *This could be kind of interesting. I enjoy the atmosphere, the food is great, and the work sure isn't too strenuous. I could get used to this.*

THE CAMERA APPARENTLY liked what it saw, and before long I had received more offers to model. Eventually someone suggested that I sign on with an agency. I decided to take some of my shots to New York, just to see if I could pique the interest of someone at a modeling agency. One agency was recruiting American models to work in Japan, so I walked right into the lobby and met a woman from the Japanese agency. I never even went into the main offices of the agency, but worked out a deal right there in the lobby, with the people booking the photo shoots in Japan.

I had no idea what the fashion modeling world was all about, but modeling was a well-established business in New York, with such prestigious entities as the Ford Agency and others taking virtually unknown women and men and making them into superstars. By the late 1990s, the term *supermodel* had become familiar. Few male models reached such heights, but many of the female supermodels earned millions of dollars working for top-name designers, well-known catalogues, and major corporate advertisers. For me, a guy planning to be a maritime lawyer, it was an exciting, new world.

Thanks to the deal I negotiated in New York, I traveled back and forth between the States and Tokyo throughout 1988–89. It was a fantastic experience, and the money was good. My time in Japan exposed me to some of the best elements of the fashion industry, and the potential pitfalls. I recognized early on that I had to make some decisions as to how I would live. Temptations of every sort surrounded me, yet the fleeting satisfaction they offered seemed to come at exorbitant costs.

When I returned to New Jersey, I worked again as a lifeguard during the summer. That fall, I received a call from an agency wanting me to do some work in Europe. Rather than going straight into law school, I decided to take the opportunity to see Europe, so I accepted the job.

My first stop was Paris. The city was beautiful, but I didn't enjoy my time there as much as I had hoped. True to their reputation, I found many of the Parisians to be a bit cool to foreigners. My not knowing the language didn't help.

Shortly after arriving in Europe, I received a call informing me that an Italian agency also wanted to represent me. I decided to go to Milan, where I had heard the people were much warmer, and certainly more receptive to American fashion models. I had also heard some horror stories of models living on canned tuna fish and bread as they struggled to develop their careers. I wasn't worried, though, because I had made good money in Tokyo. I felt that if my modeling career was a complete failure, at least I had my undergraduate degree, and I could always go back to the States and try to get into law school. I decided not to pass up the opportunity to take in the culture of Italy, and visited many of the great cathedrals, art galleries, and museums in Rome, Florence, and Venice, and toured the picturesque rural areas of Tuscany.

Work was slow at first, partially because I landed in Milan in the fall of the year. For one of my first jobs, I did an ad for a bike race. Part of the job requirement was to shave my legs so I could pass for a cyclist.

"I'm not going to shave my legs," I protested.

"Well, if you want the job, you have to shave your legs and your arms."

"No way. I'm not doing that!"

"Do you want the job?"

"Yeah, I guess."

"Well, if that's the worst thing you ever have to do in this business, you'll be okay."

I took the job and dutifully—and very slowly—shaved all the hair off my arms and legs. I felt naked! But the shoot went well and I got some more catalogue work as a result. Around the Christmas season, I received a call for another job. This shoot was a big one.

The job was with supermodel Claudia Schiffer, for a Soviet Jeans ad campaign. German-born, the five-foot-eleven blond-haired, blue-eyed Schiffer was then skyrocketing in her career, having already been on the cover of *Elle* magazine. She had been the personal choice of famed designer Karl Lagerfeld to be the "face" of Chanel, and had done the provocative and groundbreaking Guess? jeans ads, which had catapulted her to the household-name type of worldwide stardom that eludes most models.

Claudia was professional yet friendly, and we conversed easily, especially when I found out that she had originally wanted to be a lawyer and, as a young woman in Germany, had even worked in her father's law office. For our shoot, I was dressed only in a pair of skimpy white underwear and lying on a bed, my body covered strategically by a sheet. Claudia was wearing a pair of unzipped jeans, and that's all. She was naked from the waist up. The two of us were to lie in bed while the photographers snapped one photo after another. Claudia lay on top of the sheet, giggling and doing all sorts of antics that were meant to imply that she had really worn me out. My job was to feign exhaustion and pretend that I was asleep, while Claudia positioned herself next to me, on me, and around me in ways that highlighted the jeans. It was tough work, but I survived it.

Working with Claudia Schiffer shifted my career into overdrive. Modeling opportunities flowed in my direction, and calls came for jobs at much higher levels. Over the next eight years or so, I found myself in ads with some of the most beautiful women in the world, including Heidi Klum, with whom I did a Caress body wash television commercial. I played the role of Heidi's boyfriend.

In 1997, I was chosen as "Mr. November" by *Cosmopolitan* magazine, a distinction that supposedly set me apart as one of America's most eligible bachelors. In the ad for *Cosmo*, I was the down-to-earth guy who loves to work with his dad as a "hunky" fishing guide. Actually, that was not much of a stretch for me, since my dad did indeed own a charter fishing boat, and I loved working with him. Of course, the magazine portrayed me as their sexy fisherman, which was okay with me. The photos came out so well that *Cosmo* chose me to be on their "Man of the Year" cover. I was just a regular guy from New Jersey, and felt lucky and humbled to be selected.

I made some good friends in the modeling world, but I never immersed myself in the wilder, more debauched aspects of the job to get ahead. My attitude was basically "Here I am and I hope you think my image can help sell your products. But if not, that's okay." I was always professional, cooperative, and respectful, but I refused to cross certain moral boundaries that others suggested might enhance my career. I was careful not to put myself in compromising positions, or if I found myself at an event that looked as though it could spiral downward, I'd greet the hosts and then make as hasty and gracious an exit as possible. Sometimes I'd simply leave.

Little by little I established a reputation of personal integrity in the business. One person described me thus: "David is very professional; he's real, doesn't have an attitude, and is always a pleasure to have on the set. He can sure fill out an Armani suit, and he can sell a swim suit or surf trunks. He's the guy we will use for our job."

Every agency that takes on a model hopes he or she will ascend to the top financial tiers in the business, and apparently some people thought that I had the potential to work at those levels, although I never really thought of myself that way. In fact, I often wondered, *Why me?* There are thousands and thousands of attractive people out there, and only one guy gets the job. To me it felt like a numbers game, and I was the lucky one. Sometimes I'd be in New York when

I'd get a call to fly to South Africa the next day. Although I was happy to do it, I thought, *I'm flying halfway around the world to Cape Town to be in some pictures. Surely, there are a lot of local guys in that city who could do the shoot just as well or better than I could.* I never understood why they wanted me. But I enjoyed the work, and keeping myself healthy and in good physical shape was something that came naturally to me, so it was not exactly drudge work. Sure, the hours sometimes could be horrendous, and the jobs often entailed spontaneous arduous travel to distant exotic locations, but if that was the worst of it, I could handle that.

My career was going well, so I bought a three-bedroom town house in Eatontown, New Jersey, not far from my folks. I traveled so much the town house became a marvelous sanctuary for me, a place of rest and restoration each time I returned from another hectic nation-hopping trip.

Since I lived close to New York, it was only natural that television commercials should be a part of my portfolio, although my first national commercial was actually shot in Chicago. I appeared in a Christmas holiday ad for Sears clothing, presenting my female "love interest" a gift from under the tree. It was great fun, and the pay was fantastic. I joined the Screen Actors Guild and appeared in more television commercials, for which I not only earned a good paycheck but also received residuals, a pension, health insurance, and other perks. I never ruled out going back to law school, but my career was working out well, so I kept going with it. I think one of the main reasons for my longevity in this very fickle industry was the fact that I was just a regular-looking guy. I didn't do fad diets or work out constantly to keep my body buff. I was just me, an ordinary, approachable guy with whom people could relate.

Even my dad finally came to appreciate my success. At first, Dad regarded my modeling as some sort of sissy career, but when he saw how hard I was working, and how successful I had become, he changed his opinion. He was even proud of me.

I did a lot of work in Florida for a while, and didn't go back to

Italy for a couple of years. But then one day I received a call from an agency asking me if I was interested in working there again. My four-year relationship with a woman from Indiana had recently ended, so I thought perhaps the change of scenery would be good for me.

Ironically, I thought I was done with that chapter in my life, but I chose to return. That decision proved to be one of the best choices—and one of the most fateful—I would ever make.

3

=•••=

Bruna

WHILE IN MILAN IN 1996, I HAD LIVED AT THE GUISTI APART-
ments for most of that year, but when I returned to the city in
1997, a flatmate from Australia and I rented an apartment at the Residence La Darsena, just off Via Vigevano, a main thoroughfare running alongside a canal in a historic section of the city. Over the next
eight months, I worked consistently. I enjoyed the city and the Italian
people, and met new friends. A successful model's lifestyle outside
the work environment can be as frenetic as he or she wants it to be.
Advertisers constantly hold events at which it is desirable to have
"pretty people" in attendance, so it is possible for a highly sought-after
model to flit from party to party almost any night of the week.

I didn't do much of that. I hit some of the celebrity events, but for
the most part I preferred hanging out with ordinary, everyday people
like me. Some models I knew, as in any business, liked to put on
airs, perpetually giving the impression that "I'm the best." Others
leaned more toward an uneducated, rough "punk" image; some were
involved in lifestyles and activities that didn't appeal to me, and some
were simply good-looking, athletic types. I preferred to hang out with
the men and women who just wanted to make a buck, travel, and

meet interesting people; I shied away from the unsavory elements of the fashion industry.

EARLY IN 1997 my landlord in Milan informed my flatmate and me that we were going to have to move to another location in the complex because the corporate owner of our apartment planned to return soon. At first, we were not overjoyed at having to move, but the landlord made it all go as easy as possible. One day, my flatmate spotted an attractive young woman entering the flat at the corner of the hall, right next door to our new apartment.

"Did you see her?" he asked me excitedly.

"See who?"

"The girl next door to us!"

"No, I missed her," I said.

Over the next few weeks, I noticed a beautiful fair-haired young woman using the same elevator as we did. We'd nod to each other, but that was all. Then one afternoon as I was coming back to my apartment, we acknowledged each other as we passed in the hallway. She had a vibrant, bubbly smile. I watched as she continued on past our apartment to the door at the end of the hall. It was the woman my flatmate had mentioned, all right.

A number of models and other people associated with the fashion industry lived at our apartment complex, so I guessed that the woman and I might have some common acquaintances and interests. She seemed to have her own place; I never noticed her with a roommate.

My Australian flatmate and I were intrigued as we tried to figure out who she was. Once when we saw her going into her apartment with an older gentleman, my flatmate suggested that he must be her "sugar daddy." We later learned that she was a student working on her master's degree at Domus Academy, an Italian school for fashion design, and that the man was her father, who had come to visit her and see Italy.

I was hurrying out to work one afternoon, crossing Via Vigevano, when I saw her heading toward me carrying a small take-out pizza box. She seemed to be on her way home from school. We hadn't really spoken, except for a few words in the elevator, but now she was right in front of me. I felt compelled to say something. I stopped in the street and said, "Hello, I'm David, your next-door neighbor. I've seen you in Residence La Darsena." I was rather shy, but I ventured to ask, "Would you like to have a pizza together? I'll go get one." The remark sounded silly the moment it came out of my mouth, but the woman didn't seem to mind. On the other hand, she didn't offer any encouragement either.

"Sorry, it's a personal pizza," she said. "It's just for one."

"Oh, okay," I said. "Maybe some other time." I hurried to turn away and get on across the street so she wouldn't see me blushing with embarrassment.

Much to my surprise, as I was turning away, she called out to me, "But wait!"

Wait? I turned back to look at her and she smiled warmly at me. "My friend is coming over to pick me up around nine-thirty or ten tonight, and we're going to a party. Would you like to come?"

That was an offer I couldn't refuse. As soon as I got in from work and washed up, I was ready to go. Right on time, I knocked on her door.

Her name, I learned, was Bruna Bianchi Carneiro Ribeiro. She was twenty-three years old and had come to Milan from her home near Rio de Janeiro, Brazil, to get her master's degree in fashion design. Prior to her enrollment at Domus, she had done her undergraduate work in communications in Brazil, and some other studies in Italy. She told me that her grandfather was originally from Italy and had moved to Brazil, the homeland of her grandmother. Although born in Brazil, Bruna possessed Italian citizenship, too, and sometimes traveled on her Italian passport. Since Ribeiro was a common name in Brazil, she went by Bruna Bianchi, which her parents felt was a more prestigious, sophisticated name, and sounded more Italian.

I liked Bruna immediately. She was warm and friendly, a beautiful person inside and out. She had a perpetual sparkle in her eyes. She was also very bright. She spoke several languages, was cultured and sophisticated, and quick to laugh. Bruna didn't smoke or do drugs, and she seemed averse to alcohol because she had seen the negative effects it had on her father. In one of our first conversations, she confided to me that her father "drank too much."

She had invited me to the party in the hope that she might be able to fix me up with her friend. I wasn't interested in her friend, but I sure liked Bruna. She was dating another man, though, so we struck up a friendship, meeting occasionally at the pizzeria around the corner from our building. One evening, as we talked while eating our pizza, Bruna looked at me with searching eyes. I could tell that she was pondering something, but she didn't reveal her thoughts.

Our first real date was to Lake Como on a cool, rainy day. I was happy it was raining, because we had only one umbrella, so we had to stay close as we walked. Shortly after that, Bruna told me that she had ended the relationship with the man she'd been dating. "We really hadn't been dating very long," she explained to me. "And he was kind of possessive. More important, if I can feel something for someone else, I must not really care about him," she said demurely.

"You feel something for someone else?" I asked.

Bruna flashed her gorgeous smile and hugged me. I was hooked.

Our courtship was like a dream come true. Living in Milan was romantic in itself, and we did everything together. We attended some of the social events associated with the fashion business in Italy, and some of Bruna's school events, but mostly we enjoyed the simple things. Bruna loved movies, so we often went out to dinner and then rented a movie. We took day trips to Venice and Switzerland, which were fabulous, but we didn't have to do anything extravagant like that to have fun; we simply enjoyed being together.

During Bruna's spring break before her last semester at Domus Academy, she and I traveled to New Jersey for a brief visit. When I described her to my friend Bobby Chang, I told him, "I think I met the girl I'm going to marry." Bobby teased me, because I was constantly singing or whistling the old mid-sixties Jobim bossa nova hit

"Girl from Ipanema," a song first recorded by Pery Ribeiro (no relation to Bruna), and later made popular by Astrud Gilberto and Stan Getz. For months the song reverberated in my mind. Bruna was, after all, a Brazilian beauty, and we were in love.

While Bruna and I were in New Jersey later that summer, I invited her parents, Raimundo and Silvana, and her brother, Luca, to join us. They readily accepted. It wasn't the first time Bruna or her family members had been to the United States. Before Bruna and I met, the family had visited New York, Florida, and other locations.

They had never been to our peaceful little oasis in Monmouth County, however, so when Bruna's family saw it, they fell in love with the area. They stayed with me in my town house for most of the summer. During that time, they saw everything about me—good or bad—including the way I lived, the car I drove, my family and friends. I had nothing to hide, so I readily shared everything with them and their daughter. My attitude was, "This is who I am. If you are looking for someone who loves you, here I am. If you're looking for someone who owns a mansion and a yacht, that's not me."

Bruna and her family responded positively. They loved me—or at least they said they did—and they loved New Jersey, especially the clean, quiet, safe suburban area in which I lived. It was the best of both worlds: we were less than an hour away from the hustle and bustle of the Big Apple, we were within minutes of the expansive Atlantic coast beaches, and we lived in a small-town environment where people actually called one another by their first names. For better or worse, Bruna knew what she was getting into when she fell in love with me. And so did her parents and brother.

Bruna's mother and brother especially enjoyed New Jersey's proximity to New York. Ray liked the relatively quick jaunt to Atlantic City to visit the casinos. I became his "designated driver," since Ray did not have a driver's license. He gave up driving, he said, because he got too angry at the other drivers who cut him off in traffic. In Brazil, he would walk, take a taxi, or have a private driver take him to his destination. But even as a passenger, he would yell at other motorists.

When Silvana was with him, she would constantly say, "Bahinio"—his nickname—"calm down!"

Although I'm not much of a gambler—I occasionally placed a five-dollar chip on "lifeguard red" on the roulette table—I was in love with his daughter and knew she was the one for me. So, if driving Ray down to the casinos made him happy, I did it. He was, after all, my father-in-law-to-be, and he enjoyed it, so I was the accommodating son-in-law-to-be. I also took him and Silvana, along with my dad, Bruna, and one of her friends, to Yankee Stadium to see a baseball game, and when the weather turned cold, Ray and I went to a New Jersey Devils hockey game.

During that first summer that Bruna and I were together, the New Jersey real estate market was soft and prices were attractive for buyers. Bruna's parents decided it might be an excellent time to purchase some property in America. Historically, Brazil occasionally froze its citizens' bank accounts, and Ray seemed worried that something similar could happen again sometime. He wanted to invest some of his money outside of his homeland, similar to what Bruna's aunt had done by purchasing a home in Portugal. So the idea of Ray and Silvana having a place in the United States was not as foreign as it might seem.

My mom, who had her real estate license, and I offered to help Ray find the right place, but I also spoke straightforwardly to him, man to man. "I understand you may want to buy a place, but there are two things we need to make clear. I don't want you to feel pressure because of Bruna's and my relationship that you should purchase property here. And second, on the other hand, I don't want you to feel that you would be pressuring me by buying a place here." I wanted to be sure that if Ray and Silvana bought property, it was because they wanted to, not in any way because of Bruna and me.

Ray seemed to appreciate my forthrightness. He later told me, "I knew all along that you and my daughter were going to be married."

While Bruna and I were still dating, and everyone was staying at my place, her parents purchased a condo on the Jersey coast. Mom and I helped them negotiate a good price on one unit in a beautiful complex, complete with a pool and overlooking the ocean on Island View Way, in Sea Bright, New Jersey. Bruna and I frequently went over to Sea Bright to spend the day at the Ribeiros' condo, or at their pool or the beach.

Silvana was always kind to me, giving, caring, and pleasant. Yet at the same time I couldn't help noticing there was something in her eyes that seemed cold and distant. I didn't see anything weird at the time, but I realized that her son had a similar expression in his eyes. I'm a tolerant person, though, and figured that they were merely different from me. Besides, I was beginning to like the close familial relationship I had formed with all of them.

Sometimes my friends would ask me, "How can you deal with them being here all the time?"

"We get along. They are close with Bruna, and I respect that. Bruna is here, so I understand their wanting to be close to her. I love close families." To me it wasn't about butting heads or having to have my own way. I'm pretty easygoing by nature, so it was no problem for me to have the extended family members around Bruna and me. We also included my mom, dad, and my sister and her husband, Chris, in our activities whenever it was convenient for them. We were one big, happy family.

In 1999, I gave Bruna an engagement ring I'd designed myself, made from diamonds drawn from my mother's, my grandmother's, and my great-grandmother's rings—the three most cherished women in my life up to that point. The ring was a unique way to express to Bruna how special she was to me. I had no doubt that we would be together for the rest of our lives.

We discussed getting married in Italy, because that was where we'd met, but the logistics of getting our family members there would have been a nightmare, not to mention the red tape involved in dealing with the Italian bureaucracy. Eventually, we decided that it would be much easier to get married in New Jersey while her parents were visiting. There was never any real question about where we would live—both Bruna and her parents were keen on her living close to New York, but in a comfortable, safe place.

On December 17, 1999, Bruna and I were married in Eatontown, New Jersey, in a private ceremony attended only by our parents and my grandmother. Bruna was twenty-four years old, and I was thirty-one. The town mayor presided over the wedding ceremony. We had a small reception for the family at Molly Pitcher Inn, a well-known banquet location overlooking the Navesink River in Red Bank. In January 2000 we traveled to Brazil and had a big party with Bruna's extended family members and friends. While in Brazil, we went to visit the town of Bahia, where her father was born. From there, Bruna and I spent our honeymoon at a nearby Club Med resort. When we returned to the States, we set up housekeeping in the town house.

During the early months of our marriage, I continued to do modeling shoots, but I turned down all long-distance trips that would have taken me away from home for more than a few days. Bruna understood the fashion business, the travel requirements, and how, as a model, I might need to be gone for a day or two, then get to be home for three or four days. Even though we were so close to New York, and as well connected as I was with many people in the fashion industry, Bruna was uneasy about the idea of working in the city. She didn't want to make the daily commute. Instead, she began to teach an evening class in Italian at Brookdale Community College, near our home.

When we learned that Bruna was pregnant, I was overjoyed. I loved her with all my heart, and creating a new life together just made everything perfect. Other than my college girlfriend, I'd had only one other serious relationship, one that lasted about four years. That woman was special to me, and I will always cherish the memories of that time. For a while I thought that she might be "the one," but things ultimately didn't work out. We were apart for long periods of time, both of us being models and traveling a great deal.

But when I met Bruna, something in me woke up. It was a yearning to be a dad, to have a family, to raise a child with the woman I would be with forever. To me, Bruna was the right woman at the right time, and in my heart and mind, we were destined to be together and to bring a precious little baby into the world. I couldn't have been happier.

Bruna had an easy pregnancy; she wasn't sick, and she seemed to glow with the joy of imminent motherhood. I didn't really want to know in advance whether our child was a girl or a boy, but Bruna did. I acquiesced, and the ultrasound revealed that we were having a boy. "Okay, that's great," I said. "We can paint the upstairs bedroom blue." We enjoyed picking out baby clothes for a little boy, getting his nursery ready, and seeing to all the myriad details involved in preparing for a baby.

At the baby shower, Bruna stood up and in a heartfelt gesture expressed her gratitude to all of our relatives. "I thank you for accepting me, and I feel as if we are one big family," she gushed.

On May 25, 2000, we welcomed a child into our world. At the moment of his birth, the umbilical cord was wrapped tightly around his neck and he couldn't breathe. The doctors acted quickly, though, and in a matter of moments we heard the strong cries of an adorable baby boy. He was a big boy, too, weighing eight pounds, eight ounces.

We named him Sean Richard Goldman, and I was thrilled. Neither Bruna nor I had any relatives by the name of Sean, but we liked the name and we thought that it might be easy to pronounce in both America and Brazil. Our only connection to it was a John Lennon song that we liked, "Beautiful Boy." We chose Sean's middle name in honor of my beloved late uncle Richard, one of the kindest, most wonderful men I had ever known.

Several years later, I learned that in 1983, former president Ronald Reagan had proclaimed May 25 as National Missing Children's Day, calling attention to the thousands of children who are abducted internationally by a parent or a family member each year. How ironic that Sean should be born on that day.

Sean was born in a beautiful birthing room in Riverview Hospital in Red Bank, but because Bruna had suffered some vaginal tearing while giving birth, she ended up being displeased with the whole experience there. Bruna and I talked about having a couple of kids, at least, because we didn't want Sean to be an only child. After Sean's birth, she often reminded me, "When we have another child, I want to have the baby in Brazil."

Bruna's parents had come to the States for the birth, and afterward, Silvana was adamant in insisting that the Brazilian medical facilities were better than those in the United States. I didn't agree, but kept my opinion about Silvana's rantings to myself, since Sean was a beautiful, healthy baby. I knew from my travels that people came from all around the world to the United States to be treated by our top-quality physicians and hospitals. So if Silvana was convinced otherwise, it really didn't affect me.

I was too busy adoring our newborn son. Every time I looked at our beautiful baby boy—with his perfectly formed tiny fingers and toes; his tufts of soft, fine hair; his cherub's cheeks—I gave thanks to God for a healthy baby. I was ecstatic, and delighted to be a dad.

As I gazed into Sean's barely open eyes, it hit me that most of what this little guy was going to learn about life—at least the most important things—he would learn from Bruna and me. And while I had absolute confidence that Bruna would be a loving, caring mother, I knew the moment I saw Sean that there were many things about life that he could learn only from me.

Although I didn't consider myself an expert, I had learned much from my dad and my uncle Richard. I assumed that Sean would learn best by my example, that my attitudes toward love, marriage, family, materialism, education, and faith would have a profound influence on shaping his values. What he would see in me would be even more important than what he would hear from his peers—at least during the formative years of his life—and perhaps even more important than what he might hear from other relatives. I wanted him to see good things in me.

Above all, I wanted to be a role model for him. In my modeling career, I had played many roles in advertising campaigns and television commercials. Photographers had dressed me up as everything from a rough-and-tumble sports star to a suave, sophisticated "man about town." But what I would be for Sean was no act; this was no fancy suit of expensive clothes that I would wear for a few hours and then shed for something more comfortable or convenient. No, I was Sean's dad for life! I somehow inherently understood that being a father was the most important role of my life. Especially in our day and age, when television and movies so often portray dads as inept buffoons, or obsessed absentee workaholics, or wimpy, overly permissive Mr. Nice Guys, men who have no ethics, morals, or intelligence in their heads and no courage in their guts, I wanted to be different; I wanted to be the kind of dad my son could look at and of whom he could say, "That's what it means to be a man."

I realized, of course, that I would probably make some mistakes in raising him. I could read every book from Dr. Spock to Dr. Phil and still feel pretty clueless and inadequate regarding how to raise a child. Someone once said that parenting is like trying to put together a puzzle when you're not sure you have all the pieces. It never dawned on me that parenting requires patience—and lots of it—because I didn't look at parenting as a chore. Nothing about it seemed taxing or burdensome to me. I felt that I was the luckiest guy in the world to have a wife and son in my life. I honestly believed that if I kept doing the right things long enough, my son would learn how to live right.

Sean's birth completed my world. I had traveled around the globe and seen so many things; now I was ready to settle down. Sure, I still enjoyed work, and the annual golf trip with the guys, but I had far more important priorities now. I was a dad! I knew that I couldn't be a great father "in my spare time," that the myth of quality time—"Oh, I can't always give my son a lot of time, but I'll give him *quality* time"— was just that, a myth. My responsibilities as a father now determined my priorities, and as far as I was concerned, my wife and child were my top priorities. I wanted nothing more than to be a great husband

and father. I recognized that being a dad meant more than merely bringing home a paycheck, more than merely going through the motions of being a good husband and father.

Looking at our baby boy in his bassinet, I realized I wanted to *be there* for my son. I wanted to be there when he stood up on his pudgy little legs and took his first steps, when he said his first words. I wanted to be there for his first day of school. I wanted to be there when he worked up his nerve to dive into our swimming pool for the first time. I could hardly wait to help him learn how to ride a bicycle. And I could scarcely imagine the thrill we would both feel the day he caught his first big fish off the back of a boat. This was going to be good.

As I gazed into Sean's face, I rededicated my life to my wife and to my beautiful baby boy. I had always enjoyed being at home with Bruna, but once Sean was born, I wanted to be at home even more often. I tried not to book prolonged business trips away from home, accepting mostly local modeling jobs and working in New York City whenever I could.

I did other things to supplement our income. I went to school and earned my real estate license, so I could sell real estate on the side. Bruna continued teaching Italian classes one night per week at Brookdale Community College. Bruna didn't like the idea of being a stay-at-home mom. She was ambitious and wanted a career, and I respected that. I let her know that I would support her in whatever decision she made. When Sean was about two years old, Bruna took a full-time job teaching Italian at St. John Vianney, a private school near where we lived. We knew we'd never get rich at these jobs, but we didn't care. We were in love, we were content, and we were happy.

RAY AND SILVANA were very much involved in our family life. They visited often, sometimes staying at their condo for a month or two at a time before returning to Brazil. We were always delighted to see them, and we frequently went over to their place at the beach. Silvana was a good cook—in contrast to Bruna, who never prepared a meal from scratch—so we'd often enjoy sumptuous meals as a family at their condo. Although Ray and Silvana were bilingual, they spoke mostly English around Sean, as did Bruna. Occasionally, when talking "baby-talk," they might lapse into their native Portuguese, and although Sean later picked up a few phrases, we made no real effort to teach him Portuguese.

Bruna's family members were quite generous. When we went out to eat, Ray and I usually quibbled over the check, both of us wanting to pay. "No, no. You are the son," Ray said. "When you are older, then you will pay."

How true.

In the summertime, we had numerous family cookouts, including my family members as well as Bruna's. We were a happy melting pot. Our good friends Michelle and Dan Langdon came over occasionally, and my buddy Bobby Chang, and we enjoyed their company. Especially after a few drinks, Ray always sang my praises. He told Bobby, "David is like my son. He's like my own blood."

4

Living the Dream

IN THE EARLY FALL OF 2000, I WAS IN CALIFORNIA DOING A MEN'S
catalogue shoot in the hills of Montecito, working at the home of
Michael Bay, who had directed a number of highly successful films,
including *Pearl Harbor*. During the afternoon, I enjoyed swimming
in Michael's infinity pool, but later that evening, my throat grew
scratchy, and I got really sick, with flulike symptoms. Patrick, a friend
and fellow model working on the photo session, gave me a vitamin C
drink. I felt a little better and was able to make it through the shoot.

The following week I had a job in Vermont for *Parents* magazine,
so I took my mom, Bruna, and Sean along with me. The magazine
loved having them on the shoot, and even included them in several of
the photos. It was early October, and the fall foliage in Vermont was
spectacular.

Bruna and I planned to visit Brazil with Sean shortly thereafter. I
was scheduled to go on an annual golf outing to Myrtle Beach with
some of my friends, so it seemed like a good plan for Sean and Bruna
to go ahead without me, and for me to join them later in Rio. But
when I arrived back home from the golf trip, I wasn't feeling well. I
went to our family doctor, who gave me some antibiotics to combat

the flulike symptoms. I started on the medication, but one morning I noticed a strange tingling in my fingers and toes. It felt almost as though I had an inflamed sciatic nerve. I thought perhaps I had pinched a nerve playing golf, so I went to a chiropractor. The chiropractor said, "This isn't something I can fix. Something more is going on here."

I mentioned my condition to Bobby Chang, who had been along with us on the golf trip. Bobby was the head of the cardiothoracic division at Weill Cornell Medical Center, affiliated with New York Presbyterian Hospital. Bobby described my symptoms to some friends of his who were specialists, and they thought I might have contracted Lyme disease or something similar. Bobby suggested that I see Dr. Nancy Nealon, a neurologist friend of his in New York. I was feeling worse, so I agreed.

I took a New Jersey Transit train to Penn Station in New York, then boarded the subway to Dr. Nealon's neighborhood. By the time I got out of the subway car, I could barely shuffle along the street to the doctor's office. My feet felt as though they were encased in cinder blocks. Arriving at Dr. Nealon's office, I could hardly move or swallow. The neurologist began with some simple clinical exams. She then asked me to hold my arms upright as she tested me. She pushed both of my arms down using only one finger on each. I was diagnosed with Guillain-Barré syndrome. "This is serious, David," she told me. "This syndrome attacks your central nervous system. It causes your own immune system to turn on you and could kill you. We need to get you into the hospital right away."

The neurologist made some calls, and the hospital admitted me that same day. The doctors immediately began treating me with high doses of immunoglobulin, a blood-based substance that looks almost like a thick hair gel, which they dripped into my system intravenously, blocking the antibodies causing the problem. As the gunk filled my veins, they swelled up as though I had phlebitis. It was extremely painful, but time was of the essence. My system was already paralyzed; I couldn't move and I was struggling to keep from choking. Fortunately, my body responded quickly to the treatment, but recovery was a slow, tedious process. I entered the hospital in early October and was not released until Thanksgiving.

AFTER LONG CONVERSATIONS with Bruna, we decided that it was best for her and Sean to stay in Brazil until I was able to leave the hospital. Bruna adamantly opposed staying in Brazil at first, but it was for the best, and I was useless in my condition. She called my mom crying and telling her how much she wanted to come home to be with me. "David is my world," she told Mom. But it was the right thing for Bruna and Sean to stay where they were. I hated not seeing them, but my concern for their well-being overshadowed my loneliness and feelings of helplessness as I lay nearly paralyzed, hooked up to the monitors above my hospital bed. Sean, of course, was still a baby, and Bruna was breast-feeding him. I didn't want them to be around the hospital, where they would be exposed to sickness and germs. Besides, I still had to go through the rehabilitation process to gain proper function of my limbs and my dexterity. This wasn't going to be pretty. I missed them terribly, but it wasn't worth taking a chance.

The colder fall weather was setting in, and I knew Bruna and Sean were cozy in Brazil with Bruna's parents, it being summer in South America, and there was nothing pressing them to come home sooner. Although we had contracts to close on a new home in October, the sellers were gracious enough to extend the date. The buyer of my town house was understanding, too, which alleviated the stress and the rush to move while I was still in the hospital. When I was discharged from the hospital in November, Bruna, Sean, and I had a sweet reunion.

Fortunately, I had a good health insurance policy through the Screen Actors Guild, so the bulk of my hospital bills were covered. My recovery and rehabilitation period stretched for nearly eight months. During that time, occupational and physical therapists came to our home every week to work with me. One of the exercises I did to help improve the dexterity in my hands and fingers was to play with an old-fashioned Erector set. Sean often sat in my lap as I worked with the nuts and bolts, turning screws and fitting the metal pieces of the set together. Sean's eyes sparkled as he watched me, so occasionally I'd let him help put one of the pieces in place. Before long, we were building model cranes, cars, and trucks together.

During my rehabilitation, I spent hours on end with Sean every day; both of us were learning to walk, he for the first time, and I for the second; I was learning how to keep my balance without the use of crutches or help from someone else. I regained my upper body strength rapidly, but my legs remained weak, and I was unsteady on my feet. Sean imitated me, trying to pull himself up by holding on to a table in our den. Near the end of my recovery, Sean took his first steps unassisted, but for about two months before that, we were pretty much on the same level. We spent hour after hour together on the floor, playing with his toys, or with him sitting in my lap as we watched television, or with me reading books to him. Looking back on that time now, I am so thankful for it. Those many days on the floor together were a special bonding season for Sean and me. I was his captive audience, and he was mine. I was happy to be able to spend so much time with my best buddy in the world. As it would later turn out, this bonding time between us was more crucial than I could ever have imagined.

BRUNA BECAME CONCERNED about both my physical condition and how we were going to make it financially. "Don't worry; I'm going to get better," I promised her. I had saved some money before we were married, so I knew we could live off that for a while. In addition, we had a small income from some property we owned in Brazil. When we got married, Bruna's grandmother had given us an apartment in Brazil as a wedding present. Bruna's father managed and rented it out for us, and that income helped provide enough extra money to support a nanny to help take care of Sean. Bruna had found one when in Brazil, a young woman who stayed with us for about six months. When she decided to move on, Bruna found another. In Brazil, a full-time nanny earns around three hundred dollars per month.

Some of my friends teased me about having a nanny, given our relatively middle-class income, but I didn't mind. I knew Bruna had been raised by a nanny, and also that she didn't relish doing domestic chores. I wasn't sure if she even knew how to do such chores. I felt that if having a nanny helped Bruna to focus on other things she wanted to do, then the cost was well worth it.

When I came home from the hospital in November 2000, we closed on our new home in Tinton Falls. The house was a gingerbread-style dwelling nestled between the trees, with a pool and a deck in the back, on a picturesque piece of property overlooking Swimming River, a peaceful, quiet, navigable tributary eventually leading out to the Atlantic Ocean. From the front, the home looked like a modest Cape Cod–style, two-story dwelling, with a side entry and a below-ground garage in the basement. But from the back, the house opened to a natural vista, a thick jungle of lush, green trees, with spring-fed ponds and several dams and waterfalls cascading to the river. I sometimes quipped that it looked like a place Tom Sawyer would have loved. One of the many aspects of the house that appealed to us was that it was located in Monmouth County, with some of the best schools in the state. When Sean was old enough to attend school, he'd be able to get a good education.

When Bruna first saw the house, she was ecstatic. "Oh, I can plant a garden right over here," she squealed as she pointed to the side of the house. In fact, she never planted a flower, or picked up a twig in the driveway. Nor did she ever attempt to clean the house, do the laundry, or cook a meal that didn't come out of a package. The nanny cooked quite often, and we ordered a lot of takeout. Mom and Dad came over to visit often, and they usually brought with them wonderful food, including Mom's famous chicken and dumplings or tuna that Dad had caught. On other days, I cooked. I often brought home and prepared the "catch of the day," and we had delicious fresh fish for dinner. Bruna never gave any indication that she wanted to learn how to cook, but I didn't mind.

During the latter part of my recuperation, I constructed a deck and dock down by the river. It was excellent therapy for me, and a good way to build my strength back up. By late spring of 2001, I was getting back on my feet and returning to work, so gradually Bruna's financial concerns evaporated. Although I didn't know it at the time, she would occasionally say something to her friends such as "Oh, I know David will never be rich." As far as I was aware, Bruna found our modest, comfortable lifestyle appealing, and we were both content with it.

I began to model again as well as sell some real estate. Because I could set my own hours, we quickly fell into a pattern of me being "Mr. Mom," staying at home more frequently with Sean. He and I did everything together, having breakfast at some of New Jersey's popular diners, going out in the boat, and playing in the Tom Sawyer–like environment of our backyard on the banks of Swimming River. When I had to meet a work obligation and couldn't look after Sean, Mom or Dad was right there. As Sean grew a little older, he came to love jumping off the dock into the slow-moving river. He and I occasionally camped out in our own personal Shangri-La behind our comfortable suburban home. We were living a dream come true.

Bruna liked my being home, but she also liked it when I took modeling jobs. My career somehow helped her feel more important or prestigious. When I appeared in a catalogue, she would often take it to school and show my shots to her friend Michelle Langdon and their fellow teachers in the break room. "Oh, look at my husband!" she would gush.

Bruna never expressed concern about my working so closely with such beautiful women. Part of that stemmed from her own self-confidence, but beyond that, she knew that I was absolutely faithful and 100 percent loyal to her. I adored her, and never gave her any reason to be jealous.

As I had done earlier, because I was trying to be home more often,

I continued to turn down the big-bucks fashion shoots that would have taken me away from my family for prolonged periods of time. I still worked a lot in New York, but I recognized that the drop in our income would be severe. To generate more money, I looked around for some additional entrepreneurial opportunities. About that time, two of my friends, Jim Freda and Gene Quigley, had established a pretty good business with a Jersey Shore deep-sea-fishing charter boat service, Shore Catch Guide Service. Jim and Gene kept saying, "Dave, we need you. You're the guy. You know this business; you grew up doing it with your dad. If you aren't going to be traveling so much, why don't you consider joining us? We have more business than we can handle. You can still do modeling when you want, and we'll help cover your charters when you have to be away."

I secured my captain's license and became a partner in the fishing charter service. The boat business was a way for me to make a more consistent living for my family; it was sure money. If the weather held up, I was guaranteed a day's pay. Besides, being out on the sea again was refreshing and the business was a natural fit for me. I loved taking Sean out in the boat with me when possible. Bruna enjoyed going out on the boat, too. While Sean and I fished, she would relax and sunbathe.

Bruna's brother had attended the famous Lee Strasberg Theatre and Film Institute in New York and had made some minor appearances in Brazilian telenovelas. Bruna dreamed of doing something similar—on a much grander scale, of course. She studied acting at the Actors Training Institute, a local school in Red Bank. She often came home from her acting classes boasting, "I'm going to be the next Catherine Zeta-Jones!" I thought she was just being cute; I didn't think she was serious. Maybe I should have believed her.

Life was good. We weren't living in a mansion, but we owned a lovely home in a beautiful part of New Jersey. We never missed a mortgage payment. We drove matching late-model Jeep Cherokees, mine gun-metal gray and hers silver. We enjoyed going to Broadway shows and ball games in New York City. I also always made time for a special "date night" with Bruna each week. Although we were not rich—a fact I later discovered really bothered Bruna—we were young and in love and having fun as a family.

We traveled frequently and took wonderful family vacations. Before we were married, we went on several "mystery trips" together. A mystery trip was one that I planned for Bruna, giving her only the barest amount of advance information to help her prepare for our destination. "We're leaving on the twentieth, and you need to pack summer clothes for at least ten days," I'd say. Bruna loved the intrigue and suspense of it all. "Oh, come on," she'd beg. "Tell me where we're going! Tell me, please."

"Nope, I'm not going to tell you, but you're going to love it." We went to Turnberry Isle, a beautiful resort in Aventura, Florida, and to Montreal, where we enjoyed the romance of the old city. We enjoyed traveling to places as close as New York and as far away as Europe and Brazil. Bruna loved these mystery trips so much that we did something similar with Sean when he was old enough to understand that we were going someplace fun. When we visited Disney World over Valentine's Day in 2004, we concealed our destination from Sean until he saw the huge Disney arch over the park's entranceway. His eyes lit up. I'm not sure who enjoyed it more—Sean, Bruna, or me!

As WAS OUR custom, during the late spring of 2004, I often took Bruna's parents and my dad, along with Sean, out on my boat to go fishing. We'd have a ball. We'd catch the fish, clean them, and then bring them home to Silvana to cook for dinner at their condo, or back to our house, where I'd prepare one of my special seafood dishes.

The night before Bruna and Sean left for Brazil that last time, we attended the carnival sponsored by St. Leo's Church. Looking back now, it was another of those occasions when I should have seen the signals. Besides enjoying the rich food and the kids' rides, Bruna seemed especially happy to see her friends. "Oh, that's so good," she said later that night. "I got to say good-bye to everybody."

I assumed that she was simply referring to the end-of-the-school-year good-byes. Or, possibly, she meant that she was saying good-bye because she wouldn't see her friends for a few weeks while she was visiting Brazil. I never dreamed that she was saying good-bye to them permanently.

We had a swing set delivered the morning of Bruna and Sean's departure, and since their flight was later in the evening, I spent most of the day outside in the yard putting it together. Sean had a plastic shovel and helped me dig the holes for the posts.

Meanwhile, my dad and mom took Bruna and her parents to lunch at the Turning Point Restaurant in Little Silver. Now that I think about it, the restaurant's name seems pretty prophetic.

My dad later recalled that at lunch that day, Bruna brought up a rather unusual story involving a close friend from college, a Brazilian woman who had married an American citizen and subsequently obtained her U.S. citizenship. The couple was splitting up, but rather than divorce her husband, the woman merely remained separated. She then returned to Brazil and married a doctor in her home country, without ever being divorced in the United States. It was strange fodder for lunchtime conversation, especially on the day Bruna and her parents were flying off to Brazil with Sean. But it was just another story mixed in with the usual banter, and none of us gave it much thought.

When the family members returned from their lunch, they found Sean and me outside enjoying his new swing set. All too soon, it was time to get ready to go to the airport. Sean and I went inside and I bounded up the stairs to the master bedroom, where Bruna and her mother had laid open on the bed four large suitcases. I must have surprised them, because the moment they saw me they both stopped packing in mid-movement and the expressions on their faces were those of two kids caught with their hands in the cookie jar. Although I didn't ask, almost immediately Bruna blurted out an explanation of why she was taking so many clothes. "Oh, we have to pack extra suitcases because we will be attending a wedding in the mountains so we will need warm clothes as well as our summer things," she said.

"Okay, if that's what you need"; it sounded logical to me.

Bruna changed into a Jennifer Lopez–style outfit, a tight-fitting, stretchy, comfortable sort of casual elegant ensemble. Her mom dressed comfortably as well, in khaki pants and a buttoned blouse, and a pullover in case she got cold on the plane. Raimundo, as always, was dressed in black, replete with a baseball cap, his usual look. There was nothing about the way the family dressed that evening that would have given me any hint that this trip was anything other than a normal family vacation.

BY THE TIME I loaded Bruna's four suitcases into the Jeep, along with her mom's and dad's bags, there was barely any room in the vehicle to sit, much less to get everyone safely secured with a seat belt. I've always been a seat belt advocate, so it was only natural for me to encourage the others. "Buckle up, everybody."

Bruna's mom squeezed into the backseat and pulled four-year-old Sean onto her lap. She stretched the seat belt out as far as it would go and then wrapped the belt around both herself and Sean—not exactly a safe way of traveling. I started to protest and then decided simply to hold my tongue. We'd safely made the forty-five-minute drive to Liberty International many times before; we could probably do it one more time. This would be the last time we'd ever make the drive as a family.

5

My New Reality

MOM'S NATURAL, WELL-INTENTIONED FATHER'S DAY GREETING ripped my heart wide open. I hadn't even realized that it was Father's Day. On past Father's Days, I always got a card from Bruna as well as one from Sean. On our first Father's Day after Sean's birth, Bruna gave me a framed collage that included Sean's first lock of hair and his footprint taken in the hospital the day he was born, along with the inscription "Sean's First Important Things for Daddy on His First Daddy's Day, June 18, 2000." Bruna also included Sean's blue hospital bonnet, worn in those first hours after his birth, and even a sealed snippet of the umbilical cord. In the top left corner of the collage was the hospital record of Sean's birth: "Baby Goldman, May 25, 2000. Born at 3:26 P.M.; weight: 8 pounds, 8 ounces; length: 21 inches. Mother: Bruna; Delivery doctor: Dr. Karoly; baby doctor: Dr. Appulingan." That first Father's Day gift from Bruna instantly became one of my most cherished possessions.

For Father's Day 2004, however, Bruna had left no cards for me to find, no special pictures of Sean—only the ragged knife edge of her words saying that she was not coming home. Still trying to process the basic information—that my wife was walking out on me for no apparent reason, and that she planned to separate me from my son, whom I loved—I stumbled around our home, the tears blurring my vision. I could barely carry on a conversation with Mom right now.

"Breathe, David, breathe," I said aloud to myself and the empty house. The sound of Bruna's voice on the phone nagged at me. I had never heard her so cold. And where did she get all that information about what I shouldn't do? Bruna was a bright woman, but she was not a legal expert. And what about Sean? Did he know what his mother was doing? How was she explaining this to him? Surely he couldn't possibly think that I didn't want him to come home. I could still see his bright eyes and his incredible smile as we put the swing set together just a few days earlier. Surely he knew I loved him and that nothing had changed about my love. He knew that, didn't he? A thousand worrisome thoughts and bleak scenarios flashed through my mind.

I shook my head and tried to pull myself together. I had to stop dwelling on such dark, depressing images. But how? How could I possibly think of anything else? When I finally composed myself enough to function, I attempted to talk to my mom on the phone. "I'm coming over," I said. "Bruna is not coming back, and she's keeping Sean."

"What? Not coming back? Keeping Sean?" Mom's voice on the phone sounded frantic. "David, what are you talking about?"

"Yes, Mom. I just got a call from Bruna, and she says she's not coming back and she is going to keep Sean with her. She wants to stay in Brazil. And she says that she is not coming back."

As I drove to my parents' home, the abhorrent situation nearly overwhelmed me. Divorce was unheard of in our family. My grandparents stayed together all their lives; my parents had been together for more than forty years; my sister and her husband had been married for more than a decade. To think that Bruna would simply up and leave was beyond comprehension. And that she would take our son, the joy of my life, without even discussing her feelings was more than I could possibly understand. Didn't she love me? Didn't she want to live in the United States? Hadn't her parents loved New Jersey so much they'd purchased property there? We were a loving family. Bruna's actions made no sense.

A few hours later I called my friend Gene Quigley. Gene and I had been buddies since our teenage years. When I told him that Bruna had left with Sean and had no intention of coming back, he tried to calm my fears. "Maybe she just needs some time away," he suggested. "Don't worry. She'll calm down. She'll come to her senses. Give her some time, and she'll be back."

I appreciated Gene's attempt to console me, but he hadn't heard that voice on the phone. It wasn't Bruna; at least not the same Bruna to whom I had been happily married for more than four years, with whom I had created a beautiful child, and with whom I had made love two nights before she departed for Brazil.

BRUNA AND I talked by telephone several times over the next few days. The conversations usually began in a friendly tone, but quickly degenerated because the content remained the same. She urged me to come to Brazil. At times she attempted to play on my love for Sean. "Don't you want to see your son?"

For my part, I continued asking her to come home, but she wouldn't hear of it. Agonizing as it was, I waited patiently each day to hear from Bruna, clinging to every opportunity when she allowed Sean to get on the phone with me. From the beginning, I resolved not to let on to Sean that anything was amiss, that his mom and I were having problems, or that I was overly concerned about seeing him. I gave no indication that he might not be coming home after the vacation. I wanted him to know that I loved him and that I missed him terribly, but I kept my part of the conversations upbeat.

When Bruna allowed Sean to talk, I could hear the excitement in his voice. "Hi, Dadda!"

"Hey, Sean. I love you and I miss you. When you guys come back, I'm going to give you the biggest hug and kiss, and pick you up on my shoulders. We're best friends forever. My heart beats for you."

"Dadda?"

"Yeah?"

"I love you forever." Sean's innocent, heartfelt words thrilled me and crushed me at the same time.

I gathered my composure. "I love you forever, buddy. We're best friends. Who's your best friend?"

"You are, Dadda."

The phone conversations shredded me emotionally, but they were my only contact with my son, so I cherished every moment of them.

OUR FRIENDS WERE shocked at the news that Bruna had run off with Sean. Nobody could understand what might have motivated her to leave me, much less take Sean away from his doting father. Michelle and Dan Langdon knew Bruna well. The Langdons have a son one year older than Sean, and the boys enjoyed playing together. Michelle expressed her sense of betrayal at Bruna's actions. "She called me and asked me to clean out some supplies from her classroom," Michelle later told me, "but I didn't think anything of it. I was just glad to help. We worked together every school day for two years, and I never saw or heard a thing that gave any indication that she was thinking of running away to Brazil."

According to her friends, Bruna had seemed happy and content. The only comment she made that expressed any hint of complaint to her friends was simply that we were not rich. When she first moved to New Jersey, she loved the town house I owned. Then when we moved to our new home, she was enthralled with that. But the area in which we lived was known for some fabulous mansions owned by extremely wealthy families, and we were not in one of them. Bruna had told one of her friends, "David will never be able to afford to buy me one of those."

Occasionally she would allude to her former lifestyle in Brazil, where she had lived in pampered affluence, complete with security guards at the gates to the family apartment and nannies and chauffeurs, as she was growing up. Sometimes she would brag to her friends, "Oh, in Brazil we drive around in bullet-proof cars." Conspicuously absent from her descriptions, of course, was any reference to the *need* for security guards and bullet-proof vehicles. Bruna's own mom and dad had gotten trapped in the middle of a shootout right outside their home one day when they went out for ice cream. On another occasion, her father was held up at gunpoint while riding in the back of a taxi. Once, as Bruna came out of a store, an assailant lunged at her with a knife. She escaped and fled in her car. In truth, life in Brazil was often not safe, but Bruna always put a positive spin on it.

If Bruna was disillusioned with our simple, quiet lifestyle in one of the most picturesque parts of New Jersey, she never showed it or spoke of it to me. Apparently she was a much better actress than I had ever imagined.

6

Reality Check

A FEW DAYS AFTER BRUNA LEFT, WE RECEIVED A NOTICE IN THE mail that her official U.S. Permanent Residence status had been approved, based on our being married. We had gone through the process of obtaining her green card, and the permanent resident status was just one step below her gaining citizenship. She already held dual citizenship in Brazil and Italy, so she could come and go as she pleased from Italy to the United States, based on the Visa Waiver program, but she wanted American citizenship, too. I had thought she wanted U.S. citizenship because she was so in love with me and happy living with me in New Jersey.

Less than a week or so after Bruna declared her intentions, our nanny showed up to do some housecleaning. As best as I could explain, I tried to inform her of what had happened and I asked her to stay on part-time to help me keep the house in shape even though Sean was not there requiring her care. She needed the job, and I appreciated the help, so she agreed to come once every two weeks to tidy up the house.

The first day the nanny was there, she found some things that she knew belonged in Bruna's closet. When she opened the closet doors, she couldn't believe her eyes.

"David," she called to me downstairs. "Can you please come up here? I need you to see something."

I trudged up the stairs to the master bedroom, and when I looked inside the closet, I understood immediately what was so disconcerting. I hadn't really paid much attention to Bruna's closet since she left. Now I saw that, except for a few old, unwanted items that Bruna never wore, all of her valuable clothes were gone. All of her jewelry, belts, shoes, and other items of value were also gone. I realized for the first time that the four suitcases I had lugged into Newark airport the night she left were filled with the best of everything she owned.

About that same time, I noticed that the second set of keys to Ray and Silvana's condominium in Sea Bright was not hanging in its normal spot, on a key rack by our front door. We had our own set of keys to their condo so we could check up on it, make sure normal maintenance was being done, and use the condo while they were away. I looked all over the house, but the keys were nowhere to be found.

The reality of the situation was now hard to deny: Bruna was not coming back. I knew I needed some legal counsel, so I started calling around Red Bank for attorneys. Mom and Dad went with me for many of the initial meetings, both for moral support and to help me remember what the attorneys said. My mind was still muddled by the shock that I had found myself in such a position, seeking legal representation so my son could sleep in his own room.

Some of the attorneys with whom I spoke did not feel my situation was their sort of case, or they felt it was outside the area of their expertise. Most were willing to recommend others I should contact. All of them offered two consistent bits of free advice: "Start taping all of your conversations with Bruna," and "Do not step foot in that country without legal representation."

In meeting with the various attorneys, one name surfaced in almost every conversation, that of a local Red Bank lawyer named Patricia Apy. "Patricia Apy is the best of the best for this kind of case," I was advised. But when I contacted her, Apy said her caseload was too heavy and she turned me down.

Eventually, she called me back. "I have an opening and can take your case, if you are still interested," she said. To me, it was almost like a sign that she was the right person for the job. Her office was a mere five minutes from my home, a fortuitous circumstance I would come to appreciate in the years ahead.

When I first met with Apy, she seemed highly professional, yet friendly and easy to talk to. "Call me Tricia," she said with a winsome smile. Tricia had a good understanding of the ramifications of Bruna's absconding with our son. Most important, she recognized that ours was not a custody case but an abduction case, and as such, if I ever wanted Sean to come home, my best hope was to file for help under something called the Hague Convention, an agreement on the civil aspects of international child abduction.

I had never heard of the Hague Convention, so Tricia explained that it was an international treaty signed by more than eighty countries, including the United States and Brazil, agreeing upon principles and actions to remedy international parental child abduction. Initially, the United States Congress, in ratifying the treaty, clearly believed that the need for guidelines concerning the return of abducted children grew out of Middle Eastern marriages in which a man married a non–Middle Eastern woman and then absconded with their child, often returning to a country in which the woman had no recourse and even fewer rights. In fact, twenty years of practice under the treaty would reveal that more mothers than fathers engaged in the wrongful removal of children, basically kidnapping their own children and running off to foreign countries, most notably Brazil, Mexico, and Japan. Japan was not a signatory to the Hague agreement, but Mexico and Brazil were.

Under the Hague Abduction Convention, Tricia informed me, children must be returned swiftly, and a custody hearing must take place where the child normally lives, which in our case meant New Jersey, not Brazil. Like her fellow attorneys, Tricia emphatically warned me against spontaneously booking a flight to Brazil in an attempt to get Sean back. "Do not go to Brazil," she said. "You cannot set foot in that country. If you do, she could drag you into a custody case or some false or criminal charges, and you will be in their jurisdiction, and you don't want that. This is not about custody. You and Bruna are not divorced; you are not legally separated. You did not consent for Sean to take up permanent residence in Brazil. She has abducted your son." Tricia further explained to me that the Hague Convention stipulated that children taken out of a country without the permission of both parents should be returned within six weeks. "Brazil is a signatory to the Hague Convention," Tricia told me, "but they are a relatively recent signer. Yours would be the first case brought for the return of an American child. What should take six weeks or fewer may take more time."

I leaned forward in my chair and dropped my jaw. "More time?" I asked.

"The average length of time for a contested treaty case and return of an abducted child is, in my experience, eighteen months to two years. But this is clearly a treaty case; the facts are unequivocal. Bruna has only been in Brazil a few weeks, and once you file may voluntarily return. I would predict that at a minimum you should expect six months to secure a return."

LATER, BRUNA'S PARENTS would attempt to use my willingness to abide by the attorney's advice as an argument against me, saying, "David was more interested in complying with his attorney than coming to visit with his own son." That was lunacy. Of course I wanted to see Sean, and would have been there at a moment's notice to bring him home, but my attorney wisely counseled me to stay out of Brazil until orders had been entered by the New Jersey court, and there were assurances that Sean would be returned to me under the rules of the Hague Convention.

Tricia's advice both gave me hope and made my stomach turn. Intellectually, I understood when she said it could take months to get Sean home, but emotionally I clung to that lower number. Indeed, even six weeks seemed like an eternity to me. Six weeks without my son? Six weeks without seeing his smile, without tossing him onto my shoulders, without taking him out for breakfast or a ride in our boat? Six weeks without tucking him into bed? How could it possibly take so long? How could we survive six long weeks apart? Six *months*? Impossible.

I recognized, of course, that getting Sean home was just the first of many steps. Bruna had not filed for divorce, and Tricia advised me not to file for divorce unless and until Sean was back on U.S. soil. To do otherwise, she said, would dramatically slow down the effort to have Sean returned expeditiously. An entirely different international legal process has to be employed to litigate divorce, then, to secure the return of an abducted child. Further, it might cause Bruna to solidify her position even further, and hope for getting Sean home anytime soon might evaporate. It might also cause the Brazilian courts to be less inclined to push for Sean's return.

Also, the focus was to bring Sean home, not to start any other costly litigation that might muddy the waters or slow the process. But I also knew that in the United States, a former marriage partner is not permitted simply to take a child to another state without the other partner's permission, much less to another nation. I felt sure that the U.S. court system would be fair.

Whatever sort of custody arrangement we eventually agreed upon, at least it would be done in the United States, in our home state, the area in which we had lived together, and would be decided by a U.S. judge. All of that seemed so very far in the future. Right now, all I cared about was getting Sean home.

Tricia cautioned me to be strong, and not to allow Bruna to sway me into doing something stupid. "She will use everything she can to get you into that country," the attorney warned, "but don't do it. She may try to woo you there with kindness; she may try to seduce you; she may try to cajole you, threaten, or accuse you. She may do anything to try to trap you into a family court custody case in Brazil. Don't be fooled."

In fact, Tricia was suspicious that I had been set up from the beginning. Although I didn't know it at the time I hired her, she would later discover that Bruna had already been laying the groundwork. Immediately upon arriving in Brazil, she had filed a cause of action, which she kept secret from me. In it, she alleged that she and Sean had already been living in Brazil for an extended period of time, and that Sean had already been enrolled in school—both misleading statements. Bruna had indeed enrolled Sean in school as soon as she arrived in Brazil, without my knowledge or consent. She also had Sean seeing a therapist, ostensibly to "help him deal with the loss of his father," thus attempting to give the impression to the court in Brazil that our situation had resulted from a planned separation. She even told the Brazilian courts that her parents had assisted her in negotiating the terms of our separation, an allegation her parents would later attempt to deny.

Nothing could have been further from the truth. If there had been a planned separation, it had been orchestrated by only one partner in our marriage, Bruna, most likely with the support and assistance of her parents. When Bruna disclosed to me in one of our early conversations that she had enrolled Sean in school and that he was seeing a therapist, I was appalled. "Bruna, what are you doing?" I asked.

"Oh, Sean loves school, and he is seeing a wonderful therapist."

I later discovered that she knew exactly what she was doing, and was following a well-orchestrated plan to give the impression to the courts that she and I were legally separated.

WITHIN A WEEK or so after Sean's abduction, following Tricia Apy's instructions, I began recording Bruna's telephone calls to me. When Bruna realized that I was not cooperating with her plans, the calls took on a less friendly, more aggressive tone. "You need to come here," she urged. "We need to take care of all this here. Why should I come there? You are the one alone." At times she begged me, at other times she cajoled me, but the message remained the same. "Come here and sign over custody of Sean to me." She promised that if I did so, she would bring Sean home for visits every few months. But then she dropped some frightening hints.

"We can do this together and do it friendly, but if you are not going to come here, things are going to change."

Still surprised at Bruna's new tone, I countered, "You're threatening me, too?"

"I'm not threatening you," she answered. "I'm telling you."

7

Angels and Demons

WORK WAS GOOD THERAPY FOR ME, ESPECIALLY DURING THOSE first few days after Bruna's calls. Getting in my boat and heading back out to sea was a tonic for my soul as well as my body. I'm not sure that I was such good company for my charter customers, however, during those early days after Sean's abduction. I was often sullen and moody, trying my best to help my clients have a good time and catch the big fish they sought, but becoming melancholy if not downright morose as the six-hour charter went on. Thanks to stories like *Moby-Dick*, fishing captains are often perceived as a crusty Captain Ahab types, or like the cantankerous shark hunter Quint in the movie *Jaws*, so maybe my new clients weren't surprised. Actually, most modern captains are pretty nice guys, and I felt bad that some of my clients thought I was an unfriendly sad sack.

About ten days after Sean had been taken, I was down at Sandy Hook Bay Marina preparing my boat to go out when a guy who looked to be about my age showed up. "Hi, I'm Mark DeAngelis," he said. "My father and I are on your boat today." I checked in Mark and his dad and we boarded the boat.

Mark was about my height, and looked a bit like the actor Toby McGuire, with a light, scruffy beard. Winsome and articulate, Mark was quick to engage in conversation as we headed out to sea. He told me that he worked on Wall Street, as do many of our Shore Catch clients, given our proximity to the Big Apple, and that he and his fiancée, Denise, had just moved to our area less than two weeks earlier, to a suburban section of New Jersey that was much less stressful than New York City and ideal for raising a family. When he mentioned the location where they had purchased their home, I recognized it immediately. It was only a short distance from my house.

Once out at sea, we found the fishing slower than usual, so after about thirty minutes or so, Mark and his father and I struck up a deeper conversation. Although I was unaccustomed to sharing my feelings with strangers, for some reason—maybe it was the father-and-son thing, I don't know—I felt willing to open up a bit with Mark and his dad. Before I knew what hit me, I was pouring my heart out to them. I apologized for not being more on my game, and admitted that I had been going through a difficult time.

I didn't volunteer the details of what had happened right away, but as the day went on, I shared more openly with them about what Bruna had done, how she had walked out of our marriage without any warning and taken our son to Brazil. I could tell that Mark and his father were taken aback by the story, and although they offered no solutions, they were empathetic and kind in their encouragement to me. Despite my emotional condition, we did end up putting a nice catch together, with Mark's dad landing a thirty-pound bass. Mark and I stayed in contact, and fished together again several times, and he never failed to ask me about what progress I was making in getting Sean home. Clearly he took more than a casual interest in my situation. He became a good friend, and one of my staunchest allies in my efforts to bring Sean home. Although I'm fairly certain that Mark DeAngelis would not claim to be a saint, I'm convinced that he was heaven-sent. Sometimes angels have beards.

■ ■ ■

AFTER HER RECENT threatening tone, Bruna's phone conversations remained somewhat cordial, albeit stilted, as she continued trying to coax me to travel to Brazil. When I suggested, instead, that she return to the United States, she became irate, screaming at me over the phone about how miserable she had been in New Jersey. "I don't want to live in New Jersey anymore!"

"Why are you screaming at me, Bruna?" I asked.

"I don't want to live in that place. Please understand this!" That's all she would say. When I suggested that if she had wanted a divorce or a separation, we could have talked about it had she been more open with me, she grew defensive.

"Bruna, you're the one who ran off to Brazil with Sean."

"I ran off to Brazil with Sean because if I was there, and I told you that I wanted to separate, I knew you were never going to give me the separation. That's why."

The phone calls continued with a tone of pseudo-friendliness, although I could tell that Bruna was growing impatient.

One day in July, shortly after I once again refused to acquiesce to her demands, I came in from a fishing charter and was cleaning my boat when my Nextel Direct phone squawked. The only person who had that number was Bruna. But it wasn't Bruna on the phone.

"We know who you are. We know where you live," an ominous-sounding male voice growled. "Prepare to die." Click. The phone went dead.

I stared at the phone in amazement. *Is this some kind of joke?* I asked myself.

Then, a few days later, I received another such call. Again it was a man's voice in a poorly disguised accent. The threats were much the same.

It happened again a few more times.

I called Tricia Apy, and she contacted the FBI. Federal agent John Marley and one of his colleagues came to my home to discuss the situation with me. The agents told me to get out of my house right away. "You have to take this seriously," Agent Marley warned. "This is what we call a conditional threat. If you stop doing what you are doing, they will probably let you alone. But if you don't, they may try to do something. We can't really do anything until an actual attempt has been made and there is proof."

Great, I thought, *so an attempt on my life or worse has to be made before they can take action.* "Well, I'm not going to stop until I get my son back home," I said.

John nodded. "Okay, fine. Then you should leave your house for a while."

I moved out of my home and stayed with my parents for a few days. Then, thinking that I might be putting them in danger, for a couple of weeks I slept on my boat in parts of the bay where I knew I'd be hard to find. During that time, I'd stop by the house every so often, just to pick up my mail or some fresh clothing. On several occasions I found evidence indicating that somebody had been snooping around my house. Someone had been trying to pull mail out of my mailbox slot. A couple of times I came home and found cigarette butts, still burning, on my front stoop. It was clear that somebody wanted me to know he or she had been there.

I admit that at times I let the circumstances get the best of me and I succumbed to imagining all sorts of outlandish scenarios. For instance, it seemed within the realm of possibility that someday I might flip the switch on my boat and trigger an explosion. I quickly discounted such negative thoughts and attributed them to watching too many movies. I decided that I would not live in fear, and after a few weeks I moved back home, with a Louisville Slugger baseball bat and a can of mace. These people had already stolen my son. I was not going to allow them to steal my life as well. If they tried to kill me, I wouldn't go down without a fight.

■ ■ ■

I COULD NEVER have imagined that fateful evening as I took my family to the airport and kissed them good-bye that our fairy-tale love story would disintegrate into an incredible tale of deception and tragedy, a bitter legal battle between Bruna's family and me waged over international borders. Nor could I have guessed that the nightmare would continue for so long.

People often say there are two sides to every story. But if that was the case, Bruna would have trumpeted her charges on the first and every subsequent page of her court filings. Had there been any abuse in our marriage, neglect, drugs, alcohol, or infidelity, she would surely have spelled this out in court documents against me. But she didn't. She couldn't. There were no skeletons in my closet.

On August 26, 2004, the Superior Court of New Jersey granted the first of many orders for Sean's return. The court order demanded that Bruna return Sean to Tinton Falls within forty-eight hours of receiving the notice. It also froze Bruna's personal bank account, which contained around three thousand dollars, as well as the Ribeiros' New Jersey bank account, containing slightly more than nineteen thousand dollars. Nor were the Ribeiros permitted to sell or transfer their beachfront condominium until further order from the court in New Jersey. The court order essentially granted temporary custody of Sean to me, pending any final decisions that might be entertained after his return. Moreover, the court order clearly stated that any violation of the order or retention of Sean could constitute the crime of kidnapping.

When Bruna failed to comply with the court order, on September 3, 2004, I asserted my rights as the "left-behind parent" under the Hague Convention on International Abductions in an effort to enlist Brazil's assistance in returning my son. Although I didn't fully realize its importance at the time, the date of the filing was crucial. To compel the return of an abducted child under the Hague treaty, the left-behind parent must formally assert his or her rights within one year of the abduction. I had filed with the U.S. Department of State requesting Sean's return approximately six weeks after he failed to return home and I filed the application with the Brazilian court less than four months after his abduction. With the help of Tricia Apy, I hired a Brazilian legal firm to represent me in Brazil. Because Brazil had signed on to the Hague Convention only as recently as 2000, there were few lawyers in that country with any experience handling Hague cases. The junior partner in the three-attorney firm with the most experience in Hague litigation, Ricardo Zamariola Jr., had joined his partners, Marcos Ortiz and Roberto Andrade, only a little more than a year before Bruna absconded with Sean. Ricardo was a mere twenty-four years of age when he and his partners, who were only five and four years older than him respectively, fought their first case involving the Hague Convention, winning the return of a child born to a Swedish father and a Brazilian mother. Soon after, before he was even a full partner in the firm, Ricardo helped Marcos on another Hague Convention case, this one involving a Brazilian couple living in the United States. When Tricia called and left a voice mail for Ricardo asking him if would be interested in my case, the Hague Convention had never been tested in a case involving a Brazilian and an American citizen. Ricardo took the case and asked for a fee of fourteen thousand dollars plus expenses. At the time, this sounded like an astronomical figure. Before it was over, I'd consider a fourteen-grand attorney's bill a bargain.

Although the youngest member of his law firm, and the one with the least experience, Ricardo Zamariola was brilliant. Level-headed and a quick study, and extremely fluent in English, he was perfect for the case. None of us could have imagined when he signed on in September 2004 the depths of the legal, procedural, political, and diplomatic battle we were entering—not to mention the wrenching emotional roller-coaster ride we were about to take.

EVERY DAY DURING the next year, from September 2004 to September 2005, I anxiously awaited a phone call saying that the case had been resolved, that Bruna was bringing Sean home, or that I could go get him and bring him home. No such call ever came. Instead, all we got was one legal maneuver after another on the part of Bruna and her parents, with multiple filings and conflicting arguments lodged in the United States and Brazil simultaneouly, as one month turned into another without my child. Nearly twelve agonizing months dragged by, months filled with protracted litigations by Bruna and the Ribeiros' attorneys. Finally, in August 2005, the Superior Court of New Jersey entered final custody orders against Bruna in both countries, finding her to be in willful contempt of the New Jersey court orders in failing to return Sean. At the same time, the court found Bruna's continued retention of Sean to be "actionable" under the International Parental Kidnapping and Crime Act of 1993, as well as under New Jersey laws regarding interference with custody matters. This meant that I could bring charges of kidnapping against Bruna.

But I didn't. Why? Because I had already filed for assistance under the Hague Convention, and since my case was pending in Brazil, my attorneys advised me not to seek criminal prosecution—not yet—because such an action might be used as a defense by Bruna to the obligation to return Sean home. It was crazy! But I dared not allow myself to wallow in the legal morass. I decided to let the attorneys wade through that mess. I tried my best to focus on work. I now realized that I was going to incur massive legal bills, so I needed to work as much and as often as I could. I took some modeling jobs when they came, but mostly worked at the fishing business. Besides, going back out to sea was good for me, almost therapeutic. I actually developed a reputation for taking my fishing clients out for exceptionally long trips. Why not? I had nothing to come home to, so I didn't mind spending a few extra hours out on the sea. My clients thought I was giving them a bargain, giving them more for their money, but in truth, they were giving me a valid reason not to go home to my empty house.

As day after day, then month after month, clicked off the calendar, I felt frustrated that I was so helpless in the face of the overwhelming opposition. I was in an entirely new place, a position of vulnerability that I had never before known. Even doing my best, I could make no headway toward getting Sean home. I needed help. I had to open myself to others who were willing to help, and that was an awkward feeling for me.

FOR MORE THAN a year, the Brazilian courts had stonewalled us when dealing with our case. All the while, Sean remained in Brazil, and I had little contact with him. Finally, in late September 2005, my attorneys informed me that a judge in Brazil was ready to consider our case. I immediately dropped everything and booked a flight to Brazil.

I felt nervous excitement as I parked my Jeep at Newark's Liberty International Airport, although it was a bittersweet feeling. The last time I'd been there, I'd lost my wife and son. Still, the anticipation that I might be returning with Sean buoyed my spirits. Ricardo, my attorney in Brazil, was encouraged because a federal court in Rio de Janeiro would finally be hearing the case. Bruna and her supporters had tried desperately to have the case decided in family court as a simple custody case. They argued that because I had initially signed the authorizations consenting to Bruna's traveling with Sean to Brazil, her actions could not be considered "wrongful." They consistently tried to argue that this was nothing but a custody dispute, best decided in Bruna's city of Rio de Janeiro. But I had never granted her any authorization to *keep* Sean in Brazil; he had never lived there.

That was a crucial distinction. It wasn't illegal for Bruna to have taken Sean out of the country; it was illegal for her to have retained him in Brazil without my consent, especially after the court ordered that he be returned. As such, the case was not a custody matter but an abduction case, to be considered under the stipulations of the Hague Convention. Hague cases were always to be handled in federal court rather than family court, and the Brazilian courts finally concurred. This was the good news. The bad news was that the Brazilian courts had basically ignored the return order we had obtained on the basis of the Hague Convention more than a year earlier.

Flying into Rio, seeing the outstretched arms of *Christ the Redeemer*, the 130-foot-high statue of Jesus standing atop the peak of 2,300-foot-high Corcovada Mountain, which overlooks the city and the sandy beaches and sea below, I still had to force myself to shake off worries that I might be flying right into a trap. Bruna and her family members had broken off communication with me for the past nine months and had shut down my contact with Sean, not allowing him to call me, not accepting my calls to him, not even allowing e-mail exchanges between us.

Nevertheless, I was hopeful, almost to the point of being naïve. I went to the hearing assuming that I would be reunited with Sean and be able to bring him home. I knew of Brazil's reputation for protecting the rights of the mother, and especially protecting their own citizens. In their minds, I was the "gringo," the American coming into their country to rob a child from a Brazilian mother. But I was undeterred. After all, I was right. The law was on my side; we had an order from a U.S. court demanding Sean's return, and the power of a major international agreement supporting us. Sean had to be coming home.

I assumed that my opposition was merely Bruna and her parents—a formidable team, to be sure, but people with whom I had always gotten along well. Surely, we could work out this crazy matter in some equitable way. I had no idea at the time that Bruna was not acting alone. In reality, my legal battle would be against one of the richest, most powerful, most influential families in all of Brazil.

Soon after my arrival in Rio, I met my attorney, Ricardo Zamariola. I was surprised at how young he looked, but it didn't take long for me to realize that he knew his stuff and had a good handle on the legal aspects of our case.

The initial hearing I attended in Brazil was conducted completely in Portuguese, a language I hardly understood. Neither Bruna nor her parents—the kidnappers, as I had begun referring to them—

attended, yet they were allowed to keep my son. Not only did they not attend the hearing, they refused to allow me to see Sean.

My attorneys brought me before any and all of the judges who would see me prior to the hearing, a normal procedure and common practice in Brazil. Then, once we were in the courtroom, I sat there trying my best to comprehend what was going on. No offer was ever made by the court to provide an interpreter, and Ricardo was busy enough taking notes or speaking on my behalf, so I sat through the entire ordeal barely understanding a word. The decisions, however, I understood.

On October 5, 2005, a Brazilian federal judge, Fabio Tenenblat, said that although it was clear that Sean's home was the United States and he had indeed been wrongfully retained in Brazil, and that his abductors were violating court orders entered in New Jersey as well as the stipulations of the Hague agreement by retaining him, he was there in Brazil with his mother, and the mother is the most important parent-child bond. The judge admitted that it had taken far too long for the courts to get to the case, but the judge also said Sean had, in the meantime, acclimated to living in Brazil, and therefore he should stay with Bruna.

The judge referred to a clause in the Hague treaty that gives the court discretion to permit a child to remain in the second country when the left-behind parent has waited a year to request a return and the abducting parent can demonstrate that the child was settled in his or her new environment. The judge pointed out that Sean was at-tending one of Rio's best schools, had a number of friends, and was a "normal, happy child." Therefore, he would allow Bruna to keep him in Brazil.

It was a ludicrous ruling, and was completely inconsistent with treaty law around the world, but a firm one nonetheless. I was ap-palled and upset, and fought hard to hold my tongue. I knew that any outburst on my part would be used against me to show that I was an unfit parent, and would play right into the hands of the kidnappers.

I returned home frustrated and discouraged, and, worst of all, without Sean. While in Brazil, I had not been permitted to see my son, nor had I been allowed to talk with him by phone. It was clearer than ever that the Ribeiros were no longer my loving in-laws, but had transformed themselves into my opponents and were playing hardball.

Before leaving Rio de Janeiro, my attorney and I filed an appeal to the judge's ruling based on the fact that our legal challenges under the Hague, in which I had sought Sean's immediate return, were well within a year of his abduction. In fact, we had filed for help under the Hague Convention rules in September 2004, fewer than six weeks after the abduction. I wasn't asking the Brazilian courts for any favors; we weren't asking them to bend any laws or to make mine an exceptional case; all I was asking was that they do what was right. There were no gray areas; there were not two sides with equally strong positions. The Hague Convention demanded that a child abducted by a parent be returned within six weeks. Our court order in New Jersey demanded that Sean be returned to the United States within forty-eight hours. That had been more than a year ago, and Sean was still in Brazil.

It was also at this point that it became clear to both of my attorneys that the issues in our case were greater than simply those in my case. As my appeal was prepared, it was obvious that one of the weaknesses of our position was caused by the lack of support by the Brazilian government in upholding their own treaty obligations. The Brazilian Central Authority, which administrates the Hague Convention in Brazil, had decided when I originally filed that they would not actively assist in the case if I hired a private lawyer. Since my application had been sitting in Brasília with no action for two months, I had no choice but to secure the assistance of Ricardo. As we began the process of taking an appeal, Tricia knew that the support of the Brazilian Central Authority and the United States embassy would be crucial to success. Tricia traveled to Brazil to collaborate with Ricardo on the appellate case, but particularly to meet with our consul general, Simon Henshaw, who understood that not only were the courts not applying the treaty, but the Brazilian government wasn't supporting the treaty in the way that it should. He was a passionate advocate for the increased support of the Brazilian authorities, and as a result of his advocacy, the BCA decided to review and actively support our appeal.

I returned to an empty house physically and emotionally exhausted. I dropped my things at the door and went into the kitchen to get some fresh food for Tuey, our family cat, who, like me, was still awaiting Sean's return. I glanced around the house to make sure everything was okay, and everywhere I looked, pictures of Sean beamed back at me. But they weren't new pictures. The most recent ones had been taken in the spring of 2004, nearly a year and a half ago. My eyes gravitated toward a photo of Sean and me riding a roller coaster together at the Point Pleasant boardwalk the day before his departure for Brazil. I wondered how much he had changed since then, and what he looked like now. I wondered if he still remembered me or even thought about me.

I trudged up the stairs toward what had been Bruna's and my bedroom. I stopped briefly in front of Sean's bedroom door. I dared not go into his room, where his shoes remained neatly lined up awaiting his return. I couldn't bring myself to look into the baskets filled with his toys. I pushed past the doorway to my bedroom and fell onto my bed, wishing this nightmare could end, praying for Sean's well-being, and for his quick return.

BETWEEN AUGUST 2004 and January 2005, I was afforded little contact with Sean. I sent him cards and gifts, but I doubt that he ever saw them. Some were even returned unopened.

During one of my early, brief phone calls with Sean, I was reminding him how I'd always carried him around on my shoulders at home when he stunned me with a remark: "There's another guy who carries me on his shoulders now."

"Oh, really?" I tried not to sound too surprised. "Who is this?"

"My friend."

"What's his name?"

"John," he replied. I heard Bruna in the background telling Sean to be quiet, and the next thing I knew, the call was disconnected.

I didn't know who "John" was, but the notion of someone else trying to replace me in my son's life angered and repulsed me. That was also my first clue that perhaps in addition to running off with our son, Bruna had also stepped outside our marriage and become involved with another man.

In January 2005 my attorneys and I became concerned about Sean's whereabouts. The Ribeiros' lawyers continued to misrepresent where Sean was living, saying emphatically that he and Bruna were living with them. That January my attorneys asked for the specific whereabouts of Sean, and eventually were told that Bruna had gotten her own place, with her parents' help. At no time did they tell the Brazilian or U.S. courts that Bruna had moved in with her Brazilian paramour, a man named João Paulo Lins e Silva, and she had taken Sean with her. All I knew was that from January 2005, my contact with Sean was severed.

SOME OF MY friends tried subtly to encourage me to move on, to let go of Bruna, yes, but also to let go of Sean. I couldn't do that, and I quietly recoiled from anyone who suggested such a thing. "That's easy for you to say. It's not your son who was kidnapped and is being held in a foreign country." My friend Jim Freda later admitted that at times he thought the situation was hopeless, but didn't want to discourage me. A devout Christian, Jim vowed to pray for Sean and for me, and I have no doubt that he did.

Other friends semiseriously suggested that we form a kidnapping party of our own, that we go down there and bring Sean back without the blessings of the Brazilian courts. Although I never seriously considered such an action, when I contacted the U.S. State Department for help and advice, they adamantly warned me against attempting to get Sean home that way. "If you go down there and break any laws in Brazil by attempting to kidnap your son and bring him home, if Brazil presses charges, we will have no choice but to send you back to face those charges in Brazil."

Great. Thanks a lot. The U.S. authorities were basically saying, "We will uphold the law if you rescue your son, but we can do nothing to force Brazil to uphold the same law when one of its citizens kidnaps your American-born child."

A more compelling reason for my not attempting to smuggle Sean out of Brazil was that I didn't want to put him in harm's way. I had already received death threats, and should we try to pull off a covert raid of some sort, wrenching Sean away from his captors and whisking him out of the country, he could easily get hurt. I didn't want to endanger him by putting him at risk of physical harm, not to mention the emotional trauma that might result from such a rescue. No, I had to do it right. I had to bring Sean home through legal, governmental procedures. I was his father. The courts would have to be on my side.

But they weren't.

Over the coming years, each time I got kicked in the teeth and sent home empty-handed, it convinced me all the more that I was perhaps facing an evil far beyond that of Bruna. I was soon to learn that I was correct.

8

A Friend Indeed

SOCIALLY, I FELT A BIT AS THOUGH I HAD BEEN MARKED WITH A scarlet letter. People who had heard rumors about Sean's departure but who didn't know me looked at me suspiciously, no doubt wondering what I had done to cause my wife to run off with our child. Ordinary, mundane activities such as going to the grocery store or to a gas station got to be awkward, furtive affairs. I wanted to get what I needed and return home as quickly as possible. Although I had done nothing wrong, people looked at me as though I had. Sometimes disparaging comments that were made about me got back to me. Bruna's orthodontist, for example, who had fitted her with braces after we were married, learned of her actions when I requested her billing records. She had gone to him prior to the abduction, accompanied by her parents, had him do one last adjustment, and then her mom paid off the bill. Later, the orthodontist and his wife were out to dinner with mutual friends of ours. During the conversation, someone suggested, "David must have done something really mean or have been a really bad guy for his wife to take off with his child like that." Those kinds of comments seared into my heart, but they were unavoidable. Most people assumed there were two sides to every story, so there must be something missing, something that I wasn't telling, or some bizarre element or piece of the puzzle that had not yet been discovered but that would eventually make sense of the entire matter.

Although I knew that no such missing puzzle piece existed on my end, it was futile to attempt to explain that to others.

Friends who knew me well were certain that I had done nothing to precipitate Bruna's actions, but they seemed nonetheless nervous and flustered around me, not quite knowing how to act. For my part, I wanted to prove to them that their confidence in me was not unfounded, that I had not done anything to cause Bruna to leave the way she had. I had honestly been a loving husband and a doting father. The problem? I wasn't rich, and apparently Bruna wanted somebody who was.

As much as I needed the support of friends, and to be with other people simply to maintain some sense of normalcy in my life, I tended to avoid parties and other social gatherings as much as possible. It always felt awkward, even when I attended birthday parties or other functions that Bruna and Sean and I would previously have enjoyed. I didn't feel that I could pretend to be happy while my son was being held captive in a foreign country, yet at the same time I didn't want to be a "downhead," a wet blanket on someone else's festive occasion. I knew every time I did something with our old circle of friends, the conversation would eventually turn to Sean and whether there was any update on his situation—often there wasn't. Consequently, if I couldn't gracefully get out of attending a function, I'd stop in for just a few minutes and then try to make as hasty an exit as possible.

When friends asked me to go out with them, I declined. About the only place I would go in the evenings was to my folks' home. I could feel myself changing from the upbeat, happy-go-lucky prankster I once was to a morose, contemplative loner. And as much as I recognized that the sadness was destroying me, I felt helpless to overcome it. Instead, I grew more and more sullen and reclusive.

One night, about a year after Bruna's departure, my friend Al Applegate called asking me to go out to dinner with him. As usual, I immediately began making excuses as to why I did not want to leave the house. "Get dressed," he said. "It's my birthday. We're going out to dinner and I'm going to have a couple of drinks. You are my designated driver. You have no choice." I rarely drink, but occasionally I'd have a beer at a barbecue or a drink with some of my boat captain buddies after being out to sea. I could probably count on my fingers the number of adult beverages I'd consume in a year. But Al was a social drinker, and after all, it was his birthday. Perhaps subconsciously, I was glad he was using the occasion to pry me out of the house.

We went to Buona Sera, a restaurant in Red Bank. After dinner we moved to the bar area, which was crowded with people. I became engrossed in watching an NBA basketball playoff game on television, while Al enjoyed a few beers. About that time, the bartender turned a shot glass upside down in front of me, the traditional signal that somebody had bought me a drink. He pointed across the large square bar toward a table at the side of the room, where an attractive young woman was sitting with a friend. She smiled at me and waved discreetly. I nodded and waved back in appreciation and mouthed the words "Thank you."

I looked back at the bartender and said, "Get her a drink, please, or refill whatever she has, and I'll take another cranberry juice." The bartender acknowledged the drink order, and in a few moments delivered a fresh drink to the smiling woman. Although I was not afraid to talk with strangers, especially pretty ones, I normally didn't initiate such encounters. I certainly didn't attempt to make eye contact, but when I looked over and saw her again, she was still smiling at me.

A few minutes later, the young woman pressed through the crowd at the bar and stepped over to where I was sitting. I smiled at her, held up my glass of cranberry juice, and we struck up a conversation.

"Hi, I'm Wendy," she said pleasantly. We went through the basics of "What's your name?" and "Where are you from?" As it turned out, Wendy had not in fact purchased that drink for me. It was an elderly gentleman sitting next to her and her friend Mary who had done so. The man had overheard Wendy and Mary talking about me, so he'd bought me the drink on her behalf! "He said he was tired of listening to us just talking about you and wanted to see if he could initiate some contact." Wendy laughed as she told me the story, and I chuckled along with her. She was easy to talk to, friendly, and kind. Her smile seemed to light up the room.

She told me that she worked in procurement—acquiring property or services and negotiating contracts with suppliers—for a large corporation about an hour north of the restaurant. "What do you do?" she asked.

"I'm in advertising," I said. I always felt awkward saying, "I'm a male model," when I first met someone. "And I sell a bit of real estate, and I also have a charter fishing business."

We talked easily for a while about our lives, and she told me that she had been married previously, so it seemed natural to ask her if she had any children. "Yes, I do," she replied without hesitation. "I have two boys. Do you have kids?" she asked.

"Yeah, I do," I answered. "I have a son who was kidnapped."

Wendy's jaw dropped. "What?"

"My wife kidnapped my son and took him to Brazil. I haven't seen him for nearly a year." I attempted to briefly explain to her the nightmare in which I had been living.

Wendy seemed fascinated but didn't quite know how to process the story I had just shared with her. We talked a little more, and she introduced me to her friend, Mary, a bright, married soccer mom, who was employed as an investigator for a consulting firm that worked with the government. I could tell that Mary was probably good at her job, because she had a million questions for me. Much to our surprise, our conversation revealed that Mary lived around the corner from me, a mere two minutes away from my house. With the many people from all over the area at Buona Sera that night, how ironic that I would meet one of my neighbors!

When Al and I were ready to go, we said good night to the women. Before we left the restaurant, though, Wendy gave me her business card and we exchanged phone numbers. There was something special about this woman who had just suddenly been dropped into my life; I wanted to stay in touch with her.

I drove Al home, happily fulfilling my designated-driver duties. Al thanked me for going out to dinner with him, but I was equally appreciative to him for getting me out of the house. I had no sooner arrived back home, and fed Tuey, when the phone rang. It was Wendy. She lived about forty-five minutes away, so she was going to stay overnight at Mary's. "We're still wide awake, and Mary wanted some coffee, so we're at Dunkin' Donuts not far from your house. Can we get you anything? We're going to pass right by your place."

I looked at my watch. I'm not a big coffee drinker, especially at that hour, and I didn't want to eat or drink anything that would make me feel more anxious than I already was. I had turned into a bundle of nerves since my life became so filled with turmoil. In fact, after the realization set in with my friends and family that Bruna wasn't coming back and had actually abducted Sean, several of them suggested that I seek professional help and go on antidepressant medication. That was not for me. I am not a depressed person by nature. I was dealing with a cause-and-effect situation; I wanted to keep my wits about me. I needed to remain sharp, and I didn't dare dull my senses. That's why I avoided caffeine. But I was happy that Wendy had thought of me.

"I'll have a hot chocolate."

"A hot chocolate?"

"Yes, that's all."

Within a few minutes, the women were knocking at my door, Wendy toting a large cup of hot chocolate. I invited them in and they accepted.

Something about Wendy intrigued me. And Mary was an inquisitive dynamo, so I knew there would be no problem maintaining a conversation with them. More than anything, I was glad not to be alone. Mary had dozens of questions about Sean and the abduction. I could tell that she was trying to figure out: *Who is this guy who seems nice and polite? And why did his wife really run off with their son?* I showed her and Wendy my photos of Sean, and we sat around the living room talking for another hour or more. As they began to understand the ramifications of the story, they were shocked. I showed them various court documents and the orders for Sean's return so they could see that I was telling the truth. As usual, I felt the need to prove that I had done nothing wrong, and the women seemed sympathetic.

I didn't mean to sound overly dramatic, but at one point I said, "Getting Sean home is my mission. This is my life right now."

The women nodded in understanding.

I looked first at Mary, then at Wendy, and said, "You don't know what you are getting into by becoming involved with me."

We became friends, good friends, in fact. Living as close as we did in the neighborhood, it was easy for Mary and me to stay in touch. Occasionally, she'd invite me over for a meal with her family, or would sometimes drop off food at my house. Usually Wendy was with her during those times, so it was always an opportunity to reconnect. Later, as I made trip after trip to Brazil in my attempts to get Sean back, Mary watched my house and was kind enough to feed Tuey.

As Wendy's and my friendship blossomed, so did Wendy's involvement in the quest to bring Sean home. She didn't completely understand the complexities of the Hague Convention or why the rulings in our case did not result in Sean's immediate return, but she believed me when I told her that I had not done anything to cause Bruna to abscond with our child. That meant a lot to me.

I WASN'T ALWAYS the easiest guy to get along with during those dark days. Commercials on television featuring children just broke my heart. I even had difficulty being around my sister and brother-in-law's children, who lived in South Orange, New Jersey. I dearly love those two kids, one a mere eight months older than Sean and one a year younger. But it was too hard to be around them. They would always ask me about Sean and Aunt Bruna. There was no getting around reminders of my son.

I tried my best to come out of my shell, but it wasn't easy. Often when I was out with Wendy and we were having a nice time, I'd suddenly notice some young children somewhere, and just the sight of those kids would tear me up inside. "I have to go," I'd say abruptly. Seeing other children sent pangs of grief searing through my heart and reminded me afresh that I should be with my son and my son should be with me.

Similarly, in the early stages of getting to know Wendy, I avoided being around her children. They were good kids, but one was nine years old, and the other was five, only a year older than Sean. At first, Wendy expressed sympathy for me, realizing perhaps how difficult it was for me to see kids because it would immediately make my mind turn to Sean. After a while, though, I'm sure that dealing with my fragile emotions got tiresome for her.

WENDY AND I tried to have a normal relationship, but it wasn't easy. For instance, the summer after we met, she invited me to go to Boston with her to visit her family, but I didn't feel that I could do it. I just wasn't ready yet. Although I enjoyed her company, and we got along great—she was attractive, caring, a hard worker, and, like me, a Yankees fan—I felt that I could not make a serious commitment as long as Sean was still being held in Brazil. And then there was the delicate matter that I was not yet legally divorced from Bruna, even though she had blatantly compromised our marriage. Moreover, my attorneys continued to caution me against filing for divorce until Sean was safely back in America. Wendy understood all this, but it was no less difficult for her. By default, I was asking her to put her life on hold until mine came together.

"It's your life and you have to move on," Wendy gently nudged me. "You have the best lawyers, and you're constantly pursuing every open door in your efforts to bring Sean home. If you're doing everything you can, that's all you can do," she said. "While you're doing all you can, you still need to live. It's okay for you to try to find some happiness yourself."

After about a year, I knew that I was falling hard for Wendy, but because of my internal struggle I couldn't bring myself to tell her that I loved her—and especially not with any sense of a permanent commitment backing up those words. Wendy noticed my reluctance to put my feelings into words and sometimes playfully challenged me about it. "David, why don't you ever tell me you love me?" she teased. "I know you do," she said as she poked me in the arm.

Without thinking, I replied flatly, "The last time I told a woman I loved her she ran off with my son."

Wendy flinched and then recoiled. "Hold on. That's not me. That's not who I am." She wasn't going to let me get away with that.

EVENTUALLY I GOT to the point where I could enjoy playing and interacting with Wendy's children without it creating enormous emotional turmoil for me, but I was still holding back: For the longest time, I avoided introducing Wendy to my family members. We reached a pivotal point when my grandmother, whom I loved dearly, passed away in 2007 without ever meeting Wendy. I knew that my grandmother and Wendy would have been good friends, had I been willing to bring Wendy around the family more. After that, I didn't want to make that mistake again. I introduced Wendy to my sister and her children and to my parents. They soon became close allies and advocates in the fight to get Sean home.

My grandmother's death really hit my dad hard, especially with Sean not being there. "I'm seventy-five years old," he'd say. "Who knows how long I'll be around?" Although unspoken, the implication of Dad's question was not lost on our family. He was wondering, *Will Sean get back home before I die?*

THE AGONY OF being torn apart from your child, enduring year after year without contact, is nearly impossible to convey adequately. Prior to Bruna abducting Sean, he and I had done so many things together.

Now, as our separation endured, dragging on to become years, it was heartbreaking to think about what we were missing out on together.

I missed his first tooth falling out. I missed celebrating his birthday with him; I was robbed of being able to enjoy his first day of school, not to mention Christmas and Hanukkah seasons and Father's Days. In truth, I missed every single day that Sean was away—they were all special to me. I was unable to enjoy all the milestones of his early childhood. Most of all, I was denied the great God-given privilege of being a parent to him in the everyday details of life.

I missed his voice. Occasionally, in the beginning, I would be allowed to speak to my son by telephone, but those contacts were closely monitored. After the Ribeiros realized that I wasn't giving up and the litigation began, when I called their home, as soon as someone recognized my voice they would hang up the phone. Gifts and birthday cards I sent to Sean were returned unopened.

Little was happening during the dark years between 2005 and 2008, as our appeals were delayed in the courts. I was like a dead man walking, going through the motions of life. I felt as though my life were in limbo. I continually pressed my lawyers for information, but often there was no new information to be had. Sometimes it would be weeks before I received responses to my phone calls and e-mails. I understood that there was not much movement in the case, but every day was another day of anticipation, every day I lived with a dagger in my heart. Nothing was happening, but my determination remained the same. I just didn't know what else to do. Where could I turn to find help?

I found my solace at sea. Work continued to be therapeutic for me, and I booked as many charters as possible, but I was living my life on hold, perpetually ready to run off to Brazil at a moment's notice. If I had a charter booked and my lawyers called to inform me of a hearing in Rio, I would drop everything to go. When that happened, my partners would try to cover for me, but if they themselves were already booked, I would have to cancel the charter. Sometimes, when clients called to book a charter, I would forewarn them that there might be a chance I couldn't do the trip. Some understood and were compassionate; others chose to book elsewhere. I understood this, of course. Some people planned their entire vacations around the charter fishing trips; others came in from hundreds of miles away, and had to make hotel reservations and other travel arrangements. Others simply didn't want to risk booking their business associates on a fishing trip that might not happen. So at a time when I needed every extra penny to pay my lawyers, my business suffered.

Coming back to my home was always painful. I could still see evidence of Sean everywhere I turned; I could still smell his scent. Every time I opened the door, I would recall how he used to charge out to greet me, running into my arms at full throttle. I used to look forward to coming home to his hero's welcome every day after work. Now, to enter a dark, empty house was heartrending.

I couldn't eat; I couldn't sit still during the day. I worked myself to exhaustion, yet when I lay my head on my pillow at night, sleep eluded me. I'd toss and turn, wondering what else I could do, whom else I could appeal to for help. Did anybody have any solutions? Was there something I hadn't considered that might lead to Sean's return? My mind raced constantly, searching for an answer, even when I shut my eyes and tried to sleep. What little sleep I was able to get was always fitful, and usually punctuated by what felt like electric shocks throughout my entire body, as my rest was interrupted by thoughts of Sean and what I might be able to do next in my attempts to get him back.

The television was my comfort at night. I didn't watch it, but I kept it on all night long, hoping the sound would lull me to sleep. I needed to hear something other than my own thoughts.

Our back yard "Shangri-La," complete with the ponds, trails, and the new dock I was building, remained just as it was the day Sean left. I couldn't bring myself to walk through it, much less finish certain projects, such as the walkway we were building along the river's bank, or try to add more to it in anticipation of Sean's eventual return. Now it was a grim reminder of the fun Sean and I used to have there.

Shortly after Sean was abducted, I snipped one of the fragrant flowers that blossomed in June down by the river. I love that sweet fragrance, and I knew Sean loved it, too. I could recall him picking one of the flowers and taking it up to the house to give to his mom. Now when I saw those flowers blooming, the sweet fragrance was a pungent reminder of what once was. The first time the flowers bloomed after Sean was gone, I cut one of them, placed it a Ziploc plastic bag, and put it in the freezer so I could show it to Sean when he came home. Each year that he was gone, when those flowers bloomed, I did the same.

Anyone who has ever lost a loved one or gone through a divorce knows that horrible feeling in the pit of your stomach. My loss caused my stomach to churn even more, because there was no sense of closure. Certainly, I was thankful that Sean was still alive, and I was pretty sure that he was physically healthy and well, but we were supposed to be together. It was only with the help of family and friends that I was able to continue living, but the constant pain of Sean being gone was almost unbearable. For some reason, the pain seemed to manifest itself physically on my right side, and wherever I'd go, it was always there. Like an exposed nerve, at times when I'd least expect it, the pain would take me by surprise, sear through me, and level me.

9

=■■■=

Contact!

Occasionally I'd hear that Bruna had sent an e-mail to one of her former friends in the United States. One of her oft-repeated excuses for running off to Brazil was that she and her family were so prominent in their community. "David always encouraged me to go to New York to work in the fashion industry, but I didn't know anybody there. Here, in Brazil, in my community, I am *known*." Of course she could easily have become known in the New York fashion world had she wanted to, especially through some of the friends and contacts I had made.

In late 2007, nearly three years after Bruna had abducted Sean, Wendy received word at her company that a new person was joining their team, a young woman who would be spending some time working in the American office and then returning to the company's corporate offices in her home country. The woman was from Brazil.

Wendy wasn't looking forward to working with her. Unfortunately, Wendy's attitude toward Brazilian women had been severely skewed due to my situation. The Brazilians she had heard about most in recent years were those who had abducted Sean.

Wendy had been employed at that same company for twenty years, and although the firm had corporate offices and a strong presence in Brazil, not once during that time had she ever worked with a colleague from Brazil. Ironically, when the new woman showed up on the job, she was stationed in the office adjacent to Wendy's. It was almost as if somebody had put her there on purpose. Wendy acknowledged her presence, but didn't go out of her way to be overly friendly toward her. She noticed, however, that the new woman was bright and had a friendly effervescence about her.

One day Wendy came back to her office to find the Brazilian woman standing nearby outside her door. "Hi, Wendy," she said warmly. "I want to introduce myself. My name is Pamela." She stretched out her hand toward Wendy's. "I know you are really busy," she said, "but I just wanted to say hello."

"Oh, hi, Pamela. Thank you," Wendy responded, shaking Pamela's hand, further surprised at the woman's warm personality. "Glad to meet you. Let me know if you need any help with anything."

Over the next few months, Wendy and Pamela got to know each other, and Wendy often helped Pamela with unusual English words or phrases. Their friendship spilled over to after-work hours, and the two sometimes went out for coffee or went shopping together on their days off. In January 2008, Wendy opened up a bit and told Pamela about Bruna abducting Sean.

"I can't believe it!" Pamela railed. "How could she do that?"

Surprised by Pamela's reaction, Wendy gave her more of the ugly details.

Pamela was appalled. She helped Wendy discover Orkut, a social networking site similar to Facebook. Designed by a Google employee, after whom it was named, Orkut was one of the most popular Web sites in Brazil. Using it, Pamela quickly found Bruna's profile page.

The text was all in Portuguese. Pamela translated Bruna's profile information for Wendy. Under her "passions," Bruna had listed "J.P. and Sean."

"Who is J.P.?" Pamela asked Wendy.

"I don't know."

"Well, it says here under Bruna's marital status that she is married."

The women began searching Bruna's "friends" for anyone with the initials J.P. Pamela found a man named João Paulo, so the women clicked into his account. In João Paulo's profile, under his "passions," he had listed "Bruna and my son, Sean." J.P.'s marital status was "married."

Pamela was reading the content aloud in Portuguese when she let out a gasp. "Oh, my God!" she cried.

"What? What!"

"Wendy, Bruna is married to this guy, and he is calling Sean his son!"

"Who is this guy?"

Pamela continued digging into J.P.'s profile, and with every bit of new information she discovered, she let out another gasp. "Oh, my! Oh, my!"

"What?"

"Do you have any idea who this guy is?"

"Of course not. I've never heard of him before."

"He's an attorney and he practices international family law." Pamela's shock suddenly turned to fear when she discovered J.P.'s last name: Lins e Silva. "Wendy, these are some of the most powerful people in Brazil. His grandfather, or great-uncle—I can't recall which—if he were alive today, he would be the president in Brazil. He was the head of the most powerful political group in the country." Pamela told Wendy that the Lins e Silva family was known and feared throughout the country.

"I have to call David," Wendy said. "Please stay here online so you can read this information to him. We'll put him on speakerphone, and I want you to tell him everything." Wendy dialed my number.

That same day, I had driven my mom to Jersey Shore Medical Center, where she was scheduled for heart surgery. I was waiting for her to be prepped when I saw Wendy's number on my phone.

"David, I know this is a really bad time," Wendy said, "that you have taken your mom to the hospital, but I have to tell you something." She rattled out the story so fast I barely had time to comprehend the significance of her words. "I'm sitting here with Pamela," she said, "and we found Bruna online on a site called Orkut, and she's remarried!" She conveyed the information as Pamela translated the Orkut profiles.

My head was spinning. With my mom about to go into heart surgery, I find out that one of the most powerful families in Brazil was now taking part in the illegal holding of my son. This was too much.

"I have to go," I told Wendy. "I'll call you later."

WHILE MY MOM was in surgery, I stayed in her room, waiting, pondering all that Wendy had told me.

Bruna and her family had severed all direct communication with me. My mom had tried to stay in touch with Sean by sending him notes in e-mails she sent to Bruna. Occasionally, Mom would receive a response, ostensibly from Sean. The replies were always brief, curt, and didn't appear to be the responses of a young boy to his grandmother. It was clear that someone besides Sean was responding to my mom's messages. So it was a huge surprise when, about an hour after I had talked with Wendy, Mom's cell phone rang. I answered the phone and heard Sean's voice on the line. At that point, we hadn't spoken in months. The family in Brazil refused all of my calls. Now, suddenly, as if out of the blue, he was on the phone! I wanted to shout for joy, but as always, I tucked my emotions deep inside.

Sean didn't seem to recognize my voice at first, apparently thinking that he was talking to "Pop-Pop," my dad.

"Hey, Sean! It's Dad," I said with as much control as possible.

"Oh, hi, Dad." Sean sounded more reserved than usual.

"Hey, buddy, I love you."

"I love you, too."

"I was just thinking about you and me camping out back. Do you remember playing together in our backyard?"

"A little," he answered honestly.

"I miss you, Sean."

"I miss you too, Dad."

As soon as someone in Brazil realized that he was talking to me rather than my mom, the line went dead.

The surprise phone call was, of course, bittersweet. I was elated just to hear Sean's voice and to be able to talk to him, however briefly, yet at the same time I could tell that his memories of life at home in New Jersey were starting to fade, replaced by the misinformation being drilled into him by his grandparents and the Lins e Silvas. *How long?* I wondered. *How long must this go on before I can get my son home?*

SHORTLY AFTER THAT, my attorneys confirmed what Wendy and Pamela had already discovered about Bruna. We learned, long after the fact, that on September 1, 2007, after Bruna had somehow obtained a Brazilian divorce, she had married Brazilian lawyer João Paulo Lins e Silva, whose father was considered one of the country's premier attorneys in the field of family law, specializing in matters pertaining to international child abduction. We learned that the elder Lins e Silva had even presented a lecture to his peers as a legal authority well versed on aspects of the Hague Convention regarding international child abduction. It was astounding! Although I had no hope of ever being reconciled with my wife, I did find it strange that she could marry someone else when her divorce was not recognized in the United States. Technically, we were still legally married in New Jersey.

Moreover, she had married a family law attorney, someone who had to have known better than to condone the abduction of a child from one country to another. Ironically, the Lins e Silva family was Brazil's preeminent legal family when it came to dealing with Hague cases. When anyone in the United States called the International Academy of Matrimonial Lawyers in an attempt to find an attorney in Brazil who was skilled in family law and could help in an abduction case, the Lins e Silva law practice was the one most often recommended.

Pamela helped Wendy set up her own Orkut account, so she could monitor Bruna's activities on her profile page. About a week later, Wendy noticed that it appeared that Bruna had made a change to her profile, in the section under "passions." Wendy asked Pamela to translate. Bruna now listed "J.P. and my children, Sean and Chiara."

"This wasn't here last time, was it?" Wendy asked Pamela.

"No, it wasn't," Pamela said.

"Maybe J.P. has a child by another marriage," Wendy suggested. Pamela went onto Bruna's site, read the notes on her "wall," and translated the Portuguese for Wendy. "It looks like she is pregnant and they are having a girl and they are going to name her Chiara." They couldn't tell how far along Bruna was, but there was no doubt that she was pregnant.

ALTHOUGH ONE OF Bruna's complaints about life in New Jersey was that she had to work, in one of her early calls describing how great life was for her in Brazil, she disclosed that she had opened a fashion *attillie*, a business in which she could design and sell clothes. She was back in Brazil little more than a year before her mother helped her set up a children's clothing boutique in Ipanema. She had studied design in Milan, so it made sense that she would want to use her education and skills, but the hypocrisy of her saying that she didn't want to live in New Jersey because she had to work irritated and insulted me. Teaching school and being home early each afternoon, and having holidays and summers off, was much easier than running her own business every day.

In her court papers, she had tried to turn this around, claiming, "I was forced to work and pay for our family's health insurance." We did in fact change our health plan from my Screen Actors Guild policy to her school's plan a couple of months before she abducted Sean.

When I first became aware of Bruna's statements regarding our health insurance, I wondered, *Is getting health insurance through a spouse's employment such a horrible thing?* Then, after talking with a number of friends, I realized that it was not at all uncommon for a married couple to secure coverage through a spouse's workplace. A relative of ours was in the insurance business, but because his wife was a public school teacher and her group health insurance provided better coverage for less money than his company offered, he had gone with her policy.

Then I thought that perhaps in Brazil, health insurance was purchased differently than in the United States, that people there regarded me as a loser because we changed our policy and obtained our health insurance through Bruna's employment the last few months she lived in America. It was certainly one of the Ribeiros' caustic complaints about me once Bruna left. When I asked my lawyer in Brazil how most couples handled health insurance there, he replied, "Exactly the same. The couple usually opts for whichever insurance gives them the best coverage and price, whether it is through the husband's employment or the wife's." I realized again that Bruna was simply grasping at straws, trying to find some excuse for her actions.

She ran off with our child! Why? Because we got our health insurance through her employer instead of mine? It was a foolish and frivolous smoke screen.

Beyond that, to think that she could possibly have supported our family on her salary, teaching at a small private school, was ridiculous. Yet she perpetuated the notion in Brazil that she was the main breadwinner in our family.

NEAR THE END of May 2008, Wendy went on Orkut again and found a picture from one of Bruna's boutique fashion shows for her line of little girls' clothing. Sean was in the picture and Bruna was obviously pregnant. Wendy later discovered information about a party for Sean in which J.P. was referring to Sean as his son. The more Wendy uncovered, the more frustrated she became at me for allowing Bruna any hold over my life.

Actually, nothing that Bruna did surprised me anymore, and in some ways nothing, apart from her keeping Sean from me, affected me. By that time I had emotionally detached myself from her. My concerns were for Sean and Sean alone. If anything, Bruna's actions made it easier for me not to suffer over the end of our marriage. How could I express any emotion for this person who had done such horrible things not only to me but to her own child? The cruel, selfish person with whom I was now dealing was so unlike the woman to whom I'd thought I was married. In some ways, Bruna's infidelity and her stone-hearted attitude made it easier for me to focus on Sean.

When Wendy found out that Bruna had opened a boutique and was now pregnant, she pressed me to move on as well. "Bruna has moved on with her life. But what about us, David? Where are we? What are you going to do? Are you ready to move on with your life?" I understood her frustration, but I was too consumed with my concern for Sean to be completely aware of the torture I was unwittingly inflicting upon her. She obviously saw a possible future with me, as I did with her. But I had difficulty focusing for long on anything other than getting Sean home—and Sean was not yet home.

BETWEEN JUNE AND August 2008, Bruna's and J.P.'s Orkut sites were quiet, and Wendy and Pamela found no new information. In fact, they assumed that Bruna had already given birth to her baby, and had taken a maternity leave from her boutique. Then, in mid-August, Wendy checked Orkut again and found a photo of Bruna showing that she was still very much pregnant. "Wow, she's going to have that baby any day now."

10

The Unspeakable

ALTHOUGH FRUSTRATED WITH THE LACK OF FORWARD PROGRESS in our relationship, Wendy never pushed me too hard, perhaps because she knew of my intense, passionate, all-consuming commitment to bringing Sean home. But she often tried to refocus my attention on us, on our future, if we were even to have one together. At times her frustration simply got the best of her, and she needed some space. But I wouldn't let that space grow too large; I was persistent in trying to keep us together. I believed then, as I do now, that having Wendy in my life was a godsend.

I hadn't been ready for the family trip to Boston that Wendy had proposed earlier in the summer, but eventually I realized the truth of her words: that I needed to love and to let people love me. Our first trip together finally came at the end of the baseball season, when Wendy and her children and I drove to Baltimore to see the Yankees play the Orioles. I had never been to Baltimore's Inner Harbor, located a short distance from Orioles Park at Camden Yards. So the trip was a milestone for me. Most of all, it was a pivotal point in Wendy's and my relationship.

■■■

THAT SUMMER, ANOTHER young woman from Brazil, Vanessa, came to work at Wendy's company. Like Pamela before her, she was placed at a desk right next to Wendy. Wendy had to laugh. She was now working between two Brazilian women. Throughout the summer, Wendy and her new Brazilian friends periodically checked Bruna's online postings.

On August 29, Wendy's birthday, the Friday before Labor Day, nobody was at work except Wendy and Vanessa. During a break, Wendy suggested that they go on Orkut to see if there was any new information. She discovered that one of Bruna's friends had written on her Orkut wall, "Bruna, don't worry, we'll take care of the store while you're gone."

"What does that mean?" Wendy asked.

"She must have had the baby," Vanessa said, "and her friends are helping with her boutique while she is attending to the baby and not working."

Wendy didn't mention anything to me about having perused Bruna's site that day.

That Labor Day Monday, while I was out working a tuna fishing charter, Wendy returned to Bruna's Orkut site. She went to J. P. Lins e Silva's profile and used an online translation site to translate from the Portuguese. One of the comments on J.P.'s wall intrigued Wendy, but the computerized translation seemed stilted and strange, so she e-mailed the Portuguese message to Vanessa and asked her for a better translation.

About an hour later, Vanessa e-mailed Wendy back. "My God, Wendy! Someone died in João's family . . . maybe Bruna. I don't know for sure!"

Vanessa sent her translation of the choppy message to Wendy:

Unfortunately, I could [not] go to the death ceremony (Mass of the Seventh Day). I was in a meeting at work.

I would like to give you a strong hug! But you need to know that I am praying for you. I am praying to ask God to give you strength and wisdom so you will be a winner.

I hope you can fight for your life and health, because you have a long life to live. There is a lot of wonderful things to happen in your life. This kind of thing happens in anyone's life and you need to understand that. You need to have hope.

Our future depends if we face the obstacles in life or not; think in positive things, believe in God. God gave you your daughter as a gift and I know that you will do better. I hope that God can give you help and hope in your heart!

Vanessa and Wendy exchanged a flurry of e-mails. "Something is not right," Vanessa said. "I think Bruna might have died."

"What! What are you talking about?"

Vanessa explained more of the context of the message to J.P., and although they couldn't be certain, it seemed that something tragic had occurred for which the friend was offering condolences and apologies to João Lins e Silva for not attending a Catholic mass held seven days following somebody's death. It appeared that the somebody who had died was Bruna.

Wendy called me around 5:00 PM. I was still at sea with my clients, returning from a fishing excursion. "Where are you? How much longer till you're back?"

"Still at sea, coming around. We're coming around the tip of Sandy Hook right now."

"I might have something to tell you," Wendy ventured.

"What?"

"I'm not going to tell you, because I'm not sure yet."

"Does it have anything to do with us?" I asked.

"Kinda . . ."

"What did I do?" I asked, half joking.

"Nothing," Wendy said.

"Okay, I'm going to lose you, because my cell phone service is fad-ing in and out. Keep your phone on and I'll call you back later. I have to go," I said.

While I was piloting the boat in to the marina, Wendy received more information by way of e-mails from Vanessa. "Wendy, Bruna died!" Vanessa sent Wendy a link to a newspaper article telling the story. "She died after having the baby; she bled to death. The baby lived, but Bruna died."

Wendy reeled at the news. Finally, she asked, "Are you sure?"

"Yes, that's why I sent you the newspaper article."

Wendy called me again and again, but my phone sent her messages to voice mail. When she finally got me, she sounded very serious. "David?"

"Yes?"

"I have to tell you something."

"What?" I said.

"Do you know how people sometimes say, 'You need to sit down before I tell you this'?"

"Yeah," I offered, wondering what in the world Wendy was going to tell me.

"You need to sit down," she said.

"Okay, I'm sitting. What's wrong?"

Wendy's voice was strong. "Bruna's dead."

"What!"

Wendy's words streamed together. "She's dead! She died having the baby!" She launched into an emotional outburst of sentences while I was still trying to process her initial statement. A million thoughts pummeled my mind all at once, but, almost like a computer sorting out the unimportant information, I sifted Wendy's information down to all that mattered. I didn't ask about the circumstances surrounding Bruna's death or any other details. There was only one question that mattered right now. When Wendy calmed down enough to hear me, I asked, "Are you sure?"

"Yes!"

"How are you sure?"

"Vanessa found the article in *O Globo* [a major Brazilian newspaper and media conglomerate] and she sent me an e-mail link to the article stating that Bruna had bled to death during childbirth. The baby lived, but Bruna died."

"I'm calling my lawyer," I responded. "I have to call Ricardo." Although my heart was pounding madly, I knew the importance of getting in touch with Ricardo in Brazil as soon as possible. My thoughts raced. *How could this go on any further? I have to get down there to Brazil. Sean needs me. My son is suffering. His mom just died. He's been apart from me for more than four years. He needs me. I have to get there to comfort him. I have to be with him. This time they have to let Sean and me see each other.* I was shaken, but at the risk of sounding callous, I must confess that when I heard the news, my first thoughts were not about Bruna. Certainly I was distraught and disturbed by her death. I didn't know the details, but I was sorry that Bruna had died. *How awful!* She had just turned thirty-four the week before. Nevertheless, my concerns were for Sean. My son was now bereft of both of his parents. This situation was getting worse and worse for everyone involved.

I wondered why my attorneys in Brazil didn't know that Bruna had died. She had died on August 22; Wendy and Vanessa discovered the message and news article on September 1, a full ten days later. Clearly, Bruna's family members did not want the news of her death to get out too quickly—especially to America. But none of this mattered to me at the moment. We had to get a plan together.

I didn't have Ricardo's phone number with me, so I called my sister to get the number and then called Ricardo in his office in São Paulo that night and asked him if he had heard anything about Bruna's death. He had not; he had not seen it in the newspapers, and he'd received no notice from the court. Apparently the Lins e Silvas had been successful in squelching the news. Nevertheless, he immediately responded, "It's over."

Driving home, I was overcome with a flood of emotions. It was now late into the night and I was exhausted from a fourteen-hour day at sea. This new information was a lot to come to grips with, to say the least. Memories poured over me, memories of how Bruna and I had met, the first time we expressed our love for each other, and so many wonderful, joyous experiences we and our families shared. What had happened? And what was yet happening? I had to shake it off, had to stay focused, to keep myself in the present. I couldn't go back there in my thoughts, trying to relive the past. It was too draining, and it was of no use anyhow. I needed every ounce of sanity, energy, and strength to do whatever needed to be done to help Sean. Yet I had a feeling that something bigger and more powerful than all of us was taking control.

I promised Ricardo I would get to Brazil as soon as possible. Then I called Tricia Apy in New Jersey and informed her of Bruna's death. "We're done," she said. "We're done. We have to be done, because a fit biological parent always trumps a third party."

After speaking to Ricardo about the Brazilian law covering such matters, Tricia said, "It's over. You are the surviving parent. They have no choice now but to send Sean home." I thanked Tricia for her assessment and positive comments and hurried to make travel arrangements to Brazil. Within three days, along with my mom and my friend Tony Rizzuto, I was on my way.

I thought it would be especially good to have Mom accompany me, since Sean would benefit from another warm and compassionate family member with maternal instincts. Mom had loved Bruna at one time and was deeply saddened by her former daughter-in-law's death. Although she disliked flying, she wanted to make the trip with me.

During the long ten-hour flight, anxious reminders of past trips haunted me. I couldn't help recalling the time my dad and I went through the "dog and pony show" of meeting judges and attending one of the many court hearings regarding Sean in Brazil. One particular judge arrived at the federal superior court thirty minutes late, wearing big gaudy sunglasses. She acted as though she were a rock star. When it was her turn to speak about our case, she huffed, "I've been too busy to read all this paperwork, but I've received a beautiful photo collection of this boy and his mother. My own mother died less than a year ago, and I still lie awake at night missing her. The mother is the most important bond in a child's life. My decision will be for the boy to stay with his mother, and I'll figure out a way to make a legal decision for this to happen."

Unbelievable! She openly admitted that she had not read the files, but her mind was already made up. While she spoke, women in white waitress outfits served coffee and biscuits to her and the other judges, right there in the courtroom during the hearing. *What kind of place is this?* I wondered. Clearly, the narcissism and sense of entitlement were not exclusive to Sean's captors. Even as we flew to Brazil following Bruna's death, I worried that we might encounter similar attitudes among the authorities whose decisions affected Sean and me.

WE ARRIVED IN São Paulo the morning of September 7, 2008, and made our way to Rio, talking in subdued tones about how we now hoped that this long, painful ordeal would finally end and we could bring Sean home with us.

After several unanswered calls to Bruna's parents and to Lins e Silva, we contacted the attorneys representing Sean's captors to see if we could arrange for my mom and me to visit with Sean, to express our condolences to the family and to comfort Sean. The kidnappers refused to allow Mom or me to see Sean at all. Nor would any of the family members accept our phone calls.

"David flew here and tried to take Sean back," they claimed. "We haven't even had time to mourn yet, and he's already taking us to court."

In fact, they had already been to court on two separate occasions since Bruna died, in an effort to get my name removed from a Brazilian birth certificate they had obtained for Sean. When Ricardo sought to enter a plea on my behalf, we discovered that Lins e Silva had already petitioned the Brazilian state court on August 28, less than a week after Bruna's death. He asked the court to declare him Sean's legal guardian and to remove my name and all references to my family name from Sean's Brazilian birth certificate, and to change Sean's name to Sean Bianchi Lins e Silva. The petition asserted that I had "abandoned" Sean, so that upon his mother's death he was in effect an "orphan."

Nevertheless, Lins e Silva's efforts must have been quite convincing, because shortly after arriving in Brazil, I was hit with shocking news: the courts had already granted João Paulo Lins e Silva temporary guardianship of my child! Later I saw television interviews with Silvana in which she referred to Sean as "Little John," as though he were João Paulo Lins e Silva's son. More than a year later, when the Ribeiros returned some of the clothes they had purchased for Sean, on the labels they had designated him as "Sean Bianchi." *Poor Sean*, I thought. *It's a wonder my son can even remember his real name: Sean Richard Goldman.*

It was as though, immediately upon Bruna's death, Lins e Silva— a man with no blood relation to my son, and whose retention of him after Bruna's death was determined by the court to be unlawful, was attempting to erase my existence and disconnect me from Sean. To lend credibility to Lins e Silva's application, the Ribeiros had joined him in the request.

Ricardo informed me that Lins e Silva was arguing something he and his father, Brazil's leading family law attorney, called "socioaffective paternity," claiming that because Sean had been living with him in Brazil for four years, Lins e Silva was now the most qualified person to raise my son. They said that Sean should not be returned to me because for the past four years I had not had a relationship with him. That argument would be tantamount to saying that because Jaycee Lee Dugard was kidnapped in 1991 when she was only eleven years old, and lived with her kidnappers, Phillip and Nancy Garrido, for eighteen years, the kidnappers were therefore the most qualified to raise her! Or that since Elizabeth Smart was apparently so frightened she didn't make any real attempt to flee her abductors, Brian Mitchell and Wanda Barzee, they should be allowed to keep her.

Essentially, the Lins e Silvas had convinced the court that if you kidnap a child and keep him away from his biological parent long enough, he should stay with his kidnappers, because those are the people he knows best and with whom he is most comfortable. To me, it was an absurd argument, yet without any attempt at providing notice to me, the Brazilian court permitted the filing to proceed.

The request to issue a new birth certificate for Sean was outrageous in my opinion, and that a court in any country would seriously consider such a thing when I was still living and making every effort to have Sean returned to me was a mockery.

I talked to Wendy by phone and tried to describe the twisted turn of events.

"Please, David," she pleaded with me. "Get out of that crazy place and just come home."

"I can't leave yet," I said. "I have to file an amended application with the Brazilian Central Authority, under the Hague Convention abduction rules, naming this new guy, João Lins e Silva, as an additional kidnapper wrongfully retaining Sean in collusion with the Ribeiros."

Bruna was dead. Despite the Brazilian court's willingness to entertain the most ridiculous motions by the Lins e Silvas, we had another chance. I couldn't give up now.

11

Unending Nightmare

Mᴏsᴛ ᴏғ ᴜs ʜᴀᴠᴇ ᴇxᴘᴇʀɪᴇɴᴄᴇᴅ ɴɪɢʜᴛᴍᴀʀᴇs ᴀᴛ ᴏɴᴇ ᴛɪᴍᴇ ᴏʀ another in our lives. They can be frightening and upsetting, but usually the dawn of a fresh new day dispels the power of the images that haunted us the night before. The nightmare that began the day Bruna informed me that she and Sean would not be coming back, however, lost none of its power as it reran in my mind almost every night while I tossed and turned and tried to sleep. Worse yet, when I awakened the next day, the nightmare would still be there, and Sean was still in Brazil, now living with a man who claimed that he had more rights to raise my son than I had, even though he was not a blood relation to Sean. This same man, in collusion with my former in-laws, continued to defy the laws of two nations and a major treaty agreed upon by eighty nations.

Tᴏɴʏ Rɪᴢᴜᴛᴛᴏ ʜᴀᴅ to get back to New Jersey to work and to take care of his three daughters. My mom and I stayed in Brazil from September 7 to September 20 and were rebuffed at every attempt to see Sean. Mom even wrote a letter to Silvana, as one grandmother to another, expressing her deep sadness at Bruna's passing. She received no reply. Through Ricardo, I repeatedly attempted to set up a time when I could at least speak to my son, to hear his voice and see his face. The response from Bruna's Brazilian husband and her parents was always the same. Through their attorneys, they denied any contact between Sean and me or Sean and my mom, his paternal grandmother.

Knowing the law, Ricardo told me that I *should* be able to see Sean. I knew better than to get too excited. I hadn't seen the law followed in Brazil yet. Nothing in this case so far had gone as it *should* have, whether under Brazilian, U.S., or international law. Worse still, the recent court proceedings and personal rebuffs we'd received had given us even greater cause for concern and had reinforced our belief that the unending appeals and court filings allowed by the Brazilian legal system could stymie justice from ever being served. When Ricardo learned that Bruna's Brazilian husband had not filed for custody of Sean, but instead had filed to actually replace me on a birth certificate issued for Sean in Brazil, he was irate. "This procedure is clearly an invalid application of Brazilian law," he railed. "There are ex-wives, there are ex-husbands, but ex-parents do not and cannot exist!" Nevertheless, the request was received and processed by the Rio de Janeiro State Court. The only assurance Ricardo could provide regarding the potential outcome of this action was that it *should* not be successful. I was learning the hard way that what *should be* and what *are* may often be two separate matters when it came to Brazil's judicial system.

For example, in Brazil, a public prosecutor is assigned to analyze every case and submit a formal written opinion to the court. In a strange sort of ritual, both defendants and plaintiffs are allowed to meet with the prosecutors or judges presiding over a case. Some would refuse Ricardo's request to meet with us, while others accepted.

The meetings were always conducted in Portuguese, without an English translator. Although I was picking up more and more of the language, my Portuguese was still grossly inadequate, so usually I sat mute while Ricardo and the judges or prosecutors discussed my case.

For one such meeting, I flew from São Paulo to Rio early in the morning. After waiting in a hallway for several hours, we were finally able to meet with the public prosecutor, a woman I guessed to be a few years older than me.

Following a cordial introduction, Ricardo and the woman began discussing my case, while I sat in an adjacent chair saying nothing. I listened intently as Ricardo presented the facts, going step by step, and relating his argument to the rules of the law. The public prosecutor suddenly cut him short and smiled at me. Gesturing toward me as she continued to smile at me broadly, she said in Portuguese, "He will never see his son again. The boy will remain with Mr. Lins e Silva, who is more qualified as a father, and the boy has been here for so long that he belongs here. Have a nice day. Good-bye." She had no idea that I could understand her evil comments. She got up, indicating the meeting was over.

I rose as well, hoping against hope that I had misunderstood what I'd heard, but I could tell from Ricardo's body language that I was close enough in my comprehension. I refused, however, to sink to the level of Sean's captors or those, like this woman, who were protecting them. Instead, I pointed to a photograph on her desk. The picture was of a boy about thirteen or fourteen years old. *"Sua Fighlio?"* I asked. Your son?

The prosecutor grabbed the picture and kissed it, then with both hands pressed it to her heart as she exclaimed in Portuguese, "Yes, yes. My beautiful, beautiful son. I love him so much. He is my world, my baby, my angel." She seemed fully aware of the hypocrisy and cruelty she was demonstrating.

Ricardo realized that even if I didn't understand every word, I had a grasp of what was going on. He hurried me out of the office and offered an apology. He was beginning to feel personally ashamed for his country's behavior.

AFTER NEARLY THREE exasperating weeks, I felt desperate for help. While sitting in a hotel room in São Paulo, I decided to write a letter to my elected officials in New Jersey, and to the local media outlets in my home state and New York. In the letter, I outlined the events that had brought me nearly to despair after more than four years of struggling against a confusing and seemingly one-sided legal system in Brazil.

After explaining that Bruna had died, I closed the letter with a plaintive plea for help:

> I am engaged in a battle to regain custody of my son, who needs me more now than ever. Unfortunately, I am fighting against people with substantial influence at high levels in the Brazilian judiciary system, government and media. It is imperative for my success that I have high-level support within the government and media of my own country. I need this now more then ever. I find it impossible to believe that the United States will passively allow the child of a U.S. citizen to be abducted and naturalized to another country.
>
> So now after four years of trying desperately to be with my son, I find myself sitting in a hotel room in São Paulo since September 7th, hoping and praying to be reunited with my son, ready to bring him home and resume our life as father and son. We have much healing to do. I have never lost hope the day would come for us to be together again. I will never give up, but I need help.

I e-mailed the letter from Brazil on September 20, 2008.

Although I got no response from my elected officials at that time, I did hear from Jeff Pegues, a reporter with WABC News in New York City. Mark DeAngelis had talked to a friend who knew Jeff and was willing to contact him about the story. Jeff was interested. "Can you come up to New York?" he asked Mark. "I want to film an interview at our studios and get this on the news tonight."

Mark met with Jeff that day, and together they got me on the phone from Brazil. Jeff did a brief feature on WABC-TV, including some still shots of Sean and me and audio clips from the phone interview, on the eleven o'clock news on September 22; he was the first major media person to pick up the story. He clearly saw the gross miscarriage of justice and pressed his superiors for permission to get more involved in the case, but they were willing to invest only limited resources. Jeff was really passionate about covering the story, and presented any new developments as his station allowed. I was grateful for his diligent efforts. At last I was not alone.

Shortly after we began to get some media attention in the United States, I received an invitation from *Domingo Espetacular*, a *60 Minutes*–style investigative news show in Brazil. Since Mom and I were still there in the country, I agreed to appear on the program, along with her and my Brazilian attorney. We met the journalist and crew at Ricardo's office and taped for a couple of hours. But before the interview was aired, Sean's abductors managed to get an injunction from a judge putting the kibosh on all media coverage. No one was allowed to talk about the case in the Brazilian media.

The Lins e Silva family continued to pressure the media to suppress the story. They correctly assumed that the Brazilian public would not support their actions if they knew the truth. They dug up an obscure code, known as the "Secrecy of Justice," in Brazil's civil law. The code guaranteed that because the case involved a minor, the details could not be divulged to the public. The code was sporadically enforced at best, but the Lins e Silvas clutched that code and used it as a club in their efforts to suppress the story. Not only did they attempt to shut down coverage of the story in Brazil, they also complained that I was violating the law by going public with the story in the United States.

Attempting to elicit sympathy, João Lins e Silva claimed that keeping a lid on the story was in Sean's best interests. His father, Paulo Lins e Silva, wrote a telling letter to the American ambassador to Brazil complaining that television networks were giving me time to tell my story. Lins e Silva feigned a position of claiming the upper ground, saying in essence, "It's so unfair, because we in Brazil obey the law, and we cannot speak to the press because of the Secrecy of Justice Code. We are bound to silence on the case."

I couldn't believe my ears when I heard this nonsense. Just when I thought I had seen the most outlandish misinterpretation of justice by them yet, the Lins e Silvas astonished me with their audacity once again. And in Brazil, when this family spoke—or didn't speak—the media, the courts, the government, and the many people under their influence usually bowed to their wishes.

FOR THE FIRST four years following Bruna's abduction of Sean, from 2004 to 2008, I struggled like a lone swimmer floundering against one powerful, irrepressible wave after another as round after round of legal machinations continually knocked me off my feet, picked me up, tossed me around, and pounded me back to the surf. I had worked day and night for several long years now trying to bring Sean home. Looking back, I see that in some ways it was good that I didn't really know the full extent of the powerful forces against me.

Bruna's new father-in-law, Paulo Lins e Silva, was an expert in international parental child abduction. In one of his scholarly lectures, he had described how a clever lawyer could work the Brazilian legal system to have endless delays in the courts to keep a child in Brazil indefinitely. He had also warned of the psychological abuse the abducting parent inflicts upon an abducted child, a process known as "parental alienation." In one of his conference speeches, Paulo Lins e Silva described for his audience how the abducting parent "will use the child as an attack missile against the left-behind parent." The senior Lins e Silva was presenting the plan that he and his son had put in place against me, and even at the time of that lecture they were practicing his thesis of parental alienation on my son.

Mark contacted a Brazilian attorney whom he had come to know through my case. The attorney was not working for me, but he was disgusted at the way we were being bullied by the Brazilian legal system. "I want to help," he told Mark. "Let me check and see what can be done."

A few weeks later, he called Mark back. "I don't think it looks good," he said.

"What do you mean?" Mark asked.

"Mark, you have no idea what you are up against. You have no idea of the extent of the conspiracy to keep that kid in Brazil. These people are vicious. They are well connected in high places, and they have enough money to drag this case out for years."

I was a "nobody" with exhausted resources fighting against a rich, powerful, influential family. I felt as though I were David against Goliath. Occasionally, I'd meet people who cared and wanted to help, but there was no way to marshal their efforts. The opposition was overwhelming; what could one person do?

As I had already been doing for several years, Mark DeAngelis and I called and sent messages to our representatives in the U.S. House and Senate. They indicated that they felt sorry for what was happening, but the most they could do was refer the letter to the Office of Children's Issues at the U.S. Department of State, which would in turn write back and say that they were doing all they could. Indeed, we later learned that sixty-six American children had been abducted to Brazil and none had ever been returned to the United States. The people in the government offices weren't being rude or indifferent; it appeared that they simply had no tools with which to help; they had no answers and no clout to find the answers.

Representatives from the U.S. embassy in Brazil continued to write letters to Brazilian authorities after General Henshaw was reassigned, asking them to recognize my paternal rights and return Sean according to the stipulations of the international agreement to which Brazil was a signatory. All to no avail. For the first time in my life, I understood what people meant when they said many foreign governments regard the United States as a "paper tiger." We will make pronouncements, write letters, pass resolutions, and have all sorts of meetings, but there are no teeth in the words. Despite the power of the United States, we could not or would not force Brazil to be accountable; consequently, we could not force the people who kidnapped Sean to comply with the court orders and return him. *We're supposed to be a superpower, and yet we can't get a helpless abducted child out of Brazil, a country that is supposed to be a friend of the United States.*

During the first four years after Sean's abduction, I had made five separate trips to Brazil, hoping the rule of law would be followed and I would be able to see my son and bring him home. In every instance, my efforts proved futile. Again and again, I returned home feeling as if somebody had kicked me in the teeth.

Every day was another day of separation between us as father and son. Sean was growing older, he spoke mostly Portuguese now, and the indoctrination he was receiving at the hands of his captors was bound to have had an effect on him. If only there were some way to get the public's attention, maybe we could put some pressure on the Brazilian government to do what was right. But time was not on our side.

LIVING CLOSE TO New York proved advantageous in the never-ending effort to secure media coverage for our story. Being a private person, I was hesitant to reveal my life to the media and the public. However, I soon saw the power the media possessed, and realized it might be the only way to get the assistance I so desperately needed. I knew I was taking a chance, but I had nothing to hide, and truth was on my side.

Bruna's death, and my four years of frustration combined with my futile efforts to get Sean back within a few weeks of her funeral, did what nothing else could do—it piqued the interest of the media. Her untimely death caused the story to become more poignant to the producers, editors, and other media gatekeepers who decide what the public will be offered each day on television or in the newspapers.

Mark and I had a friend who knew a producer for the CBS show *60 Minutes*. The producer was intrigued by my story. "Fascinating story. I'd love to do it," she said, "but as you know, *60 Minutes* takes months and months of research before bringing a story to air, and David needs an outlet where he can get the story out to the public now." To her great credit, the CBS producer said, "NBC's *Today* show would be perfect for this story." She even placed a phone call to a friend who worked at *Today*. The NBC producers had also picked up on the story as a result of Jeff Pegues's piece on WABC, and were already looking into it.

Through that friend, we forged a connection to NBC. They offered to have me on the *Today* show for a six-minute segment on September 24, 2008. Mark and I believed that NBC would do a good job covering the story, so we quickly said yes. My mom and I had flown home a few days before the interview. Tony Rizzuto sent NBC some photos I had on my computer, for some background images of Sean and me. Mark researched the ratings during the early morning broadcast and discovered that the show regularly reached more than five million viewers. Surely somebody in an audience that large might be able to help us.

Mark brooded over the potentially enormous audience, wondering how we could interact with them once they heard my story. The obvious answer, besides people responding directly to the network, was a Web site. There was only one problem: we didn't have a Web site.

The night before I was to appear on *Today*, Mark called our friend Bob D'Amico. Bob possessed the skills to put together a Web site, but could he actually create one literally overnight? "Do you think we could get a bare-bones Web site up and running in time for David's interview on the *Today* show?" Mark asked.

"When is he going to be on?" Bob asked.

"Tomorrow morning."

"You're kidding, right?"

"We don't need anything fancy, but we do need a page that tells people how they can help."

Bob offered to try. He worked all night long, putting together the content for the Web site. We called it "Bring Sean Home." Bob provided a short summary explaining the Hague Convention policy on parental child abduction and telling the story of how Bruna had retained Sean in Brazil, where he was now being held by his grandparents and Lins e Silva, while I was being treated with disdain by them. Bob also included information about how visitors to the site could reach their congressperson, and templates for letters requesting that our government and the government of Brazil become more involved in getting Sean back home. Bob was amazing; he put in links to various sources of information on parental child abduction, and specific ways people could put pressure on the Brazilian government and our own. He created the entire Web site, www.bringseanhome.org—not greatly different from the one that exists today—and got it online and ready to go by the time I pulled up to NBC's offices and studios at 30 Rockefeller Plaza in New York.

We asked the producers at NBC if they would be willing to mention our Web site during or after the interview, and they readily agreed. That was about all that NBC consented to at that point. Whether the network was concerned about potential lawsuits or something else, I'll never know. I do know that the producers warned me ahead of time regarding what I could and couldn't say during the interview. For instance, I was "advised" not to refer to Bruna's family as kidnappers. What else should I call them? They were holding my son in a foreign country and thumbing their noses at court orders from our country and at an international agreement signed by eighty countries. Was I supposed simply to refer to them as estranged or disgruntled former family members?

Nor would NBC allow me to say Lins e Silva's name, or imply that he or his family was involved in the abduction of my son. "Why am I even doing this interview?" I asked. Did the long tentacles of the Lins e Silvas stretch all the way to New York?

I was not pleased with all the stipulations regarding the interview, but I reminded myself that it was an opportunity to reach millions of people, and that nothing we had tried so far had netted any results. I did my best to remain calm and focused, and decided to work around all the barriers.

I was nervous enough already; I didn't need any more pressure. I wasn't comfortable opening myself up to the public, but I realized that I was up against something much bigger than I had imagined. We had no other choice. We needed the public's interest in our case, which would, I hoped, result in some sort of outcry to rectify the situation. I wasn't worried about being interviewed on "live" television; I knew the truth and had nothing to hide. I had six minutes to tell about four and a half years' worth of pain. The interview might be my one chance to plead for help to such a large audience. This was an important and pivotal opportunity, with Sean's future hanging in the balance.

I found myself seated across from *Today* host Meredith Vieira, as Lee Cowan of NBC News opened the segment by presenting a brief summary of the story, showing video clips and photographs of Bruna, Sean, and me as a happy family. Lee then told how, four years earlier, Bruna had called me from Brazil to say that she would not be returning and that I would not be able to see my son again. Lee concluded his segment by informing the audience about Bruna's death.

Meredith Vieira picked up the story from there and conducted a brief interview with me, discussing Sean's Brazilian birth certificate and how Lins e Silva was seeking custody of my son, even though Sean was an American citizen.

I answered Meredith's questions honestly and straightforwardly, but at several points I was on the verge of tears and had to fight back my emotions. Trying to think and speak coherently and succinctly after seeing the opening montage of Sean's photographs was more difficult than I had imagined. I emphasized how this sort of abduction could happen to anyone's child, and how easy it was, due to the slowness of the judicial process in Brazil, for an abductor with enough money and influence to get himself or herself declared the parent.

Meredith seemed truly concerned, and came across to me as sincerely empathetic. Near the end of the interview, she asked, "Has this government done enough to help you?"

I answered honestly that our government was perceived by many in Brazil as a paper tiger—lots of noise, but no action.

Meredith closed the segment saying, "Well, maybe somebody watching, maybe a lot of people, will be able to express their outrage and help you." She referred viewers to the network's Web site for more information and, as she had at various points throughout the interview, to our brand-new Web site, Bring Sean Home, whose address appeared on the screen.

As it turned out, the nearly seven-minute interview segment was well worth doing. I breathed a sigh of relief, glad that it was over but grateful for such an amazing break, and elated to have been able to make so many people aware of Sean's abduction. Now I could only hope that somebody would help.

The response to the *Today* show went through the roof, which demonstrated to the network that people had further interest in the story. More than a thousand people contacted our Web site. The people who visited the site, and NBC's, were irate at the gross injustice with which I was dealing. Many people blogged about the case or sent e-mails to their representatives in Congress. Others wrote to Brazil demanding Sean's return.

One of the most fortuitous results of doing *Today* was that it set up a meeting for me with Benita Noel, a senior producer for NBC's popular newsmagazine program *Dateline NBC*. On the air since 1992, the program was anchored by Ann Curry, and one of the coanchors was Meredith Vieira. Benita and Meredith were interested in pursuing my story for a possible special presentation on *Dateline*.

ON SEPTEMBER 25, 2008, my attorney filed the amended application with the Brazilian Central Authority, adding the name and conduct of João Paulo Lins e Silva, along with those of Sean's maternal grandparents, as having wrongfully retained Sean in Brazil, and seeking Sean's immediate return to the United States as stipulated by the Hague Convention. Things were basically starting all over again. Now I was trying to get my son away from what the Brazilian courts themselves eventually referred to as "the second kidnapper."

On October 13, 2008, the senior Lins e Silva was scheduled to present a talk to his colleagues and fellow attorneys, and to some U.S. State Department officials, at a conference hosted by the International Bar Association in Buenos Aires. The subject? International child abduction. Apparently nobody at the IBA was aware that Lins e Silva's own son, João, was complicit in and named as a kidnapper in a child abduction case, and that Paulo was the architect of the legal strategy that continued to separate Sean from me and keep him in Brazil. What gall!

When we learned about the conference, Mark posted the information on our Web site, noting the audacity and hypocrisy of Paulo Lins e Silva in speaking on the subject of child abduction while his own family was holding Sean. People in the United States and Brazil posted blogs saying, "This isn't right!" Many took it upon themselves to mention the IBA's address, encouraging others to notify the IBA about Lins e Silva's involvement in an international abduction case. "The IBA needs to know this guy has ties to an international abduction case! And he is one of your speakers?"

Although the reasons were never publicly disclosed, the International Bar Association removed Lins e Silva from its conference program. Lins e Silva was furious. Whereas previously he may have arrogantly spoken of me as a gnat to be brushed away or crushed beneath his shoe, now he had been hit where it hurt: in his ego. Lins e Silva was not about to take such an insult lying down.

12

===== ▪ ▪ ▪ =====

To See My Son

DURING THE YEARS OF THE ABDUCTION, I WAS WILLING TO DO anything to see Sean. From late 2005, when our first appeals were filed, my attorneys went back and forth with the kidnappers' attorneys, trying to arrange for any reasonable conditions for parental access, including a mutually agreed upon location where I could visit Sean, even if it meant going to a neutral country or doing so in a non-Hague country, a nation that had not signed the Hague Convention.

They would throw something out and we would say, "Okay."

Then they would say, "No."

At other times, they would present a potential location and say, "We want you to meet with Sean here."

"Yes, I'll go anywhere, under any circumstances," I would say. "I want to be with my boy."

Then they'd say, "No." Or they wouldn't return calls, and the process would simply stop, or they would return to the demand that I come to Brazil.

I jumped at every potential opportunity they dangled in front of me, only to have the chance to see Sean snatched away again and again. Inevitably, every obsequious inch I budged in their direction was met with new conditions for visitation that included their hardened demands that I give up my fight to regain my son. The constant anguish, the perpetual, stabbing emotional pain I felt from longing to be reunited with my son, was nearly unbearable. Through it all, I refused to give up hope, or to acquiesce to the fear that I might never see him again. But it was always there, lurking in the shadows, and it was an awful awareness with which to live.

Finally, in early October 2008, my attorneys secured a court order from the Federal Court of Rio de Janeiro granting me visitation rights with my son during the weekend of Friday, October 17, through Sunday, October 19. This would be my sixth trip to Brazil in my quest to see Sean. As I boarded the red-eye flight from Newark to Rio on October 13, I was thrilled; it was a visitation of only forty-eight hours, but for the first time in four years—the longest four years of my life—I was going to see Sean face-to-face. Yet reality poked holes in my idealistic balloon. I knew anything could happen in Brazil—or nothing could happen.

Nevertheless, I had scraped up the money to buy another airline ticket. Accompanying me were a couple of people from *Dateline NBC*; the show had now decided to follow the case. I was glad to have their interest, but nothing could distract me from my main purpose in returning to Brazil so soon after the fruitless trip following Bruna's death—I was finally going to be able to spend some time with my son.

I was excited, but a little nervous at the same time. How would he respond to me? After all, Sean and I hadn't seen each other in more than four years, and I had no idea what his captors had told him about me—although, judging from their allegations claiming that I had abandoned him and never wanted to be with him, I could guess that most of it wasn't good. I packed an extra suitcase, filled with gifts, photos, and some of Sean's favorite toys—at least, they had been his favorites four years earlier. My son was now eight years old. I figured that even if his tastes had changed, the pictures and toys might bring a smile to his face, or help evoke pleasant memories of our life together in New Jersey.

Similar to weekend visitation privileges for a divorced parent in the United States, the Lins e Silvas and Ribeiros were ordered by the federal court to an 8:00 PM start time for my visit on that Friday. That seemed odd to me; perhaps the relatives wanted Sean to be fatigued at the end of the day when he first saw me. I couldn't be sure, but if that's all I could get, I'd take it.

I arrived in Rio and checked in at the Marriott hotel across from Copacabana Beach. Under different circumstances, this might have been a lovely place to vacation. Now the dark, cloudy weather that enveloped the city seemed unfriendly and foreboding. I settled into my room and tried to wait patiently, hoping to hear from Ricardo soon. I was ready to go at a moment's notice, because, as I had already learned, the Brazilian courts could be quite fickle, and the best laid plans could be ignored, changed, or totally obliterated.

Shortly before 7:00 PM, Ricardo called from court. Things had changed. João Lins e Silva, Bruna's Brazilian husband, who had been given temporary guardianship of Sean after Bruna's death, had filed a last-minute appeal to prevent me from seeing my son. The judge denied the appeal but stated that since the hour was late and it was raining, Sean should be handed over the next morning, at 8:00. There were no restrictions in the judge's order regarding where Sean and I could go or what we could do. I would soon find out, however, that the Lins e Silvas and Ribeiros had their own rules, which trumped the orders of the court. They insisted that the visit take place at Lins e Silva's residence and that Sean not be "exposed publicly," in other words, seen openly with me in public. If that stipulation were to be violated, I was warned, the visitation would be revoked. I had no interest in making a public display of Sean; I wanted only to see my son and spend time with him. The NBC crew was not to come along. Later that same night, I received a call from the U.S. ambassador to Brazil promising me that an embassy representative would accompany me to the visit location, just in case.

I showed up as instructed, on Saturday at 8:00 AM, at the address João Lins e Silva had given to the federal courts. I was to meet Sean at the apartment complex in the gated community where Lins e Silva and Raimundo and Silvana Ribeiro supposedly lived.

"Wait here till we know everything is safe," Ricardo said. "I will come for you."

Along with a U.S. consular officer, I waited in the backseat of a van while two Brazilian justice officials, accompanied by two agents of the Federal Police, went inside to get Sean. I anxiously peered out the windows, waiting for any sign of my son. A hired bodyguard kept watch nearby, just in case. I was glad he was there. I hadn't forgotten about the death threats I'd received in New Jersey. I was aware of another father who, while attempting to see his abducted child, was brutally beaten. The assailants were mysteriously never found. Stranger things had happened in Brazil, where a foreigner who couldn't speak the language and didn't know the good guys from the bad guys might "accidentally" get caught in some stray gunfire. Now here I was, on their territory, in front of the gates leading to their apartment. That was part of the reason why Ricardo thought it best that I remain in the van until Sean was released for the visit.

I waited. And waited. Watching the minutes tick away on my watch, I tried to pass the time by reviewing some pictures and short home movies I had brought along to show Sean on a small-screen Sony digital camera. An hour passed, while Ricardo paced back and forth on the sidewalk next to the van. One hour turned into two. I put away the home movies and attempted to quell my restlessness by shutting my eyes. Only for a second or two. I didn't want to miss the moment when Sean appeared.

Three hours dragged by.

Finally, word came down. Lins e Silva was not there and nobody knew where he was. He was gone. João Paulo Lins e Silva, the second kidnapper, had left his new baby girl, a mere month-old infant, his own child, with my former in-laws and had departed, apparently taking my child along with him. Sean was gone.

I was furious and devastated at the same time. How can these people jerk around the law like this? Yet, almost in the same instant,

I thought, *Okay, this guy just defied a federal court order not only from the United States but from the federal court in Brazil. This is a federal case, and he is interfering with court-ordered custody terms. Surely they are going to go after him and bring him to justice. More important, they will bring Sean back to me.*

Although I was angry enough to jump on the first plane out of the country, I decided to stay in Rio and wait. Maybe I'd get to see Sean after all. Maybe I'd get to bring him home. Maybe the tide would turn.

It did. It got worse. I stayed out of sight, holed up in my hotel room, waiting to hear from my lawyer. Throughout the day, somebody at the hotel's front desk kept calling, urging me to come downstairs. "There are men here waiting to see you," the desk clerk said nervously. "They need you to come down here."

"Tell them to forget it," I said. "I'm not coming down." Ricardo had warned me that the strange men at the front desk might be trying to serve me papers for a trumped-up court case. Indeed, the Lins e Silvas were now filing lawsuits against me! It was insanity, but Ricardo assured me that they were serious, that they were trying to intimidate me because they knew the law was not on their side. To me, it certainly appeared that the Brazilian courts were on their side. With my not being able to see Sean, it was as though the courts were thumbing their noses at me, saying, "Mr. Lins e Silva has been raising the boy. He is the father figure. You? You don't matter." It made no sense. Even some Brazilian government representatives were now beginning to encourage the courts to send Sean home. One had to wonder how the Lins e Silvas possessed such powerful clout with the courts. But they and the Ribeiros were people of means and political influence, so they felt that they were above the law; they had an enormous sense of entitlement. They were somebodies, and I was a speck of lint, an irritant to be brushed off.

I also wondered why João Paulo Lins e Silva would fight so ferociously to keep Sean in Brazil, especially now that he had his own daughter to care for. Surely he must have considered how he might have felt if his child had been abducted. Although it was sheer speculation, and I may never have incontrovertible proof, the obvious answer was that he had a vested interest in keeping Sean, since he and his family might well have been part and parcel of the planned abduction from the beginning. Moreover, we later discovered, by João Paulo Lins e Silva's own admission, that he had met Bruna on at least two other occasions prior to her leaving the United States with Sean in June 2004. In a rambling, error-filled letter to the National Council of Children and Adolescent Rights, Lins e Silva wrote that he and Bruna had commiserated about their "unhappy marriages" prior to her abduction of Sean.

I met Bruna again through a mutual friend from college right after she returned to the US. At that time I was separated from my first wife.

We had similar stories, we weren't happy in our marriages for a few similar reasons and maybe through this life experience we understood each other very well. In less than six months after we met again, we were living together. And I never imagined how happy I could be at Bruna's side.

For a reason that can be explained, life brought us together three times, and without the first two we never could have really been together. The third time we were certain that we were made for each other, to be together forever.

In the days following the intentional interference with Sean's and my visitation, J. P. Lins e Silva petitioned the federal court, attempting to justify his absence by saying that he did not know the visitation was to take place on Saturday morning until I arrived to visit Sean. Of course, that was ludicrous, since he had been served papers to that effect and even had appealed the decision after I had arrived in Brazil on the very evening my visit with Sean was to take place! In his explanation to the court, he then tried to shift the blame for his actions onto me. He contended that it was actually a good thing that Sean had not been there, because I had shown up with "more than ten journalists, reporters, and TV cameras." He claimed that pedestrians in the area thought somebody was shooting a soap opera since there were so many cameras and crew members. This, said Lins e Silva, was grounds for my visitation to be revoked, based on the previous stipulation that prohibited Sean from being seen with me in public.

His explanation was sheer lunacy! Especially when the federal court called the court officials who had accompanied us on the visitation day to testify, and they both confirmed that there was not a single camera (other than mine), not a single journalist or a reporter with me that Saturday morning.

João Paulo Lins e Silva was chastised by the federal court for "malicious intent and an act offensive to the dignity of justice" for his deliberate attempt to alter the veracity of the facts. He was to be "investigated" to discover whether the crime of disobeying a court order had been committed.

I could have answered that one for them.

Lins e Silva got a slap on the wrist and was still permitted to practice law in Brazil. Talk about impunity. Clearly, he and Bruna's parents were trying to break me emotionally, physically, financially, and spiritually, but it was not going to work. Never!

AFTER MY FAILED attempt to see Sean in Brazil, the NBC representatives flew back home. I was alone in my hotel room late at night when someone knocked on the door. I got out of bed, went to the door, and looked out the peephole. I realized the person outside was someone trying to serve me with legal papers. I refused to open the door.

The person trying to serve me with the lawsuit continued to harass me throughout my stay. I called Ricardo and he said to accept the papers. When I was finally served, on October 24, 2008, I was appalled to see that the Lins e Silvas were suing *me* in Brazilian court for defamation of character and libel! (You can't make this stuff up!) They claimed that by going public with the story, I was disparaging their good name.

It was late at night, but I called Mark DeAngelis and told him about the suit. He went ballistic. The following morning, he called the U.S. embassy in Brazil and reached Ambassador Sobel's assistant. Nobody there knew anything about the Lins e Silvas' legal threats. "Do you realize these people are trying to intimidate David in his hotel room, serving him with lawsuits?" Mark asked.

"No, we are unaware of anything like that."

"We're worried about his safety," Mark continued to rail. We had heard stories of others who had met with unfortunate fates when they bucked the Brazilian legal system. "You need to protect this guy. He is at risk down there."

The Lins e Silva family was formally accusing me in the lawsuit of hiring a helicopter to harass the family by flying over their property. It was ridiculous. I was scrimping and saving every penny I earned, trying to keep up with the legal bills, translation fees, and the travel back and forth to Brazil for weeks at a time. I could barely afford a plane ticket to go down there, much less pay to hire a helicopter to harass the family holding Sean illegally.

I remained ensconced in my hotel room, not really knowing for sure if I was in any danger. After a few more days of the absurdity, I realized this was another failed trip that was exhausting my emotional and financial resources. After discussing my options with Ricardo and with Tricia Apy, I booked a flight back home—once again leaving without Sean.

NOT ONLY DID the Lins e Silvas file charges against me for slander, and for founding the Bring Sean Home Web site, but they even sued me on behalf of Sean's half-sister, Lins e Silva's daughter, demanding money from me in their lawsuits. This was ironic, since one of the Ribeiros' and Lins e Silvas' smear tactics claimed that I really didn't care about Sean, that I had abandoned him, that I had never tried to be with him until after Bruna passed away, that my "real motive" was money. Attempting to prove their assertion, they pointed to the

$150,000 settlement of the litigation against the Ribeiros for damages related to their involvement in the abduction.

After the New Jersey court had entered final orders for custody and monetary sanctions against Bruna for her continuing kidnapping of Sean, the damages case against the Ribeiros remained pending. The Ribeiros continued to argue it was all Bruna's idea, that they had no advance knowledge of the abduction and could do nothing to stop it. They stated their support of Bruna was simply the act of loving parents. The Honorable Paul Kapalko of the Superior Court of New Jersey disagreed, and ordered that the case for damages proceed. In December 2006, on the day the case against Bruna's parents was to go to trial, their lawyers approached mine with offers of settlement and promises of negotiating the conditions under which Bruna could return, and we could address issues of custody and divorce. My attorney worked for days on forms of orders to facilitate access with Sean. While eventually Bruna refused to agree to any access arrangements, the Ribeiros, still admitting no wrongdoing or collusion in Bruna's abduction of Sean, offered to pay me $150,000 in return for dropping their names from my civil suit and allowing them access to their assets in New Jersey, which had been frozen since August 2004 because of their involvement in the illegal removal and retention of Sean.

I was willing to have the Ribeiros sworn in and to have them testify under oath. Finally, some justice might be served. When I received word of their last-minute settlement offer, my first response was "Absolutely not! I don't want their money. If we take their deal, they will walk away free and clear. They'll sell their condo and we will have no leverage."

Tricia agreed, but pointed out that a trial, and the inevitable appeals that would follow, could take several years and would leave an aspect of the New Jersey case still unfinsihed, which could be exploited in the Brazilian case. The only reason we had initially frozen the assets was to encourage Bruna and her family to see the consequences of their illegal behavior and bring Sean home. Any money awarded would have been long since spent on the costs of the trial, and I was already deeply in debt. She basically advised me, "Take the settlement; it will cover some of the costs you have incurred, and we can keep fighting to get Sean home." No part of the settlement absolved anyone of the responsibility to comply with the orders of the courts of New Jersey or released Bruna from paying the financial judgments that had already been entered against her.

Frankly, had I not accepted the settlement, I would not have had the resources to pay my attorneys, and I would have lost my battle for Sean's return by default, because the Ribeiros and the Lins e Silvas could far outspend me. As much as I was reluctant to do so, I accepted their settlement offer.

With Bruna's parents' names dropped from the case, they could get their money out of the New Jersey bank and could legally sell their beachfront condo, valued at approximately $500,000, which they promptly did. The money I received from them went directly to my attorneys, to help defray the skyrocketing legal bills I was racking up because of theirs and Lins e Silva's actions in stonewalling Sean's return. Now they had the audacity to give the impression that by accepting that settlement I was trying to get money out of them. The settlement did not affect my legal case against Bruna. Nor did it exonerate her actions in abducting our son. It also did nothing to affect the stipulations of the Hague Convention demanding that Bruna return Sean to the United States.

Ricardo summarized point by point the sad state of affairs in a letter that proved Lins e Silva's error-filled claims wrong: "The truth about that agreement: it was an act by which the financially superior party used its economic power to exclude itself from a lawsuit, considering that the financially weaker party needed resources to keep fighting for a greater cause."

For the Lins e Silvas to accuse me of pressing this case for the sake of money rather than my love for Sean was both ludicrous and insulting. For them to file charges against me, demanding that I pay them damages for their sullied name, was beyond the pale.

Yet the court in Brazil entertained the charges, forcing me to incur still more expenses to defend myself against them. Listening to the Brazilian prosecutor describe the charges against me—that I had hired a helicopter to harass and stalk the kidnappers' families by hazing their homes—I got the impression that even the prosecutor was somewhat embarrassed to make the case. When he asked me about the helicopter, I answered truthfully, "I have no idea what you are talking about." The case dragged on for months, and eventually was dismissed.

FOLLOWING MY APPEARANCE on *Today* and my return trip to Brazil, Mark succeeded in stepping up our media campaign. He booked me for interviews with Dr. Phil McGraw and Greta Van Susteren, and orchestrated a letter to then senator Barack Obama, who was in the heat of a campaign himself, running for the presidency. Apparently somebody in the Obama campaign took the time to check out my story, because Senator Obama wrote back, "The United States is working to pursue Sean's return under the Hague Convention on the Civil Aspects of International Child Abduction." It was similar to the responses I had received from New Jersey senators Jon Corzine and Frank Lautenberg, and congressmen Rush Holt and Frank Pallone. But would any of them be effective? At that time, I could never have imagined that the future president of the United States might one day play a role in helping to bring Sean home.

One of the truly special media connections we made was with Bill Handelman, a kindly gentleman and journalist for the *Asbury Park Press,* one of the more popular local newspapers on the New Jersey coast. A former sportswriter, Bill was a bright guy with a big heart. The story of Sean's abduction touched him deeply, and after a front-page story on Sean and me, Bill was first in line when I had news of any kind to present to the public. When Bill first interviewed me at my house, he was already fighting a losing battle with kidney cancer. Nevertheless, he felt compelled to tell the story of Sean's kidnapping and the subsequent miscarriages of justice we endured. Bill and I talked frequently and became close friends. He passed away in June 2010; he was sixty-two years of age. I wish he could have met Sean.

Also, for the first time, a magazine in Brazil was willing to break the stranglehold the Lins e Silvas had imposed on the media in that country. Dorrit Harazim, who wrote for *Piaui* magazine, a publication similar to *The New Yorker*, interviewed me and then wrote a five-thousand-word feature, "A Father in a Foreign Land," in which she boldly told the story of Sean's abduction. The response from her readers was one of shock. They were appalled that such a thing could happen in their country, but apparently not surprised.

We hoped that Harazim's efforts might encourage other reporters to look more closely at our case and to increase public awareness about it in Brazil. Few journalists in Brazil were willing to oppose the Lins e Silvas, but an undercurrent of disgust was rife among those who knew the truth. I believed it would be only a matter of time until, like a seething volcano under enormous pressure, one small crack would allow the whole thing to blow sky high.

Following Harazim's lead, a legal publication and Web site in Brazil, *Consultor Juridico*, ran a 3,500-word story detailing how the case had landed in the Brazilian judicial system. The pressure mounted.

Perhaps the sudden media interest opened some eyes at the U.S. embassy in Brazil. I was out on my boat with clients the week before Thanksgiving when I received a telephone call from Clifford Sobel, the U.S. ambassador to Brazil. A good man, and an often mentioned potential candidate for the U.S. Senate, Ambassador Sobel became proactive and took a special interest in getting the U.S. embassy in Brasília to exert as much pressure as possible to get Sean back to New Jersey.

I was surprised to receive the ambassador's call, but extremely grateful. He reassured me that they were working on my case and that we had "the full support of the United States." I wasn't sure what that meant, but I expressed my appreciation to him. He reiterated that this was a clear-cut child abduction under the terms of the Hague treaty, and he emphasized to me that he understood how every week must feel like an eternity after four years of fighting to get Sean home. "It is a priority for the embassy to have this remedied," he assured me. I thanked him for his call and returned to my fishing clients.

On December 1, 2008, Dr. Phil McGraw conducted a brief but hard-hitting television interview with me discussing the events since Bruna had died. The *Dr. Phil* show was syndicated throughout the world, so I hoped that someone somewhere might see it and be able to help me. Steve and Karen Bott, two friends of Bruna's and mine, were also interviewed, and they expressed their total surprise at Bruna's actions. Dr. Phil was outraged at the lack of response on the part of the Brazilian courts, and he asked Tricia Apy, also on the broadcast, what could be done. She encouraged his viewers to contact their elected officials and the U.S. State Department, Office of Children's Issues. Many did. The pressure was building.

Anytime I did an interview, I always tried to make the point that Sean and I were not the only parent and child victimized by international child abductors. I would tell how nearly three thousand American children were known to have been abducted. My situation may have been one of the most visible at that time, but we were merely one instance in the greater tragedy. Indeed, since Sean's abduction, more than sixty other children had been spirited away to Brazil by their own parents or relatives. This problem was a worldwide tragedy, and each year the number of abducted children and left-behind families was growing.

On Saturday, December 13, I joined Wendy, Mark, and a small group of demonstrators organized by our Web site to pass out flyers in front of the Brazilian consulate in midtown New York. At first, I felt a little awkward out there on the sidewalk distributing flyers to strangers as they walked by. But it didn't take much to remind me that while most people were busy Christmas shopping or getting ready for Hanukkah, I was getting ready to endure another joyless holiday season without my son. That motivated me to get a flyer into the hands of every person who happened by. Most people took the flyers; some crumpled them up and tossed them in the nearest trash can; but others paused to read the information, and a few stopped to talk about the case. I don't know how much good it did, but it was another bit of ratcheting up the pressure on Brazil to do the right thing.

The Lins e Silvas were powerful people, and I often wondered how far their influence reached. While we were conducting the rally in front of the Brazilian consulate, a South American reporter was interviewing me when her cell phone rang. "Hold on," she said, as she took the call. A voice on the reporter's phone threatened her with serious consequences if she continued the interview. Suddenly, her face turned white and she stopped the interview immediately and disappeared. Apparently, someone inside the consulate had contacted the Lins e Silvas about the rally and the interview, resulting in the threatening call to the reporter warning her to stay away from this story. I never heard from her again.

Jeff Pegues of WABC-TV covered the demonstration as a follow-up to the segment he'd done in September. People were increasingly interested in what was going on with the case. Word was getting out, although it was a painfully slow process.

I struggled through another holiday season without Sean, trying desperately to smile, to keep from being a downhead around Mom and Dad, my sister and her family, and Wendy and her kids. My house remained dark throughout the holidays; I put up no Christmas decorations; I lit no menorahs. To protect myself from becoming deeply depressed, and to help overcome my disappointment at not being able to celebrate the holidays with Sean, I focused my efforts on helping NBC get the home videos and photographs of him that they needed for the special they were working on. About that time, I received word that the *Dateline* feature would air in late January 2009. Rather than being one of several stories on the show, the producers had decided to do an hour-long special on our case alone. This could be the big break we needed.

13

=== **■ ■ ■** ===

Date with Destiny

DATELINE NBC's PROGRAM TOLD IN DETAIL THE STORY OF SEAN'S abduction, my struggle to get him home, and the uphill battle I still faced. Meredith Vieira hosted the entire program, which included background material on my early modeling career, how Bruna and I had met and married, and how she left with Sean. Meredith again interviewed me, asking poignant, probing questions that allowed me to make my case.

At the close of the program, Vieira asked the toughest question of all: "Does it ever cross your mind that you won't see your son again?"

"I can't think that," I replied quietly. "No, no; this is so wrong on every level. He's got to come home."

"How can any of this be possible?" Meredith asked.

"It's sick. Who can help me? Who can help? I just need help."

Meredith looked at me intently. "How much do you miss that little boy?"

"I miss him every second of every day . . . and in my sleep. The time we had together was the most special . . . precious moments . . ." I paused momentarily, feeling my emotions getting the better of me, struggling to maintain my composure. "I can never describe the love I have for my son."

The program aired on Friday night, January 30, 2009. Approximately six million people viewed it, many of whom were becoming aware of my plight for the first time.

The number of people who signed our online petition encouraging government officials to bring Sean home swelled from three thousand to more than twenty thousand almost overnight. Soon that number bumped up to more than sixty-five thousand. The effects were felt all the way to Brazil. Patricia Suarez Lomego, a brave woman who worked with the Brazilian Central Authority, the body in charge of dealing with Hague Convention cases and implementing the decisions, later told Ricardo that she received more than one thousand e-mails as a result of the *Dateline* interview. She was vilified in her own country for her advocacy of justice in our case, while people all over the world bombarded her in-box wanting to know why Sean Goldman was not being sent home.

I received innumerable e-mails and telephone calls as well, expressing support. Suddenly, it seemed as though the entire world knew about Sean and me.

In Brazil, the Lins e Silva and Ribeiro families still attempted to stifle any news regarding Sean, but once the *Dateline* special aired, it was almost impossible for them to keep the information under wraps any longer.

Two people watching were particularly touched by my plea for help: New Jersey congressman Chris Smith and his wife, Marie. They were appalled at the injustice of my situation. At eleven o'clock the night the *Dateline* piece aired, while the credits were still rolling, Congressman Smith was on the phone to one of his staff members.

We had previously contacted Congressman Smith's office, urging him to get involved. Mark DeAngelis and I had both spoken to his chief of staff in New Jersey, but the conversations had yielded no fruit. There were a number of issues, we were informed, that might make it difficult for Smith to get involved, not the least of which was the fact that I did not live in the New Jersey district he represented in Congress, but in an adjoining one. My congressman was Rush Holt, whose office Mark and I had also contacted, with much the same response we had received from our other representatives.

WHEN CONGRESSMAN SMITH first heard about our case, he went to our Web site and was moved by the story. He placed a phone call to the American ambassador to Brazil to express his concern. Yet because of established protocol between representatives, he felt this was something for Congressman Holt to handle.

The day before the *Dateline* interview aired, Mark had e-mailed Congressman Smith's office and informed them that the network was planning to do a one-hour feature on Sean and me. "If you get a chance, please tune in," Mark urged.

As it turned out, the congressman's chief of staff and the congressman and his wife all watched the program on Friday night. At around midnight, Mark received an e-mail from Smith's New Jersey office, saying that Smith and his chief of staff had indeed watched the program and asking if I could come in to their district office for a meeting.

On Monday morning, February 2, Tricia Apy, Mark DeAngelis, and I drove to Whiting, New Jersey, to meet with Congressman Smith. Standing to greet us as we were ushered into his office, Smith was dressed in a dark suit with a crisp button-down blue-and-white-striped shirt. His bright blue eyes sparkled, and his sincere facial expressions highlighted every word, creating a first impression of a man who was friendly and approachable, yet somehow intense. After a few perfunctory conversational tidbits, we seated ourselves in the congressman's office and got down to business.

Congressman Smith had just begun his fifteenth term of office, thirty years of serving the people of New Jersey in the U.S. House of Representatives. He is a devout Roman Catholic, so faith and family are not mere campaign slogans for him; they are integral parts of his life. Growing up in a strong working-class family, he was taught the value of hard work. As an athlete, he played soccer, wrestled, and ran track and cross country, so he had an appreciation for come-from-behind efforts. In fact, he was known for often rooting for the underdog.

A senior member of the House Foreign Affairs Committee, Smith strongly advocated pro-life issues, veterans' affairs, religious freedom, assistance for families dealing with autism, umbilical cord and bone marrow stem cell research, and Lyme disease education and research. Congressman Smith was well-known on Capitol Hill for sponsoring legislation in support of human rights, whether that meant fighting against human sex trafficking or campaigning to have abducted American children brought home. In 2008 he had willingly gone far beyond the extra mile in his efforts to rescue two American girls who had been visiting their grandparents in the Republic of Georgia when war broke out there. Thanks to his efforts, the children were now safely back in the United States.

Of course, I wasn't aware of all this when we first met. Mark and I knew that Smith was a champion for human rights, which was one reason why we had tried to get his attention and help for some time. Other than that, I just thought he was a really nice guy. More important, he had expressed a willingness to help, and he had the where-withal to do it. The congressman later joked that he had no choice but to help—after watching the *Dateline* special, his wife got him in a headlock and said, "What are you going to do to help this guy? He needs your help."

"So today I'm just obeying my wife," Smith quipped, setting us all at ease.

To enable the congressman to better understand some of the issues of the case that *Dateline* had not touched upon, and to outline some of the help I thought we needed from an elected official, I had written a letter to him over the weekend and had sent it on ahead. The congressman, too, came prepared. When he first heard my story, he talked with Ambassador Sobel, and he was convinced that Bruna's abduction of Sean, and the subsequent retention of Sean in Brazil by her family members, was one of the clearest violations of the Hague treaty that anyone in the State Department could remember. He also seemed certain that I had done everything by the book, taking the proper steps in the correct manner to have Sean returned. "I've read your letter," he said, looking straight at me, "and I thought it was well done. Let's talk about what I can do to help."

I briefly reviewed my story, hitting many of the details the congressman already knew from watching the *Dateline* feature. I told him of Bruna's initial demands, my trips to Brazil, the refusal of the abductors to let me see Sean or even talk with him by phone after Bruna's death, the broken promises, and the failure of the Brazilian courts to ensure that I would be able to see my son. I told the congressman that another hearing was scheduled for that very week.

"Fill me in," Congressman Smith probed. "There's something going on this week, some kind of hearing that you are going back to Brazil to attend?"

"Yes," Tricia Apy replied, and reviewed the tortured legal history of the case in both countries while Congressman Smith patiently listened. "There is a federal court hearing to decide possible visitation issues for David, and believe it or not, they are still trying to decide whether the case should be adjudicated in federal courts or in their state courts." Tricia explained that the abductors were pressing for the case to be heard in state court, where they could turn it into a custody case and not a treaty case. This would get around the obligations of the Hague Convention, which demanded Sean's return—which would be a given if the case were adjudicated in the federal court. That the Brazilian judicial system even allowed the competency issue to be considered was scandalous.

We were barely five or ten minutes into our meeting when Congressman Smith looked me straight in the eye and said, "When do we go? The next time you go to Brazil, I will go with you. We will drive in the same car, go to the same places. Wherever you go, I will go; wherever I go, you go with me. We'll be like brothers."

I could not believe my ears. I literally became so emotionally overwhelmed that I stood up, reached over, and shook his hand, saying,

"Thank you! You have no idea what that means to me, to hear this from someone like you. You cannot imagine what this means to me."

The congressman's expression grew solemn and he said, "I'm sorry I wasn't here sooner."

I looked right back in his eyes and said, "I'm glad you're here now."

For the next two hours we discussed the various aspects of my case, and at the end of the meeting, Congressman Smith and I made plans to meet in Brazil on Thursday of that very week. The congressman would fly from Washington, D.C., to São Paulo, while I took the all-too-familiar late-night flight out of Newark. From there, we'd travel together to Brasília to attend the visitation hearing.

Before we left his office, Congressman Smith reiterated his astounding commitment to me. "I'll do anything you want me to do," he said. "I'll carry your bags, but bottom line, you are the quarterback. I don't want to do anything without your permission, because this is your son. This is all about you. This is all about bringing Sean home."

I left the congressman's office just blown away. "Hopeful" had been my answer to every interviewer's question about how I sized up my situation, but for the first time since Bruna's initial devastating phone call, we had attracted an ally and a champion for the cause who could and would make a difference.

I was still filled with anxiety, though, the same way I had been during every other trip I'd made to Brazil since the abduction, but I felt grateful that Congressman Smith had offered to support me. I had been so desperate for someone to champion my cause for so long; his presence could only help. I had no idea what it all might mean, or to what extent he was willing to put his name on the line for an eight-year-old boy and his dad, but as I packed the usual assortment of toys and pictures that I'd carried with me on past trips, I had real hope that I might get to show these things to Sean.

By Wednesday, Congressman Smith submitted House Resolution 125 on the floor of the U.S. House of Representatives, calling on the Brazilian government to "immediately discharge all its duties under the Hague Convention" and "to obtain the return of Sean Goldman."

Congressman Smith pushed to get the resolution passed quickly. "We need to raise the level of visibility," he said. Not only did he and his staff succeed in readying the resolution in Congress, they also collaborated with U.S. Senator from New Jersey Frank Lautenberg, whose staff was already working on a Senate resolution. We had met with Senator Lautenberg in his offices approximately two weeks before the *Dateline* piece had aired on January 17. Although the senator was dealing with the amazing circumstances of the crash landing of the U.S. Airways jet into the Hudson River, he had taken time to sit down with his New Jersey and Washington, D.C., staffs to discuss what strategy to employ in addressing Sean's abduction for what it was becoming—an issue between two countries. He offered to call Brazilian and other Latin American diplomats, and in particular to work with us in getting the U.S. Senate to support our efforts.

Senator Lautenberg and his colleague from New Jersey, Senator Robert Menendez, sent a letter to Brazilian president Luiz Inácio Lula da Silva, asking him to examine the case and take the appropriate action to reunite Sean and me. Senator Lautenberg assured Congressman Smith that before the week was over, their resolution would be on the floor of the U.S. Senate, and it was. We suddenly had caught the attention of politicians from across the spectrum.

As planned, Congressman Smith flew to Brazil on Thursday, February 5. To this day, I believe the decision by him to get on that airplane and fly from Washington to Brasília was a pivotal turning point in Sean's life and in mine.

The following day, in a tense, grueling court session that ran nearly six hours long, my attorney wrangled with the attorneys representing the abductors in Brasília's Superior Court of Justice over the circumstances under which I would be allowed to see my kidnapped son. Originally Ricardo sought to discuss *how* Sean would be returned to me rather than *if* Sean would be returned, but when our opponents refused to consider that question, the heated arguments turned toward provisional visitation. Although the debate was ostensibly about visitation opportunities, it was clear from the outset that the abductors were attempting to turn it into one about who was better equipped to raise Sean, me, the boy's father, or João Paulo Lins e Silva, the man who, with the help of Bruna's parents, was retaining my child illegally.

To make things even more intense, this was the first time that João Lins e Silva actually showed up for a hearing I attended. Throughout the day, the second kidnapper sat right across the table from me. He did not speak directly to me and rarely made eye contact, although, in my peripheral vision, I noticed him glancing at me several times during the hearing. On those few occasions when he had to look at me, he simply glowered.

He did, however, cast plenty of aspersions and provocative statements my way as he addressed the court. In one of his more repugnant utterances, he looked at me and said, "Just because you are a sperm donor doesn't make you a father."

I kept my eyes trained on the judge, and refused to respond to the pettiness of the kidnapper's crackpot statements. Instead, I spoke to the black-robed judge in calm, reserved tones.

Congressman Smith attended the hearing along with me, and although he was not technically a character witness, his very presence in the back of the courtroom seemed to enrage my opponents. The kidnapper's father, Paulo Lins e Silva, was also in the courtroom, sometimes conversing with his son and his lawyers, at other times in the back of the room, pacing and talking on his cell phone; the man was apoplectic. Officials from the U.S. embassy in Brasília and the U.S. consulate in Rio were in attendance as well. For the first time, an interpreter was provided for me.

At various points throughout the proceedings, tensions in the room rose to the boiling point, but I remained calm and forthright in my presentation of the truth. For instance, I showed the judge some of my pre-abduction family photos and read some cards Bruna had given me on past birthdays and Father's Days. João Paulo Lins e Silva interrupted, calling them meaningless cards that probably were never given to me by Bruna. He claimed that I didn't care about Sean, that

Bruna and I never loved each other, and other outright lies in an attempt to incite me to lose my temper. Instead, I looked directly up at the presiding judge and said, "I'm not here to fight this guy or to defend myself from his slanderous allegations and lies. I'm here to be with my son, Your Honor. I need your help as a matter of law to make this happen, please."

It was a long, draining, exasperating day. At the close of the session, the judge warned me emphatically not to speak to anyone about the case. Congressman Smith, however, was under no such gag order, and he spoke freely to the media outside the courtroom, and fielded phone interviews from back in the States. Before he talked to anyone about the case, though, he always conferred with me to see if I thought the interview would be helpful. "You're the quarterback," he reminded me.

Meanwhile, as I was struggling to control my anger and maintain my dignity during the visitation hearing, back in Washington, the news that Congressman Smith had flown to Brazil with me in an effort to bring Sean home was having a ripple effect. Mark DeAngelis received a call on his cell phone at about 10:30 AM from a woman named Leslie Potter, who was Congressman Rush Holt's district director in New Jersey. In an anxious voice, she told him that she needed David Goldman's phone number in Brazil because Secretary of State Hillary Clinton wanted to speak with him right away. Mark later said, "It was at that moment when I realized that we had finally succeeded in getting the case to the highest levels of the U.S. government. And it never would have happened had it not been for Congressman Chris Smith."

As elated as I was that we had finally gotten the attention of some movers and shakers in government, the potential call from the secretary of state soon paled in comparison to the results of the hearing. Following the prolonged visitation hearing, the court had granted me permission to see my son!

14

Father and Son

THE VISIT WAS SCHEDULED FOR THE FOLLOWING MONDAY, AGAIN at the Ribeiros' residence, which was ostensibly also the residence of João Lins e Silva and Sean. When the visitation was ordered, the officials from the Brazilian Central Authority were overjoyed that the agreement reached in the Superior Court would lead to Sean and me reuniting. They seemed elated, as though their job was done, since I had finally been granted access to my son. Lins e Silva dared not thwart the visit this time; too many eyes were watching.

I couldn't refrain from expressing the feelings in my heart. In a very serious manner, I looked as many people in the room as possible dead in the eye, including the officials from the BCA, and stated, "Although I'm very grateful for everyone's help that will hopefully allow Sean and me to visit with each other, this is not over." I hadn't come merely to visit my abducted son; I had come to bring him home.

ON SUNDAY, FEBRUARY 8, Congressman Smith and I had some free time, because we could not get meetings with government officials that day, so we attended church together at Dom Bosco Sanctuary, a cathedral in Brasília. It felt good to be in a place where, at least for a short time, I could let down my guard. Throughout this ordeal, I had had to remain controlled and focused. I had been tested at every turn, constantly castigated verbally and emotionally by the other side, who hoped that I would crack up or give up. They would have loved for me to have allowed that "red ball of fury" to take over, but I wouldn't let it; I couldn't. So, once inside the church, I dropped my "armor" and became quite emotional. My feeling of release wasn't because of confronting the kidnapper face-to-face. It was the culmination of suffering the unbearable agony of the previous four and a half years and knowing that my son was in such a bad place, with neither of his parents to comfort him, held by people who were too self-absorbed and cruel to see or care about the damaging effects their actions were having on him. My prayers soon turned to sobs, then a flood of tears and bellows from deep within me.

Congressman Smith sat several rows behind me and quietly prayed. I knew he was there, and his faith bolstered mine. We spent several hours praying together and listening to a choral presentation. In one of the songs of praise, which was sung in Portuguese, it sounded as though the singers were saying, "Pai Sean." I took great comfort in the song, and also in "The Chaplet of Divine Mercy," a series of prayers pleading for mercy. A number of people in the church noticed me and offered to pray for me. I gladly accepted.

NERVOUS DOES NOT even begin to describe how I was feeling as Ricardo, the court officials, and Congressman Smith and I pulled up in front of the address where supposedly I would find Sean waiting to see me for the first time in more than four and a half years. I told myself to remain calm. Sean needed to see me as his father who loved him, and to see that our relationship was natural, true, and good. I homed in on one thought: my love for my son. I let Ricardo and the embassy officials handle all the other details. We had learned since my first attempt to visit Sean that João Paulo Lins e Silva most likely did not even live at this address. It was a gated condominium complex in which Bruna's parents, Silvana and Raimundo Ribeiro, resided.

Considering the ridiculous legal shenanigans previously foisted upon me, the visitation agreement seemed tilted remarkably in my favor this time—at least it was so on paper. The agreement gave me the right to visit Sean from 8:00 AM to 8:00 PM every day, every time I traveled to Brazil, so long as I gave the Ribeiros' representatives seventy-two-hours' notice. (João Paulo Lins e Silva immediately petitioned the federal court that I should be allowed to see my son only on March 12 and 13, 2009, and then only after 6:00 PM, because of Sean's school commitments. The federal court of Rio dismissed the ludicrous request, saying that missing two days of school would not cause nearly as much harm to Sean as not being able to reestablish a relationship with me.)

More important, the agreement placed no restrictions on me, and did not forbid me to take Sean out or to be seen in public with him. Nor did it require supervision by a third party during the visitation, although our opponents pressed to have Sean's therapist present during my initial visit.

The night before my visit with Sean, I hadn't been able to sleep. The anticipation was too great. As morning dawned, I was very anxious; I didn't know what to expect, but I hoped and prayed for the best. Despite the open visitation granted to me by the Brazilian court, João Lins e Silva and the Ribeiros refused to allow Sean to leave the grounds of their complex. As much as it irritated me that we were once again being jerked around by these people, I consented. We were this close; I didn't want the relatives to whisk Sean off to some other location, as they had done previously. Moreover, the Ribeiro camp kept insisting that Sean's psychologist observe our visit. Again, as distasteful as I found any concessions to their demands, if it meant seeing my son, I would tolerate the therapist.

On Monday, February 9, I was finally permitted to see my son. I was anxious, very anxious. Sean and I met at the swimming pool in the condo complex where Ray and Silvana lived. It wasn't the ideal situation. We were smack in the middle of all the units, and I felt sure that everyone in the place—including Sean's grandparents—was glaring at us from behind tinted windows, but after four and a half years, I was thrilled to be able to see Sean anywhere. I sat down at a table by the pool and waited for him to appear, another insulting condition. I wasn't allowed in the building to call on my own child. Finally I saw him come out of the building and head toward the area in which I was waiting. He walked up the steps to the pool area and our eyes met. At that moment nothing else mattered. I restrained myself from sprinting over to him and squeezing him. Instead, I stood slowly, wearing a great big smile, and we met halfway. We hugged like any father and son would. I had to fight back the tears as I stepped back to gaze at my son. He was eight years old now, and had grown so much. His hair had lightened a bit and wafted gently over his forehead, but the bright eyes and the contagious smile were still there.

We walked back over to the table where I'd been sitting, where I had photos, candy, and gifts for him. His therapist, employed by the Ribeiros, hovered close to Sean and was practically attached to him at the hip. Sean looked at the photos, and then his bright eyes looked directly into mine. With a twisted face, he asked one of the most horrific questions I'd ever heard. "Where have you been all this time?"

Simply hearing the words come out of his mouth broke my heart all over again, but I knew I had to take the high road. "It's complicated," I told him. "The courts made things very difficult. I've actually been here many times to see you, buddy. Pop-Pop Barry came, Grandma Ellie came, Cousin George came. We all came to see you. I came many times, but things never worked out. But we're together now, so let's have some fun."

Sean looked at the therapist, who said, "I know, Sean. Two different stories. It's confusing."

"Yes, it's confusing," I said, "and we won't be able to understand everything right away, but we're together now, and we have a lot of catching up to do." The anguish in his face was painful enough to see. There was no use in explaining any further. I didn't say a word to Sean about the actions of Lins e Silva or his grandparents, who had denied me access to him all these years—in clear violation of the international treaty signed by Brazil years earlier—let alone a violation of our rights as father and son.

"Do you play basketball?" Sean asked.

I quickly snapped out of my reverie. "Sure," I said.

"Do you want to play?"

"Sure thing. Let's play some basketball."

Sean went back to the condo to get a basketball. While he was gone, I wondered if he would return. He did.

We walked over to the basketball court—well, actually, the therapist walked with Sean to the basketball court, and I walked behind them, followed by Congressman Smith and Karen Gustafson de Andrade, an official from the U.S. embassy.

Sean tossed me the ball, and we played a game of Around the World, matching each other shot for shot. We paused long enough for Congressman Smith to shoot a photograph of us both smiling together as I threw my arm around Sean. He didn't flinch; instead he nestled against me.

After a while, Sean was tired, hungry, and thirsty. I was told at the hearing that Sean and I would be able to sit down and have lunch together, but when lunchtime rolled around, Lins e Silva and Sean's grandparents had other plans. They had instructed Sean to go back to their condo to have lunch and relax without me.

Not wanting to upset Sean or cause any turmoil, I said, "It's okay, buddy. Go eat and I'll come back in the afternoon and we'll go swimming."

We said our "see ya laters" with a hug, and I gave him a kiss on his head. Trying to be as calm and normal as possible, I assured him that I would be back. As I left the complex, though, I was furious, thinking, *These people are still interfering at every single turn.*

Nevertheless, Sean and I had been together; we had played ball; he knew me, he remembered me. We had been father and son. Our bond was not broken, despite the conditions imposed by the Ribeiros. I loved my little buddy with every ounce of my being, and what was so sweet and joyous to me was that my little buddy still loved me.

▪ ▪ ▪

When I returned in the afternoon, the guards would not allow us to drive inside the complex gates. Silvana had complained that we could grab Sean and put him in the diplomatic vehicle and whisk him away to the embassy. We parked on the street and walked into the compound.

Once again I sat at the table by the pool and waited for Sean to arrive. The grandparents seemed to be in no rush for their lunch to conclude. Eventually, after about twenty minutes, Sean came back downstairs again. This time he was accompanied by a man who looked to be in his thirties. *Who is this guy?* I thought. *What are they doing now?*

The man introduced himself as Cadu. "I'm Sean's friend," he said. *Sean's friend?*

"Let's go swimming!" Sean called. We jumped into the pool like two excited friends, and I was glad the pool water obscured the tears I could no longer contain. We laughed and splashed and enjoyed being together.

We were no sooner in the water, however, than Cadu jumped into the pool as well. He kept trying to maneuver his body in between Sean and me. The man who described himself as "Sean's friend" tried to stay close to Sean, usually within a foot or two of him, sometimes closer. It was obvious that he was a plant, intentionally attempting to disrupt our visit. Knowing that we were being watched, I chose to ignore the man, awkwardly moving around him without saying a word each time he positioned his body between Sean and me.

Okay, I thought, *if he's trying to antagonize me, I'm not taking the bait.* I grabbed a beach ball and tossed it to Cadu. "Let's play catch," I said. I was there to be with Sean, and I wasn't going to let anything or anyone change that. If anyone would be the odd man out, it would be Cadu.

From an inconspicuous position nearby, Karen and Congressman Smith witnessed the whole thing. The congressman turned on my Flip video camera, clearly capturing in brief segments the actions of the intruder. The congressman came over and introduced himself to the man in the pool, squeezing his hand quite firmly as he did. "And who are you?" the congressman asked.

"I'm Sean's friend," the lug repeated.

"At your age? You're the friend of an eight-year-old boy?"

We learned that the man was a lawyer and an associate of the Lins e Silvas and Ribeiros sent to observe Sean's and my visit.

Eventually, the antagonist appeared to feel foolish, and he climbed out of the pool. He continued to watch us closely, though, and I could hear him talking on a cell phone while Sean and I played. He was speaking in Portuguese, so I couldn't easily understand him, but I could guess to whom he was speaking.

One of the main things I was happy about—and an aspect of our visit that Sean's grandparents were no doubt angry about—was that when Cadu climbed out, and Sean and I started playing with the beach ball, we were immediately in our own world. Like most boys his age, it was only a matter of minutes before Sean was wrestling with me in the water, hanging all over me, and climbing on my back. We threw that beach ball back and forth, and Sean mischievously tried to bop me when I wasn't looking. I tried not to show any surprise, giving the impression that this was all perfectly normal, but internally, my heart was pounding with joy. Despite all the indoctrination Sean had received from his grandparents and Lins e Silva, telling him what a bad person I was, my son was not at all shy around me. Within minutes of being in the water he was having a great time playing with me. He called me "Dad," and "Dada," and I called him "Son." I didn't make a big deal about our closeness; I simply acted as though his response to me was completely natural—which it would have been had we not been forcibly separated for the past four years. Inside, I was ecstatic; I felt as though fireworks were going off in my heart and mind.

Sean especially seemed to have missed my hugs. At one point he said, "Hug me with maximum force."

"Maximum force?"

"Yes, hug me with maximum force," he said with a broad smile. So I hugged him and squeezed him tightly. Sean squealed with delight. "Again," he said when I released him. "Maximum force!" So I squeezed him tightly to me again. Sean seemed to love it when I hugged him so tightly, and I have to admit, I didn't want those hugs to end.

A short while later, another boy jumped in the water and seemed on a mission to interfere. Sean and I acknowledged him and included him occasionally, but for the most part we kept to ourselves in the pool.

During the afternoon visit, I had brought food and drinks from the hotel so we could hang out and snack together when we got out of the pool. Sean especially loved Twizzlers, so I made sure I brought him a bunch of those.

We swam, played basketball, built a model robot, and looked at some family photos from Sean's years in New Jersey. Sean seemed to recall our home, some of his toys, his bedroom, and the Tom Sawyer "jungle" behind our house. He also remembered our cat, Tuey.

DESPITE THE RIBEIROS' attempts to impede Sean's and my visit, it was a fantastic few hours. I was with my son, and he clearly seemed to enjoy being with me. At the end of our time together, I walked him to the bottom of the steps leading away from the pool. We hugged, said so long, and I told him, "I love you, son. I'll see you here tomorrow." As we walked away in opposite directions, I stopped after a few steps and turned to watch Sean heading toward the building. At the same moment, he turned back to me and our eyes locked. We were father and son, and no one could deny us that. I was deeply grateful that after more than four years of separation, with little contact, and under extremely strained circumstances, our father-son bond had not been broken. Damaged, perhaps, but still intact.

I picked up my pictures and other items and prepared to go back to my hotel with Congressman Smith. I had hoped to take Sean with me, but due to the Ribeiros' and Lins e Silvas' insistence that he remain in their compound, I could not. Nevertheless, I felt good about how the visit had gone, and wanted to turn the clock ahead so I could come back to see him again sooner.

Congressman Smith noticed the strong father-son bond between Sean and me, and later confirmed what I felt. "From the moment you guys hugged," he told me, "it was obvious that this was as strong as a father-son bond could be."

He then had to fly back to Washington in time to vote on several important bills. I will always be grateful for the five days he took out of his busy schedule to be with me. During that time, we went from one government office to the next, speaking with Brazilian officials. To each person of influence we met, I showed the small collection of family photos and cards I carried with me. We even met with one of the Brazilian Supreme Court justices. She sat in her chambers, with pictures of Sean spread out on her table, and listened intently as I told my story. Congressman Smith sat through one meeting after another, hour after hour, in no hurry, as if he had nothing more important to do. To every Brazilian official we met, he urged, "You have to hear this man; you have to listen to him." He brought copies of the resolution he introduced in Congress and handed them out to every government official with whom we met. He was like Thomas Paine, the pamphleteer of old, passing out the resolution and letting the officials know "We are well aware of what's going on here, and we are not going away until justice is accomplished. There's only one parent here, and that is David."

As the congressman and I hugged good-bye, we promised to get together soon. I felt confident that Congressman Smith was returning home with a much greater appreciation for why I'd refused to give up on my son, and how harmful the continuation of this arrangement would be to Sean.

I could not have guessed, however, what a tremendous friend and advocate for Sean and me Congressman Smith would become over the next ten months. In public and behind the scenes, he constantly lobbied for our cause. Whether on the House floor, in private meetings with other legislators, in meetings with the Brazilian ambassador, or at the United Nations, he was relentless in his efforts. At times he joked that he had become my staffer, my press secretary. "I'm working for David, my fellow New Jerseyan," he often told reporters.

■ ■ ■

MY JOY OVER Sean's and my first visit was short-lived. The next day, Sean seemed much more cool and aloof. It struck me that the reason his demeanor toward me had changed overnight might be because he had been chastised for showing affection to me the day before. As the second visit progressed, Sean told me that his grandparents, especially his grandmother, had scolded and rebuked him for being so friendly to me the previous day. I was the "enemy," after all, and how dare he warm up to the enemy! They intentionally kept him up most of the night so he would be too tired to enjoy playing with me in the morning. They also excoriated him for calling me Dad.

When he came to meet me that second day, he called me David. He admitted to me, "I'm not allowed to hug you. I'm not allowed to say 'I love you,' and I'm not allowed to call you Dad."

His words broke my heart, but I knew they weren't coming from him. They were channeled through him from the people watching out the upstairs window.

At the risk of alienating my son and destroying all the good feelings we had experienced the day before, I wrapped him in my arms and looked into his clear eyes. "Look, Sean," I said gently, "I don't care what is going on up there." I nodded toward the Ribeiro apartment. "I am your father, and it's okay to call me Dad."

Sean did his best to comply with my instructions as well as the abductors' demands. For a while, he simply quit calling me anything. "Come here," he'd call, cutting himself short, to avoid addressing me purposely as Dad. I understood his struggle and didn't want to put him in an impossible situation, but I couldn't let the situation pass by unnoticed. I was his dad, and I wanted him to know that no matter what, I would always be his father and he would always be my son. Nothing he or anyone else said or did would ever keep me from loving him. Our relationship was based on "blood" and love, not court orders. That relationship required respect, despite the attempts of Sean's maternal grandparents and the Lins e Silvas to disparage me and spawn disrespect for me in his heart and mind.

During my second visit with Sean, he and I played board games at a table by the pool. How did I know where to start and what he might enjoy? Before going to see him, I had checked with some of the people at the embassy who had children around Sean's age. I asked Karen de Andrade, "What are some of the hot or trendy games that are popular among preteen kids in Brazil?" guessing that Sean might be aware of them. Karen made some good suggestions. I had also observed Wendy's kids back home; we sometimes played games together, and I noticed what they liked, so I took some of those kinds of games and toys, too.

All too soon, my few hours of "abductor-controlled" visitation with Sean came to an end. I hugged him close to my heart. "I love you, Sean," I told him. "I will always love you."

We walked over to the steps leading away from the pool area, neither of us saying a word. Just as before, our eyes connected; the father-son bond was there, and it hurt so badly that we simply couldn't go home together. I watched him leave, and waved as he stepped inside the building.

As euphoric as I felt at the close of day one of our visitation, my heart was breaking at the close of day two. Clearly his captors had intended to show him, by our confinement and the psychological pressure they were exerting on him, that my role as his dad had diminished and was nonessential, that at most I had become a guy who might come and visit now and then. They were trying to imply that because Sean and I were severely restricted in our expressions of love and our overall interaction, our relationship could reconnect only so far. I pulled strength from deep within myself and focused on my love for Sean. It was so difficult to walk out that gate, leaving my son behind. Yet I had no other legal options. I was not about to take the law into my own hands. I had never seriously considered doing so, and I certainly was not going to succumb to such a temptation now.

I returned to my hotel room and sent an e-mail to Mark DeAngelis.

Hi Mark,

Every time I close my eyes I see my son. In spite of the obstacles
they continue to put up even during the visits, my focus is on
the ultimate goal. The visits under the circumstances have been
beautiful. My son is calling me Dad, asking me to hug him with
"maximum force" and telling me he loves me. That part has
not gone out to the public or even in reports out of fear that if it
becomes public, they [his Brazilian family] will instruct Sean and
really force Sean not to behave like he did with extreme affection
and desire for his Dad.

I wanted you to know.

David

I couldn't sleep, so I watched the video clips of Sean and me playing in the swimming pool. I watched them over and over again. I was
determined that I would not rest until Sean and I could play like that in
our own pool, in our own backyard in New Jersey. The six hours I had
spent with him over those two days had zoomed by, but they were the
best six hours I'd had in a long, long time. Seeing him those days was
the most beautiful thing I'd experienced since his birth.

I STAYED IN Brazil a few more days because I was "encouraged" by
the court to undergo psychological tests. It was a requirement that
was being supported by the Brazilian Central Authority as well. Ostensibly, João Paulo Lins e Silva was to receive the same tests, and
Sean himself was to be examined. The psychological tests were really
not optional, but rather were insisted upon by the Brazilian authorities, since João Paulo Lins e Silva had petitioned the court stating
that I posed "a grave risk of harm" to Sean if we were reunited. I was
reluctant to consent to the tests, not because I feared the results but
because the Hague treaty does not require psychological verification.
Moreover, my attorneys feared that the tests could be some sort of
trap, a clever ruse to create a battery of psychological "facts," and the

information gleaned could perhaps be twisted, attempting to prove that I was in some way unfit to be Sean's father, thus manufacturing some "factual" basis to retain Sean. But I was Sean's father, his only real father, and he had been stolen from my life. Why was he not home with me? The answer to that question was the only one that mattered to me.

Tricia Apy expressed strong concerns that subjecting the treaty analysis to this psychological test could be used by the court as a pretext. Although Ricardo agreed, he was convinced that we had little choice; he contended that if we did not submit to the psychological exams, we would be giving our opponents a tool that they could leverage against us. Against my will, and with as many safeguards as my attorneys could place around the tests, I finally consented.

Apparently, the Lins e Silvas and Ribeiros were certain the psychological tests would work to their advantage. It turned out just the opposite. The Brazilian psychologists assigned by the federal court concluded that Sean had been the victim of "parental alienation." And in analyzing the strained visitations, they drew the same conclusion: that the pulling back by Sean could be attributed only to pernicious parental alienation inflicted upon him by his Brazilian grandparents and Bruna's husband. They noted, as well, after visiting the grandparents' and husband's homes that Sean did not possess a single picture of me, or any picture that showed the two of us together. In response to the psychological report, the Ribeiro and Lins e Silva families immediately hired their own psychologists in attempts to dispute the independent psychologists' findings. For their interrogation of Sean, they took him, without the permission of any court, or notice to me, to a mental institution outside Rio.

The findings of the three court-appointed psychologists became a powerful jackhammer that broke through one obstacle after another in the abductors' attempts to keep Sean in Brazil. Though written in Portuguese, the translations clearly stated that Sean was in "a wrongful retention," and that he "should be returned to the custody of the biological parent." Moreover, the three psychologists agreed that Sean had suffered "serious psychological damage" while being kept in Brazil. The technical term the psychologists used, "parental alienation," suggested that the Ribeiros' and Lins e Silvas' attempts to disparage me and undermine my parental role in Sean's life were causing devastating emotional effects in Sean. No doubt the longer he endured this sort of despicable treatment, the more chance of long-term damage—all the more reason why I had to get my son home.

15

Unexpected Help

BACK IN THE UNITED STATES AFTER SEEING SEAN, I MISSED HIM more than ever. But finally being with my son also motivated me, buttressing my will and making me even more determined not to give up the fight.

Congressman Smith had arranged a meeting with the Brazilian ambassador to the United States, Antonio Patriota, so upon hitting the ground, I didn't even go to my house, but continued on to Washington. The meeting with Ambassador Patriota did not begin well. I had brought with me the videos Congressman Smith had shot of Sean and me in the pool in Brazil, but the ambassador did not even want to see them. Congressman Smith worked the conversation around until the ambassador finally agreed to watch the videos. Meanwhile, I laid out all sorts of pictures of Sean on the coffee table in front of him. There was no use arguing with him, so I simply pointed to a picture of Sean and said to him, "This is my son." I looked the man in the eyes and said it again. "This is my son." I let that sink in for a long moment, and then said, "This is my son, and somebody who is not the father *has my son*."

The ambassador's demeanor softened, but at the end of the meeting, his only recommendation was that Congressman Smith not push the resolution he had presented in the House. Patriota clearly hoped that, with time, the problem would simply go away.

IT WAS NO less difficult to step inside my house when I returned from my trip. I knew now after being with Sean that he was no longer the little four-year-old boy whose pictures surrounded me at home. He was soon to be nine years old. I'd have to buy him all new clothes when he came back; I was looking forward to that. And we'd probably want to update his bedroom, now that he was soon to be entering preadolescence. From the day he left with Bruna, I kept Sean's room exactly as it was—with all his stuffed animals on his neatly made-up bed, his clothes hanging in the closet. His little shoes remained lined up nice and neat. His toys were in their baskets, all just as he had left them.

Nor did I remove his sandbox outside or the childproof gate at the top of the upstairs stairwell. One day, I believed, Sean would come home to me, and when he did, I wanted our home to be as close as possible to the way it was the day he departed for Brazil. As the only difference, I usually kept the door to his room closed. I couldn't bring myself to go in there unless absolutely necessary. The memories were simply too painful. Even in my bedroom, I'd often have flashbacks of Sean bounding in each morning, raising the blinds, and looking out the windows facing the river below. "Holy mackerel!" he'd exclaim, as if it were the first time he'd ever viewed the panorama in front of him. The natural setting was a source of great wonder to Sean, no matter the time of year.

"Oh, God, please bring him home," I prayed every night and every morning. "I miss him so much."

Fortunately for me, in some ways at least, I didn't have much time to sit around the house and mope. Upon my return from Brazil, I was soon shuttling back and forth from Tinton Falls to Washington and New York, attending meetings, doing interviews, traveling the media circuit, talking to anyone who might be able to exert pressure on the courts in Brazil.

It was a daunting task. In most interviews, I had only a few minutes to get my message across. I did my best to remain calm and articulate. One wrong word, one emotional outburst, could have sabotaged all of our efforts. This was serious business. I wasn't on tour, trying to promote a product; this wasn't like doing an ad for a magazine. I wasn't selling anything. Nor was this my idea of fun. I just wanted my son back.

All I could think about, as I lay awake each night with this great sense of urgency that had taken over my life, was: *Time is of the essence*. Each day that Sean was in Brazil played into his captors' hands; he was growing older and more accustomed to being there, and losing his memory of his time in the United States with his family and me.

IN LATE FEBRUARY and early March, two significant events took place that changed the playing field completely. First, in Brazil, the judiciary finally decided that our case belonged in the Brazilian federal court, not a state family court. Besides snatching the case away from Lins e Silva cronies, it put the decisions back under the Hague Convention, where they belonged.

Second, in the United States, after struggling for years to make any headway with our government, almost overnight Sean became front-page news in Washington. I'm convinced that one of the main reasons our case rose to such a high level was the behind-the-scenes efforts of former assistant secretary of state Bernard Aronson.

Bernie Aronson knew just how difficult negotiating with Latin America could be. He had served as the assistant secretary of state for inter-American affairs between 1989 and 1993 under President George H. W. Bush and during the first six months of President Bill Clinton's administration, longer than any other holder of that post. Bernie had played a crucial role in the successful negotiations to end the war in El Salvador, negotiated with the Soviet Union over Central American issues, and helped convince Brazil and Argentina to place their nuclear programs under international safeguards. Bernie understood how slow and unnecessarily cumbersome the Brazilian judicial

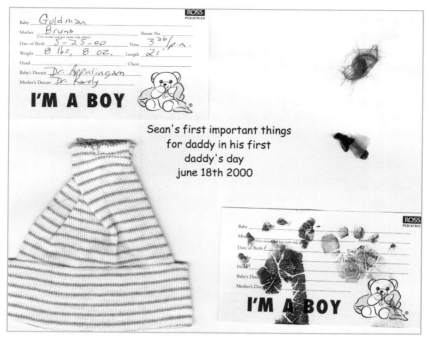

Bruna's gift to me on my first Father's Day.

Sean, me, and Bruna on vacation in Arizona, November 2000.

My birthday, July 2001.

Sean and me exploring the estuary behind
our house, summer 2001.

Boys' day at the amusement park, with Sean's best friend,
Matthew, and his father, Dan.

Sean playing in his turtle sandbox.

Sean sneaking a piece of cake on his second birthday.

Pop-Pop (Barry), Bruna, and me at Sean's second birthday party.

Bruna, Sean, and me, Halloween 2002.

Pop-Pop and his favorite grandsons, Coltrane (left) and Sean.

Me reading to Sean and two buddies at Tinton Falls Co-op Nursery School.

Sean and me playing in the leaves, fall 2002.

Thanksgiving at Aunt Leslie's. Me with (left to right) Addison, Coltrane, and Sean.

Sean the snow angel, winter 2003.

Sean and his friend Johnny, fall 2003.

Sean with his great-grandmother Phyllis.

A party at the Goldmans': (left to right) Phyllis, me, Bruna, Sean, Barry, and Grandma Ellie.

Sean and his friend Lily, Halloween 2003.

Sean's birthday at St. Leo's School, May 2004.

Sean riding a pony, 2004.

Sean and me on a roller coaster at the
Point Pleasant boardwalk, June 15, 2004,
the day before his abduction.

At St. Leo's Fair, the evening before
Sean's abduction.

Sean's and my first reunion in almost five years, at the Ribeiros' condo complex, Rio de Janeiro, Brazil, February 2009.

Later that same day in the condo pool.

Me testifying as a lead witness at a U.S. congressional hearing on international child abduction, Washington, D.C.

Congressman Chris Smith (right) at the same hearing.

A Lins e Silva/Ribeiro family "friend" interfering with and taping
a later visit between Sean and me in Brazil.

After notifying the media, João Paulo Lins e Silva and his attorney, Sergio Tostes,
drag Sean toward the U.S. consulate on the day of his release.

Thumbs up. Father and son, on their way home,
early afternoon on Christmas Eve 2009.

Five minutes after takeoff.

One hour after takeoff.

Sean at a New Jersey Nets game, January 2010.

(Left to right) Wendy, Jesse, me, Sean, Dylan, and Bernie Aronson at a baseball game in Washington, D.C., summer 2010.

(Left to right) Dylan, Sean, Zach, and Jesse at a Sandy Hook, New Jersey, beach concert, summer 2010 (guitarist Brian Kirk performing).

Best buddies on vacation, Puerto Aventuro, Mexico, Christmas 2010.

system could be, how it could be manipulated by powerful elites, and how hopeless and heartrending it could be for a lone American citizen like me seeking justice from the Brazilian courts.

Bernie regularly wrote op-ed articles about U.S. policy in Latin America for newspapers such as the *New York Times*, the *Washington Post*, and the *Wall Street Journal*. He maintained close ties to senior government leaders in both Latin America and the United States and testified before Congress on important issues concerning U.S. policy in Latin America.

Sitting at his home in Takoma Park, Maryland, on Friday, January 30, he was flipping television channels when he heard me mentioning Brazil on the *Dateline NBC* special. Bernie didn't know me or anything about me, but as he watched the program, which was already about halfway through the broadcast, he heard my plea. "I need help. I need someone to help me." He later told me that as a father, he was profoundly moved by my plea.

At about that same moment, in New Jersey, Congressman Chris Smith was watching the *Dateline* program and was equally moved by my plea. These were two men uniquely suited to helping me regain my son: Congressman Smith was the leading advocate for children in the Congress and the author of a major piece of legislation aimed at curbing child trafficking around the world; Bernie Aronson had served in the top diplomatic post for Latin America under two U.S. presidents. What are the odds that both men would view the same television program and feel compelled to volunteer for my cause? Maybe it was just a coincidence, but it seemed like something more. So many times in my struggle, people appeared just when I needed them, almost as if in answer to my prayers.

Another "coincidence" helped me immensely. Meredith Vieira, the *Dateline* correspondent who conducted the interview, was married to a longtime friend of Bernie's, Richard Cohen, a former producer for CBS News. In fact, Rich and Meredith, while still dating, had attended Bernie's wedding years before. After hearing my televised plea, Bernie reached out to Rich, asking him to pass a message to Meredith. If I thought he could help me, Bernie would be happy to do so. "Let me know how to get in touch with him, if he would like my help," Bernie wrote. Meredith made the connection, and passed the information along to me. Although I didn't even know where to start with someone of Bernie's stature, I was not about to turn away his offer of help. I had already seen the kind of effect that someone like Congressman Smith could have on the situation, simply by his presence.

I told Meredith yes, I would love to have Bernie Aronson's help, and she passed along my contact information. Bernie called me immediately. I told him I was coming to Washington in a few days to meet with Congressman Smith, so we agreed to meet at Chris Smith's office the night I arrived.

During that meeting I showed Bernie some of the swimming pool tapes from my initial visit with Sean in Brazil. He was visibly moved, as was Mary Noonan, Congressman Smith's chief of staff.

I told Bernie, "I just don't know what else to do. For the last several years, I've faced one painstakingly absurd obstacle after another by the Brazilian courts and this family."

Bernie believed it was crucial to ensure the recognition that this was a nation-to-nation issue and not merely an individual case. To do that the case had to go beyond the Office of Children's Issues of the Consular Affairs Department at State, and be elevated to the diplomatic level, where the U.S. government could make my case a major foreign policy issue between Brazil and the United States.

Although it was about 8:00 PM, Bernie called Tom Shannon, who held Bernie's old job, assistant secretary of state for Western Hemisphere affairs. Tom had served under Bernie years ago when Bernie was assistant secretary, and they had stayed in touch. When Condoleezza Rice, then national security adviser to President George W. Bush, was considering naming Tom as senior director for Latin America on the National Security Council staff at the White House, Bernie had put in a word with Rice for Tom. In President Bush's second term, when Condoleezza Rice became secretary of state, she asked Tom Shannon to move to State with her and become assistant secretary.

Bernie got Tom on the phone immediately and quickly briefed him on my story. The assistant secretary was vaguely aware of my case but had had no direct involvement in it. Bernie asked Tom if he would meet with me, and he agreed to do so the following morning. Frankly, I was amazed. I had been planning to return to Tinton Falls that evening, but I gladly tossed my schedule out the window for the chance to meet the highest-ranking U.S. government official responsible for Latin America. Mary Noonan kindly offered to let me stay with her family, and since I hadn't planned on a two-day trip, I went out and bought a shirt to wear to the next morning's meeting.

The next day Assistant Secretary Shannon and Deputy Assistant Secretary of State for Consular Affairs Michael Kirby joined us in Congressman Smith's office. After having me recount my story for Tom, Bernie said, "Tom, this has to be an issue in U.S.-Brazil relations." President Lula was scheduled to meet with President Obama at the White House in mid-March, their first direct encounter. To my amazement, Bernie asked Tom to do two things: one, to have Secretary of State Hillary Clinton raise my case when she met with her counterpart, Brazilian foreign minister Celso Amorim, to prepare for the meeting of the two presidents. Tom agreed that he would.

Bernie's second request of Tom was even more ambitious. "And can you have President Obama raise the issue with President Lula during their upcoming meeting?"

As I sat there listening, I was in awe at Bernie's boldness and the audacity of his requests. Here I was, a guy from Tinton Falls, New Jersey, and this man, whom I had only met the night before, was asking that the president of the United States and his secretary of state place Sean's return front and center in relations between the United States and Brazil. An individual case like mine is rarely broached during meetings between heads of state, much less during their first ever face-to-face encounter, when both nations want to start relations on a positive note. I understood that by any objective standard, as helpful as many people wanted to be, and as much as they were drawn to the heartrending aspects of Sean's and my story, our dilemma alone would not normally have risen to that level of attention at the State Department or the White House. Yet somehow, the right people kept stepping into place. It was almost as if somebody much bigger than us were orchestrating these relationships.

As kind and concerned as Tom appeared to be, he could not make any assurances that President Obama would raise the issue with President Lula. But he was willing to put his name on the line to encourage the president to do so.

Bernie was confident that Tom's commitment was solid, and that at least Hillary Clinton would raise my case with the Brazilian foreign minister. But he believed that the most important message that could be delivered would be president to president. To help cement that commitment, Bernie contacted Ambassador Robert Gelbard, a career foreign service officer with a long and distinguished résumé. Bob had served as U.S. ambassador to Bolivia when Bernie was assistant secretary of state. After Bob's tenure expired, Bernie asked him to come to Washington to serve as his principal deputy assistant secretary of state for inter-American affairs, the number two position in the bureau. Bob went on to serve as a special envoy to the Balkans and later as the U.S. ambassador to Indonesia. But a more recent addition to his résumé was serving as outside adviser on Latin America to the Obama presidential campaign. Bob had multiple contacts inside the administration, including Dan Restrepo, who now served as senior director of the Latin American Division of the National Security Council. Dan would be intimately involved in preparing President Obama's upcoming meeting with President Lula.

Bob immediately offered to help. Within days he had set up a meeting for me with Dan Restrepo at the Old Executive Office Building, part of the White House complex. At the same time, Senator Lautenberg and Congressman Smith kept pushing the resolutions through Congress, urging Brazil to "act with extreme urgency" to return Sean to me. Both the House and Senate resolutions passed unanimously days before President Lula's visit. The pressure was steadily growing.

On Friday, March 6, 2009, Bernie, Bob, and I met with Dan Restrepo and several of his aides. Never in a million years would I have envisioned meeting with a key member of the National Security Council staff to discuss my case in the context of the president's upcoming first meeting with the president of Brazil. Yet I was not one bit nervous. I remained focused and somehow knew exactly what to say and how to say it. After I recounted the facts, and pointed out that Brazil was holding a total of sixty-six abducted American children, Bernie asked Dan if the president would raise our case with President Lula. To his great credit, and once again to my astonishment, Dan assured us, insofar as he was able to, that President Obama would do just that.

ANDREA MITCHELL, NBC's chief diplomatic correspondent, was another point of contact. By then, Sean's story had been adopted by NBC. Andrea had been briefed on the case by Tricia, and to put the icing on the cake, Bernie urged Andrea to mention my case at the press conference following the meeting between Secretary of State Hillary Clinton and Brazilian foreign minister Celso Amorim.

As the two ministers emerged from their private meeting, they stepped to the podium, made brief comments, and opened themselves to questions from the dozens of reporters standing there. Then, as Secretary Clinton and Minister Amorim waved good-bye and started back inside, Andrea Mitchell saw her chance. "Madam Secretary, what about the Goldman child?" she shouted to Clinton.

The secretary later confirmed in a full interview with Mitchell that she had indeed raised the issue with Brazil's foreign minister. From Tom Shannon, we learned that Sean was the first item on Secretary Clinton's agenda when she conferred with Amorim. Consider for a moment just how astounding that is. The world economy was facing a global financial crisis. Brazil was the largest country in Latin America and the eighth largest economy in the world. Yet somehow my son, *Sean Goldman*, was the first issue on the table when the foreign ministers of the two countries held their first official meeting. I was overwhelmed with gratitude.

Now our strategy was to find every possible means to place Sean's case on the national agenda before the White House meeting between President Obama and President Lula. Bob Gelbard reached out to a contact at the *New York Times*, who ran a very positive story about Sean and Brazil's pattern of noncompliance on Hague abduction cases.

Bernie then contacted a friend at the *Washington Post*, who wrote a front-page story just days before President Lula's visit, stating that the Sean Goldman case was going to be a central issue in the discussions. The *Post* followed up with an editorial, "A Boy in Brazil," calling on the Obama administration to help resolve the matter, and for Brazil to "uphold the law." Our hope was that the media would feed upon the media. If NBC, the *New York Times*, the *Washington Post*, the House of Representatives, and the U.S. Senate were all highlighting Sean's story, we hoped other media outlets would pick up the drumbeat, too. And they did.

Days before Lula's scheduled visit, a reporter asked Brazilian foreign minister Amorim if he thought that President Obama would raise the case with President Lula. Amorim replied dismissively, "Oh, of course not; he's not going to." But Amorim was wrong.

Bernie met with the Brazilian ambassador to the United States to help bolster our position. His message was that this issue wasn't going to go away; if not resolved according to the Hague Convention, it was just going to escalate and damage Brazil's standing with the United States. "The law is very clear," Bernie reminded the ambassador. "Sean Goldman was retained wrongfully; the Hague Convention's stipulations have been met, and Brazil is going to pay an enormous price if you don't do the right thing here."

The Brazilian ambassador was sympathetic personally, and agreed that Sean should come home, yet he didn't think that the issue was as important as Bernie seemed to imply. But the Brazilian ambassador, like his foreign minister, misjudged the American commitment.

■ ■ ■

WHILE PRESIDENT LULA was getting ready to meet with President Obama, I was back in Brazil for another court ruling. On the Thursday before President Obama's scheduled Saturday meeting with President Lula, I received a call from an aide at the State Department informing me that Secretary Clinton wished to speak to me. In a few seconds, Secretary Clinton came on the line, and suddenly, there I was, David Goldman, regular guy from New Jersey, speaking with the U.S. secretary of state. Secretary Clinton and I spoke only briefly, but she was winsome and very kind, and wonderfully supportive. More important to me, we spoke as parent to parent.

"In the ongoing battle to return Sean to the United States, I want you to know, I have raised this repeatedly to Brazilian officials on several occasions," she told me. "I wanted you to know personally, parent to parent, we will maintain our concern and commitment to this case.

"And I feel strongly that once we are successful, and Sean is back home, we can't forget about all the other children who are being wrongly held."

"Thank you," I said. "I am under great pressure here. I just learned the [Ribeiro] family plans to rally in front of my hotel." The rally was scheduled to coincide with President Lula's visit with President Obama.

"That is deeply troubling," the secretary said. "And very unfortunate. Obviously, that should have absolutely no impact or influence on a court decision. And I think the best approach is just to ignore it, and if you have a spokesperson who is trying to help you with this very stressful situation, that they don't escalate it, and just make it clear that this is in no way reflective of what the facts are and what the best interests of Sean are."

"I don't have a spokesperson," I told Secretary Clinton. "I'm just one guy. I have the help of our consulate, Karen, who is wonderful. I just want to be with my son and bring him home. We're trapped in this complex in Rio where they have psychologists watching us. It's completely diminishing to us being father and son. I'm very grateful for your concern and your help. I do hope President Obama brings it up with President Lula. It's too wrong to continue, and it's too wrong that it's gone on this long."

Secretary Clinton's tone softened, and she sounded more like a mom than a powerful world leader. "We certainly agree with that, and I can only hope and pray that you will get a favorable decision soon."

"I do, too," I said. "That's what I've been praying for since the day I found out [Bruna] didn't want to come home. I thank you for your time; I'm sure you are very busy. I hope someday I can thank you in person, with my son by my side."

"I do, too," Secretary Clinton replied. "I would like that very much. Stay strong; I think the end is in sight."

I could only hope that she was right.

ALTHOUGH I COULD not be in Washington for the Obama-Lula meeting because I was in Brazil, we didn't want to lose any chance to make an impact, so Mark DeAngelis and Bob D'Amico decided to organize a demonstration in Lafayette Square, outside the White House, on the day Obama and Lula were scheduled to meet. The Bring Sean Home group got out the word on our Web site and organized buses to transport supporters from New Jersey and other nearby locations. On Saturday afternoon, in a cold, drizzling rain, a few hundred supporters gathered for the rally in Lafayette Square. Though the weather was dismal, their spirits were high. Many held handmade signs and called out toward the White House, "Bring Sean home!" Most wore T-shirts with the same message. Other left-behind parents carried blown-up photos of their abducted sons or daughters, emphasizing our commitment not only to Sean but also to the larger cause. Mark, Bernie Aronson, and Congressman Smith spoke to the demonstrators. In a passionate voice, Congressman Smith read an open letter to President Lula: "Justice delayed is justice denied . . . the time for action is now." Bernie spoke about the outpouring of support and affection the crowd displayed. He said to my supporters, "You didn't have to get up early this morning, board a bus, and come to Washington to march in the rain in support of David and Sean. But you are here." He closed with a moving quote from the Catholic theologian Teilhard de Chardin that he said captured the decency and power of the demonstrators: "Someday, after mastering the winds, the waves, the tides, and gravity, we shall harness for God the energies of love. And then, for the second time in the history of the world, man will have discovered fire."

Bernie later told me he met a demonstrator who had first learned about the case from the *Dateline NBC* broadcast. The man was a family court judge from Ohio and he was outraged by the injustice of Sean's continued abduction. All by himself, at his own expense, he had flown in to D.C. from Ohio that morning. Arriving earlier than the buses, and all alone, the man paraded up and down in front of the White House shouting, "Bring Sean home now!" It struck Bernie and me as a metaphor for the fundamental decency and goodness of so many Americans who had rallied to our cause: an example of the power of "love" that Teilhard de Chardin described. I often wondered if President Obama and President Lula heard that Ohio man's passionate and determined voice as they met fifty yards away in the Oval Office.

Were our efforts effective? It was hard to tell immediately. But we later got word from Bernie's sources that in a private Oval Office meeting at which the two leaders were scheduled to discuss the economy, energy, and the environment, President Obama raised Sean's case with President Lula. Although the Brazilian president did not guarantee Sean's return, he recognized that this was an issue that was of great importance to the American president.

FOLLOWING HILLARY CLINTON's public remarks and President Obama's private statements to President Lula, Alan Clendenning, bureau chief with the Associated Press in Brazil, picked up the story. Alan had been approached about covering Sean and me previously, and like many other journalists and media outlets in Brazil, he had shied away from the story, possibly influenced by the Lins e Silvas' efforts to suppress it. Now that Secretary of State Clinton had broached the subject of Sean's return, and it had made news in the United States, however, the media in Brazil could no longer ignore the story. In a real way, Hillary Clinton's brief mention of the case brought down the wall of secrecy that had imprisoned the story in that country for more than four and a half years.

16

■ ■ ■

Family Lies

I DIDN'T HEAR SECRETARY CLINTON'S INITIAL PUBLIC COMMENTS on our case until later in the day on March 4 because I was on an airplane flying across the country to appear on CNN's *Larry King Live*, which was broadcast from Los Angeles. Shortly after I landed at LAX airport, one of the producers phoned to welcome me. "We're glad you're here," he said, "and if there's anything you need, just let us know. Now, here's how the show is going to break down." He then informed me that a relative of Bruna's would also be appearing on the show, to present "the other side."

"Who?" I asked.

"A cousin from Seattle."

"Cousin who?"

"His name is Helvecio Ribeiro. Oh, I'm sorry; I see here that he is Bruna Bianchi's uncle. He will be the U.S. spokesman for the Bianchi family and for Sean's Brazilian stepfather."

Helvecio Ribeiro? I barely knew of him. He may have been Bruna's uncle, but he had certainly never been part of Bruna's life with me. And what was all this about the Bianchi family? Their name is Ribeiro. Regardless, I was uncomfortable with the relative being on the same interview with me because I knew that he could say anything he wanted and would not be held accountable, yet anything I said would be thrown back in my face by lawyers in Brazil. After I hung up with the producer, I called Tricia Apy and hastily explained the situation to her. "I'm turning around and going back home," I said, "unless you are available to go on the air from New York." As Tricia considered that possibility, I said, "And we need to get Congressman Smith on from Washington. Otherwise, I'm going home."

CNN worked out the arrangements, and both Tricia and the congressman made themselves available. I was the only guest in the LA studio, while Tricia stood by in New York, Congressman Smith in CNN's Washington studio, and the Ribeiro relative in Seattle. It was a busy news day—rescuers were searching in the Gulf of Mexico for two NFL players and their friend, whose boat had capsized during a fishing trip over the weekend; and former first lady Barbara Bush was having heart surgery in Houston—so Larry was bouncing back and forth between stories, but he gave me plenty of time to explain how Sean and I came to be separated, and that Sean was still being retained in Brazil.

Following Larry's initial foray with me, and a video clip from Hillary Clinton's supportive statement to Andrea Mitchell, Larry introduced Helvecio Ribeiro. The relative badmouthed me from the beginning, suggesting that I had been engaged in a media campaign in the United States for six months, without a challenge from Bruna's family. Ribeiro acknowledged that Bruna had kept Sean in Brazil without my permission, and confirmed that Bruna's husband wanted to keep him there.

Larry asked, "Why do you think that David should not have his son?"

"I don't question the biological right," Bruna's uncle said. "The fact of the matter is that in order to be a parent, you have to be more than just a DNA donor, Mr. King. Fatherhood is not about making home movies and taking pictures; it's about sacrifice. It's about providing support to your child. It's about being there even when you're not there. And Mr. Goldman, while Bruna was still alive, failed to do so. I'm not sure if you know that, but he hasn't paid a dime of child support so far. And he has been making allegations all over the place about us not allowing him to visit his child. They are completely untrue." Ribeiro contended that his family had offered to pay my expenses to travel to Brazil in 2006 if I was willing to meet their terms.

I sat quietly across from Larry King, inwardly fuming at this man's outrageous and insulting statements. Was he serious, claiming that I had not paid child support—to people who had kidnapped my son? Larry picked up on the contradiction, and probed further. "Why should he pay child support if the child was taken away from him without his permission?"

"Well, because it's the law," Ribeiro responded. "And also, it shows commitment. Even if it is a symbolic value, even if it is just a dime. I'm quite sure Bruna would have refused. But at least it would have [given] an indication that Mr. Goldman is really committed to making, you know, making sure that the people he claims to be the kidnappers of his son can actually provide for the child."

What? Was Ribeiro suggesting with a straight face that I pay the Lins e Silvas or the Ribeiros because they were harboring my son? The man had to be joking. But of course, he wasn't. In fact, he posited my lack of "child support" as part of the reason the Ribeiros had refused to let me see or speak to Sean.

"The law states in Brazil that a parent has to pay child support to have visitation rights. And he failed to do that. He never did that."

Larry ran another portion of Secretary Clinton's remarks and then asked Ribeiro, "So what do you say, Helvecio, to the secretary of state?"

"She's probably basing her opinions on the fact that she knows one side of the story. Probably when she knows more about Mr. Goldman's real character, she will rethink if he is actually morally fit to be a parent."

"You're saying a lot of salacious things about Mr. Goldman tonight," Larry responded to Ribeiro. "Pretty tough things." The interview with Bruna's uncle continued a few more minutes, then Larry brought in Tricia Apy and Congressman Smith. Though both of them came across as highly professional and completely under control, I could tell that they were like two mad bulldogs, just waiting to respond to Ribeiro's ridiculous and flagrantly misleading statements. My attorney responded first, when Larry asked her about the case. "Patricia, why isn't this open-and-shut?"

"It is open-and-shut," she replied without hesitation. "When this child was originally abducted in 2004, I told my client in my office that the Hague Convention on the civil aspects of child abduction applies. This child would be immediately returned, that Brazil was a signatory. I had every confidence. We are now four and a half years later on the second round of the Hague Convention and Sean is still not returned."

Larry pitched the question to Congressman Smith. "Congressman, this must be dumbfounding."

Congressman Smith was locked and loaded. "It certainly is," he replied, "and to hear one of the family members saying—first slandering David on national television, but also suggesting that he ought to pay child support to a kidnapper. The Hague Convention is all about wrongful removal and wrongful retention. Brazil signed the Hague Convention. We have a bilateral agreement that went into force in 2003. The Brazilian government has to step up to the plate. Thus far, they have not. And Sean has to be reunited with his father. This is an outrage."

At long last, Larry turned back to me. "David, what do you say? What are you saying in response to what the uncle said?"

"I think it is disgusting," I replied. "What can I say? He's attacking my moral fiber and my character, and questioning my love for my son."

Both Tricia's and the congressman's comments scored direct hits, as Tricia further explained the $150,000 settlement the Ribeiros paid to me and the statements Raimundo Ribeiro made in court admitting that they would not let me speak with my son, that every time Raimundo heard my voice on the phone, he'd immediately hang up. In court, under oath, Raimundo provided the rationalization for the family's cruelty. "My attorney has advised me that I do not have to speak on the telephone with someone who is suing me." These statements, Tricia reminded Larry and his viewers, were documented and part of the court records.

Later in the program, Larry King asked Congressman Smith why Brazil would resist fulfilling its obligations under the Hague Convention.

"Unfortunately, the federal government, only up until recently, has been very negligent, in my view. They have not done what they could have done to try to get Hague-literate judges to handle the case. And it's been handled at the state courts rather than the federal.

"And until the political pressure and the diplomatic levers were pulled, this case, which should have—as Patricia said—should have been a slam-dunk, easily adjudicated case. Clear violation of the Hague Convention on Child Abduction. Sean should have been back with his [father] four years ago or more.

"Unfortunately, it has taken raising it to the political level to get the attention of the president. I think we have gotten that attention. I have a resolution pending that has over fifty cosponsors. We expect it to be on the floor next week. We're not going to let this go. The State Department is not going to let this go.

"And when you hear the uncle talking the way he was, slandering David, I think most Americans are going to be outraged by that attitude of impunity that we have seen."

In closing the interview, Larry looked at me and asked, "Are you confident, David?"

"I'm hopeful," I responded.

As frustrating as the King interview was, at least we were getting out the message that Sean was being wrongfully held in Brazil. For more than four years, I had been begging for someone to listen to me, anyone who might be able to help my son. Some people listened, but they didn't really hear, or they couldn't understand what they could do to help in the face of such gross injustice.

Now, suddenly, people seemed fascinated by my plight. Indeed, to many people the whole idea of Sean's abduction to Brazil possessed an aura of intrigue, power, corruption, money, and conflicts between governments. Some people touted me as a modern-day David fighting against a huge Goliath, and although the odds seemed stacked against me, they recognized that I was unwilling to give up. Men sometimes told me that they wished they'd had a father who was more accessible as they were growing up, or who gave them a higher priority during their formative childhood years. Women expressed their hope that they could find a husband for themselves or for their daughters who would be there for them as I was for Bruna and Sean, and now was for my son; someone more loving, caring, and nurturing, and who had similar levels of commitment as mine. I was humbled and honored by all of these kind words.

So I continued sharing an intensely private pain on an excruciatingly public stage. Every time I told the story of Sean's abduction, the pain hurt just as much. It was like scraping a knife over a wound that had not yet had time to heal. Whatever it takes, I figured. For the first time, people seemed to be hearing what I'd been saying for more than four years. We were making great strides. But I couldn't help wondering, *Is this enough? Will our efforts be in time?*

Worse yet, every day when I woke up, Sean was not tucked in his bed down the hallway. That's all I cared about, all I ever cared about.

THROUGHOUT MARCH 2009, events were happening fast. After the blitz of publicity we received, pressure increased on the Brazilian government to honor the Hague Convention agreement. Lawmakers in New Jersey joined the U.S. Congress in condemning Brazil's actions and seeking the return of Sean. On March 16, I attended the announcement and passing of the resolution in the New Jersey State Senate in their chambers in the statehouse in Trenton. After the reading of the resolution, I was asked to say a few words, and I thanked the legislators for their support. The members of the Senate spontaneously rose and applauded me. It was another of those humbling experiences for which I will always be grateful. But Sean remained in Brazil.

Even after Secretary of State Clinton brought up our case with her counterpart, the Brazilian foreign minister, Brazil did not budge. When President Obama mentioned Sean during his meeting with

Brazil's president Lula on March 14, 2009, suddenly we were front-page news all around the world—including Brazil. Yet Sean's abductors still refused to release him. In fact, on March 15, Bruna's family engineered a protest in the streets of Rio, with people carrying banners and placards reading, "*Sean é brasiliero*," Sean is Brazilian.

IRONICALLY, WHEN THE media eventually cooled on the story, many people assumed that Sean had been returned. After all, who could imagine the Brazilian courts thumbing their noses at such international attention? Hadn't the president of the United States weighed in on this issue? Hadn't the secretary of state and both houses of the U.S. Congress agreed that Sean should be home with me?

Yet he wasn't.

Often I'd meet people in New York, or at the marina in New Jersey, who honestly believed that Sean was home. One day I went into a tackle shop in Atlantic Highlands and a man there recognized me. "Hey, David," he called enthusiastically. "How does Sean like being home?"

Another person stopped me on the street and asked, "Is Sean having any trouble adjusting to being back home in New Jersey?"

As well intentioned as those misguided queries were, they nonetheless hit me like a prizefighter's punch. I did my best to let people know the truth. "Well, Sean isn't home yet. We have to keep the pressure on the people in Brazil to let him go. Thank you for your concern."

Our case was like a whitewater rafting trip, in which you must stay in a constant state of preparedness, wearing your helmet and life jacket while keeping your oar nearby, ready for action. There would be periods of boring calm, with relatively no action, and then suddenly, almost without notice, the current would increase, and we'd find ourselves bouncing over rocks and being tossed every which way as we attempted to negotiate the rapids, working our bodies to exhaustion simply to stay afloat, and then coming out of the turmoil into another long period of inactivity. I felt such a sense of frustration during those long lags, when months slipped by with no apparent movement on the case.

THE BRAZILIAN PRESS, which had long been forbidden from pursuing the story, and had defied the court order only on occasion, now covered the story more vigorously. Some people said the gag order had been lifted; I knew that it hadn't. Nevertheless, the story kept oozing into the public.

Apparently, at some point, the Lins e Silva camp recognized this and changed their strategy to a full-court press, attempting to damage my reputation in any way possible. They unilaterally lifted their own media ban, and suddenly a flow of vitriol designed to discredit me with the public began to spew forth. At various times, their smear campaign included anti-Semitic slurs and painted me as everything from poor, handicapped, lazy, and gay to a shack dweller and a gold digger. Essentially, in Sean's captors' estimation, if they didn't approve of a person's religion or sexual orientation, or if an individual was handicapped or not wealthy, he or she should not be allowed to have children. Though I recognized that the abductors were attempting to tag me with any label they deemed derogatory in the public's mind, their bigoted aspersions still disgusted me. I never responded to or reacted publicly to any of their demeaning comments.

All the while, they tried to make Sean's abduction into an issue of nationalism, as though it were a battle between Brazil and the United States. Initially, their tactic succeeded, and public opinion tilted in their favor.

Both Ricardo and Tricia cautioned me against engaging in this war of words. Even the Brazilian media shied away from and refused to give credence to them. Although we did receive information that a public relations agency was leaking such statements to the Brazilian media in the hope that the public's opinion could be swayed against me.

The message the abductors were presenting to the people of Brazil was: "Bruna was the mother, and this David Goldman is a worthless bum. He was not a good husband; he was not a good father. He is the ugly American coming to steal a child of a Brazilian woman." After all, who would ever think that a mother could be so cruel and heartless, evil and spoiled, as to rip her child away from a doting father who loved both her and the child?

Furthermore, the Brazilian family said, "David never even tried to see Sean; he didn't even care about getting Sean back until Bruna died, because he wants Sean's inheritance."

That was more than I could take. That they would accuse me of wanting my son back only because of the pittance he might inherit because his mother had died was despicable. From the moment I learned that Bruna had abducted our son and was not coming home, I had done everything possible to get Sean home, and had spent hundreds of thousands of dollars doing so.

Even if I were all the things the Lins e Silva camp accused me of being, that would not alter for a moment the fact that I was Sean's father and he was my son. I'd heard all their accusations before, and I believed that the truth would eventually prevail. I had nothing to hide, and I knew their rantings were nothing but lies. All I could do was to keep going, leading with the truth.

The one thing that the Ribeiros and the Lins e Silvas either underestimated or possibly never considered was the enormous power of the Internet. Once the story got out, and people began discussing it online, the pressure to return Sean built exponentially.

In the United States, Mark DeAngelis and Bob D'Amico found themselves working almost around the clock as volunteers with the Bring Sean Home Web site, as requests for more information poured in, along with heartrending stories of other abducted children. We were beginning to realize that there were more victims of international child abduction than we ever imagined. Mark and Bob constantly kept our growing Internet audience informed about what was going on with Sean, and began exploring ways we could help bring home other abducted children. Like Sean's and my lives, Mark's and Bob's would never be the same.

17

Good News, Bad News

ON MAY 25, 2009, SEAN'S NINTH BIRTHDAY, I RECEIVED WORD from Ricardo that the federal prosecutor in Rio had recommended to the court that Sean be returned to me! The prosecutor stated, "This was a wrongful retention, and the boy should be under the custody of the biological parent." He cited the findings of the three court-appointed psychologists, who agreed that Sean had incurred "serious psychological damage" while in Brazil.

The news regarding the prosecutor's recommendations lifted my spirits, of course, but I had been down this road too many times to start celebrating. "I'll celebrate after Sean is home," I kept telling myself. "In the meantime, stay calm and even-keeled." I had realized by now that nothing could be depended upon, that when it came to international abduction cases, nothing was easy in Brazil. I learned that every decision, no matter how competent, sound, or seemingly final, was subject to endless, often exasperatingly inane appeals. The pattern seemed to be: get a judgment, then find some insignificant aspect of it and appeal on that basis.

The prosecutor's recommendation was certainly a step in the right direction, and hopefully a concrete development, but how could we be sure? The court would have to decide and issue a return order, commanding the Ribeiros and Lins e Silvas to return Sean to the United States and to me, and so far, we had won precious few victories in the courtroom. After so many dashed hopes, I was slow to embrace news of any kind, positive or negative. Certainly I was thrilled that the Brazilian federal prosecutor and the three court-appointed psychologists were siding with me, but I dared not get on that emotional roller coaster again. I had to stand off to the side, one step removed, and watch and wait.

All the while, the Ribeiros and the Lins e Silvas continued their massive disinformation campaign. João Paulo Lins e Silva had even gone so far as to foster the notion that Sean was Brazilian-born, based on his highly suspect contention that Bruna had registered Sean "in the Brazilian Consulate and by the First Civil Registry of Naturalized Persons of Rio de Janeiro . . . three months after Sean's birth, making him a Brazilian citizen like all of us, with all of the rights and obligations of a citizen born in Brazil, and when he becomes a legal adult, he can opt to be Brazilian or American." Clearly, Lins e Silva's rationalization was rubbish; referring to Sean as a Brazilian-born citizen was only an attempt to stir up his countrymen's nationalistic fervor, inciting the people of Brazil to stand against the "bullies from North America." The kidnappers' actions were preposterous, but there was no way I could counter them except with the truth: "Sean Goldman is my son. He was born in Riverview Hospital in Red Bank, New Jersey."

THEN, ON JUNE 1, 2009, we received the best news I'd heard in nearly five years. In an eighty-two-page written decision, Rafael Pinto, a federal judge in Rio de Janeiro, ruled that Sean was to be handed over to me on Friday, June 3, 2009! Moreover, Judge Pinto's order implied that it was urgent that Sean be returned to me, because he was being subjected to "a pernicious process of parental alienation." The judge based his ruling on the Hague Convention, but also relied heavily on the psychological reports of the three court-appointed psychologists, concluding that the longer Sean was separated from me, the more damage would be done.

While the people around me were celebrating victory and envisioning Sean's and my final and permanent reunion, I wouldn't allow myself to go there—not yet.

I dropped everything and rushed to Rio. The decision specified that to make the transition to the United States smoother for Sean, for the first month, although I was Sean's sole legal custodian, he would split the time between living with me and living with Bruna's parents. After that, I was to have full custody of him, and he would live full-time with me. These were added changes to the return order, but like so many of the arrangements involving the Ribeiros, this was not my preference, especially after witnessing their behavior during my brief visits with Sean. But if it got Sean back home, I could live with it for a month.

Of course, as soon as the decision was rendered, Sergio Tostes, the smarmy, caustic attorney for the Lins e Silvas and the Ribeiros, immediately announced to the *O Globo* news conglomerate that they would be appealing the ruling. Surprise, surprise.

Congressman Smith was on a plane almost as quickly, heading to Rio to help facilitate and observe the handover and to ensure that everything went smoothly, but got delayed in Florida and had to return to Washington. I still had no real plan for how Sean and I would make the trip home, or even how the transfer from the Ribeiros to me would be made, but Ricardo was working on it, and so was the U.S. embassy in Brasília. I talked with Congressman Smith by phone several times once I arrived in Rio, and, as always, I told him that I was hopeful. He passed that word along to reporters, with a sober warning: "The bottom line," he said, "is that child abduction is a serious crime. To allow it to continue, if Sean stays in Rio, that perpetuates the crime."

Secretary Clinton was in El Salvador for the inauguration of Salvadoran president Mauricio Funes at the time the ruling was announced. At a news conference, she brought up the favorable decision. "It's taken a long time for this day to come," she said, "but we will work with the Goldman family and the Brazilian government with the goal of ensuring this young boy's return."

Almost before the ink on the return order had dried, less than a full day later, at around 10:30 PM on June 2, Judge Marco Aurelio de Mello, a Brazilian Supreme Court justice in São Paulo, suspended the return order that had been issued the day before.

By this time, I expected the opposition to pull almost anything—influencing a Supreme Court justice was not out of the realm of possibility for Sean's well-connected abductors—but misusing the Brazilian law, by having a political party present a lawsuit to ensure that they could quickly perfect a stay of my order was a new level of manipulation. The political party sought the immediate suspension of Brazil's obligations under the Hague Abduction Convention, urging that this was inconsistent with the Brazilian constitution. Technically, the political party had filed a lawsuit in which I was not even a named party, but merely one of the left-behind parents. Further, the U.S. State Department was reluctant to even file a response, which needed to be done within twenty-four hours. However, my attorneys and the U.S. consul general, Marie Damour, were adamant that the United States had to get involved on behalf of Sean and other American children. Ms. Damour and Tricia wrote a response to the political party's lawsuit to be submitted in the Brazilian Supreme Court. Once again I had an angel on my shoulder, this time in the person of Marie Damour.

The upside was that because Judge Pinto's decision was so sound, there were no merits to any expected appeal that would be filed. Nevertheless, the announcement scuttled the planned handover. Sean would remain with João Paulo Lins e Silva, the second kidnapper.

The Supreme Court justice had issued his decision to review the return order in response to the Progressive political party's questioning the validity of Brazil's signing the Hague Convention in the first place. Since the ruling to return Sean was based on the Hague, Sean should stay in Brazil. It was asinine, but as a result of Justice Marco Aurelio de Mello's decision, the matter now had to be reviewed by the full membership of Brazil's Supreme Court, and it could possibly take months before hearings were scheduled.

I felt as though I had been stabbed in the heart. We had been so close, and now it seemed as though I were a million miles away from Sean again.

Congressman Smith was furious. The following day, June 4, 2009, he introduced HR 2702, a bill in the House of Representatives to suspend Brazil's portion of the Generalized System of Preferences, U.S. trade preferences with Brazil worth more than $2.7 billion, until Brazil complied with the Hague Convention and facilitated Sean's return. Brazil, of course, maintained that the case was being handled by the judicial system, not the government.

Although I didn't hear from her at the time, I could imagine that Secretary Clinton was equally embarrassed at the court's rebuff. She had invested her political clout in this case, had gone on record publicly applauding the return order when it looked as though Brazil was finally going to do the right thing. Then to have one Brazilian Supreme Court justice quash the whole deal was like having the rug pulled out from under her. No one appreciates that feeling, whether you are a secretary of state or a fishing boat captain from New Jersey.

The day after Justice Aurelio de Mello suspended the return order, I was allowed to spend a bit of time with Sean at the pool area of the Ribeiros' condominium complex. I showed up at the appointed time, only to be turned away. Sean was not feeling well, I was informed by the Ribeiros' messenger. He was upset and had to spend all morning with a therapist, with whom I'd had no contact. I agreed to return later that afternoon, which I did.

When Sean and I met at the compound after lunch, although he was happy to see me, he seemed listless and lethargic. Not helping matters, another of the Ribeiro spies lingered nearby. While Sean and I built Lego figures and played games at the table, a woman came and sat down, pulling her chair so close that it was touching Sean's. She glared at me as she placed a tape recorder on the table and aimed it in our direction.

I asked her to give us some space. She smugly refused and then poked Sean in the ribs and instructed him to speak. Sean was perspiring profusely and his face flushed with color. He began stuttering and stammering and finally said, "I . . . I . . . I . . . li . . . li . . . like . . . Br . . . Brazil." He looked toward the woman, who prodded him to keep going, but he shook his head no.

I came really close to losing control. I wanted so badly to destroy that monster and save my son! How the abductors could do any of the horrific things they had done and gotten away with it for so long was infuriating, but to torture my son right in front of me was more than I could bear.

I took a deep breath, gently brushed the hair out of Sean's eyes, and looked directly into them. "I know you do, buddy," I said. "It's okay."

I excused myself and walked over to another table, where Karen Gustafson de Andrade was sitting. I explained to her what had just happened at our table, then returned to the table where Sean and "the friend" were sitting. Sean and I began building a bionic robot model.

Karen came over and politely asked the woman to please give Sean and me some space.

Again the "friend" adamantly refused, adding that she was following instructions from the Ribeiros and no one else.

Karen didn't argue with her. She simply walked back to her table, where she sat and began making phone calls.

The woman glowered at me and said, "I'm moving to the other end of this table, and not because you or she asked me to, but because I want to listen to what she is saying."

Karen finished her call, picked up my Flip mini video camera, and pointed it toward the despicable woman, who was attempting to interfere with Sean's and my visit by intimidating my son. She filmed the entire spectacle, including the woman's shameless recording of our conversations.

Sean and I did our best to ignore the woman as we finished the model, but I could tell that he wasn't doing well at all. He was holding his stomach and breathing heavily.

"Sean, why don't we wrap it up early today," I said, "so you can go upstairs, get a cool glass of water, and settle down." I got up, kissed his forehead, told him I loved him, and then left. I would not be a party to the torture of my own child. That was to be our last "visit."

I RETURNED HOME to New Jersey at the end of that week, only to have Ricardo call and inform me that the Supreme Court had decided to consider the case on June 10, a few days later. I literally came home, packed some fresh clothes, and caught another red-eye flight back to Brazil. I felt almost like a puppet on a string, being manipulated by the Brazilian judges, and as I closed my eyes and tried to rest while the Continental Airlines plane rose out over the Atlantic Ocean and headed south, it did not seem too far-fetched to imagine a master puppeteer who looked a lot like Lins e Silva pulling the strings behind the court.

The hearing before Brazil's Supreme Court brought both good news and bad news. The good news was that the Supreme Court unanimously denied the bid by the Progressive Party to halt Sean's return based on their objection to Brazil's participation in the Hague Convention. The court also decided that the federal court in Rio should decide whether Sean should be returned to me. That, too, was good news, considering that the federal court had already said that Sean should be with me. The bad news? The manipulation had given the Ribeiros and Lins e Silvas what they needed—time. The abductors now had an opportunity to present an official appeal of the return order on the merits. It was unlikely that Sean would be returning home with me anytime soon.

To my surprise, on Thursday, June 18, the week of Father's Day, Judge Pinto modified his order and ruled that until the appeals could be settled, I should have full custody of Sean for six days each week— but only in Brazil.

Judge Pinto's intentions were noble; he was trying to help me. He had presented a clear and complete eighty-two-page return order. He knew the stay order was ridiculous, and he saw the urgency for Sean to get out of the environment in which he was living as soon as possible. So, by granting six-day-a-week custody to me in Brazil, he was opening the door for Sean to escape the torturous tyranny of his Brazilian family's home and was attempting to bring Sean and me together more frequently.

Unfortunately, it's a long commute from Tinton Falls to Rio. I knew no one with whom I could live in Rio, a potentially dangerous place for me, and I certainly couldn't afford to move there and leave my work. Moreover, I was concerned that after having Sean with me for five or six days a week, he'd return to the Ribeiros and Lins e Silvas and be even more emotionally tortured. Nevertheless, Ricardo, as well as some officials from the U.S. embassy, encouraged me to do it. But the idea of moving to Rio soon became a moot point. Since Judge Pinto had added these stipulations to his decision postjudgment, the ruling could not be enforced.

ON JUNE 17, in Red Bank and in Washington, crowds of people conducted candlelight vigils to note the fifth anniversary of Sean's abduction. One of the speakers at the Red Bank event was Matthew Langdon, one of Sean's friends, who urged, "Bring Sean home." In the crowd that day, with tears in his eyes, was Sean's grandfather, my dad, Barry Goldman.

That same week, Bernie Aronson wrote an op-ed article in the *Wall Street Journal* reminding readers that Sean was not yet home, and, in a not-so-subtle way, telling Brazil that if it continued to ignore its Hague Convention responsibilities, it could easily jeopardize its position as a potential host of the 2016 Olympics, a potential position on an enlarged UN Security Council, and, in general, the privileges of international leadership. The headline editor put the tag on the piece: "Brazil Helps Kidnap American Children." "They went a little overboard on the headline," Bernie said, but he and I agreed that Brazil would not like seeing one of the most influential newspapers in the world running an op-ed piece lambasting them for flagrantly violating international law. The *Washington Post* also ran a strong piece calling for Sean's return. Bernie's reminder to the Brazilian ambassador—

that as long as Sean was not returned, their reputation would suffer—
was becoming a reality.

ON JUNE 23, 2009, with the return order still under appeal, CBS
TV's *The Early Show*, in a blatant attempt to get a scoop, brought
João Paulo Lins e Silva, along with Silvana Ribeiro and her attorney,
Sergio Tostes, to New York for in-studio interviews, to air what they
asserted was their side of the story. I was invited to appear as well,
but I declined.

Had we sought criminal prosecution earlier, the abductors would
have been arrested the moment they entered the United States. They
had flagrantly harbored and provided assistance to a kidnapper, ig-
noring U.S. court orders to return Sean within two days, unlawfully
retaining him in Brazil, violating visitation privileges, and incurring
a number of other charges that could have been pressed. But while
they were here, Sean was still in Brazil, and any criminal prosecution
could have been used to defeat the Hague Petition.

The Ribeiros and Lins e Silvas possessed videos of Sean being
questioned by their own psychologist. On the basis of those interviews, Silvana Ribeiro and João Lins e Silva told host Harry Smith
that Sean wanted to remain in Brazil. "Sean wants to stay in Brazil
with the family," Silvana told Smith. "It's very hard for him to separate
from his sister."

We later learned that the abductors had videotaped Sean being
interrogated behind a two-way mirror as to where he preferred to
live. The statements made by my nine-year-old son were so obviously
coached that when Congressman Smith saw them, he was aghast.

"It looks akin to a hostage video," he observed, "where captors
scheme to coerce and extract statements from someone illegally
held." Indeed, in a very real way, Sean's existence in Brazil was very
much like being held hostage—for both of us.

The network did not request my permission to air the interviews,
even though Sean was a minor and I was Sean's father, his sole legal

guardian in the United States. Once we learned these tapes existed, Tricia contacted the CBS attorney and explained that I was the sole legal custodian of Sean under both U.S. and customary international law, and that this tape with Sean's comments and image were solicited without my consent, and could not be used without my permission. CBS's counsel immediately understood. Although CBS didn't air the full video during the interview segment with Silvana, Tostes, and Lins e Silva, they ran a teaser the night before. In it, a woman was asking Sean where he wanted to live. I was appalled and angry. I called Tricia, and she reminded CBS that Sean had been abducted and the use of such a video would support these abductors and encourage such abusive behavior by the abducting parents. Stating that it was an executive decision, CBS pulled the videos.

CNN indicated that they, too, had received the tape and intended to run it. They responded that there was "some question" about who Sean's legal guardian was and who could consent to the use of the tape. Tricia reminded CNN's producers, "In the United States of America, where your offices are located, there is no question: David Goldman is the sole legal custodian of Sean Goldman." She sent copies of the relevant U.S. and Brazilian orders, and indicated that she would be forced to recommend legal action if CNN went forward. Eventually CNN capitulated and pulled the video.

A week or so after Silvana and Lins e Silva appeared on *The Early Show*, another judge in Brazil ruled that Sean was to remain with Lins e Silva until a final ruling was reached in the case.

My stomach was churning. This case was getting sicker by the minute.

18

Pressure Points

I RETURNED FROM BRAZIL ALONE AND MORE DESPONDENT THAN
ever about the prospects for bringing Sean home. I was emotionally beaten up and drained, but no less determined to keep going.
Judge Pinto had clearly indicated that it was in Sean's best interests
to return with me to the United States. The order was solid. As Tricia
Apy pointed out, in all her years of working on international child
abduction cases, ours was as clear as any case could be. It was a textbook case in Hague 101. "Return is the only answer."

But the incessant legal maneuverings spawned by the Lins e Silvas and the Ribeiros blocked us at every turn. Every time a judge
ruled according to the facts and the treaty, the Lins e Silvas' and the
Ribeiros' lawyers found one that would throw in a procedural monkey
wrench. Sean was still trapped in Brazil, and I didn't know how to
rescue him.

The summer of 2009 was hell. Each day dragged on with little
positive news from my Brazilian attorneys. We were being yanked
back and forth by the Brazilian court system, facing one manufactured delay after another but never making real progress. From somewhere within me, I drew strength, knowing that it was right for a boy

to be with his dad, that all of heaven and earth affirmed the love of a father for his son, that by law, morality, and common sense, Sean belonged home with me.

I continued making trips to Washington, working with Congressman Smith and Bernie Aronson, trying to keep the pressure on our public officials to do something, not just about Sean but also about the scores of other American children abducted to Brazil and other countries. My goal, of course, was to be reunited with Sean, but if I could help bring more attention to the abduction issue, if I could be a voice for the other suffering families, whose pleas so often fell on deaf ears, I welcomed the opportunity. Progress, however, was frustratingly slow.

Our case had ridden a wave of media and diplomatic attention to the highest levels of government. With no new developments, attention crested, then dropped without a ripple, leaving the press less prone to delve back into the story. I continued getting requests for interviews, and there was no less interest from reporters when I gave them, but for weeks at a time, I simply had no new information to offer them. Whenever I did have something to say, I wanted it to make an impact. I knew that the media could not run headlines about Sean every day, but Sean had been the headline in my heart and mind every waking hour for the last five years. To me and to those supporting Sean's return, no news *was* news. What was Brazil doing? What was taking so long?

Our goal was to apply pressure across all fronts in any way we could to make a difference. Congressman Smith pressed the State Department to suspend or take away Brazil's preferential trading status, which gave Brazil duty-free access to the United States for many of its products. Chris worked constantly with his colleagues in the House and the Senate from both parties to build support for the legislation he had introduced, which would require better tracking of international parental abduction cases by the State Department and, most important, spelled out eighteen specific punitive responses the United States would undertake if countries failed to cooperate in

resolving abduction disputes. In July, I participated in a press conference in Washington attended by other parents of abducted children,
hoping to draw attention to Congressman Smith's bill. Unfortunately,
getting members of Congress to focus on this new piece of proposed
legislation was nearly as difficult as securing the compliance of foreign countries with their Hague treaty obligations. I discovered that
congressmen were constantly on the go: running in and out of committee hearings, voting on the floor, meeting with constituents, talking to the press, raising campaign reelection funds, and attending
political events.

On the other hand, for the other left-behind parents and me, there
was only one paramount issue: getting our children back. When one
reporter asked me to comment on what it felt like to be a father of
an abducted child, I responded, "It's an anguish that's with us 24-7.
Awake, asleep, working, walking—no matter what, it's with us." Unfortunately, that same kind of constant attention to the issue of child
abduction was not the norm for our government officials.

When I wasn't in Washington, I kept busy with work, staying out
at sea all day and returning home physically exhausted in the hope
of being able to sleep. I spent time with Wendy and her children,
and with my mom and dad, but despite Mom's home cooking, I lost
weight. I noticed more gray flecks showing up in my hair, and could
barely recognize myself in the mirror.

On September 30, 2009, we received some hopeful news. The
Brazilian court in unanimous decisions threw out three suits filed
by João Paulo Lins e Silva aimed at obstructing progress under the
Hague Convention. The next decision date was scheduled for October 16.

Back in June, Congressman Smith had urged Congressman Eliot
Engel to hold hearings on Brazil's patterns of poor compliance with
regard to returning abducted children. Congressman Engel was the
chairman of the Western Hemisphere Committee, and was also the
secretary of the Brazil caucus. Engel agreed to hold a hearing the
second week of September, timed to coincide with an upcoming visit

to the States by President Lula, who would be in New York at the
UN General Assembly and then in Pittsburgh for the G-20 Summit,
a confab of the world's top twenty industrial and economic powers.
President Obama was scheduled to attend both meetings.

We had hoped to get strong media coverage for the Engel hearing
as a result of these two important gatherings of world leaders, attended by both the U.S. and the Brazilian presidents. But at the last
minute, the hearing was canceled, with no explanation given.

Congressman Smith would not be deterred. Prior to the UN and
G-20 meetings, he was invited to a summit mix-and-mingle that both
presidents were scheduled to attend. "David, you're coming along,"
he told me. "I want to introduce you to President Lula."

Before the event, I wrote a short note on a card that we planned
to hand to President Lula. The message on the card essentially said,
"I am the father of Sean Goldman, and I implore your help to get my
boy back."

Unfortunately, due to a problem in Honduras, President Lula did
not show up at the event. Undaunted, Congressman Smith suggested
that we attempt to get the card to President Obama. The idea was to
give the note to the U.S. president, who would be seeing the Brazilian president several times over the next week. Again and again, while
others were schmoozing at the party, the congressman tried to find
someone who would pass the note to the president. Congressman
Smith asked eight separate people, including two assistant secretar-
ies, to get me in front of the president for five seconds, so I could give
him the card. "Here's a note from a father who simply wants his son
back," he told them. "You don't even need to talk about it. Just hand
the president the note." It never happened. We were a mere fifteen
feet away from where the president stood as he made his brief remarks, but the gap may as well have been a million miles.

Late that night, we dropped off the card at the Brazilian mission,
with the hope that somebody there would get it to President Lula. We
never learned if that happened, and we returned home disappointed
and discouraged.

■ ■ ■

BEHIND THE SCENES at the same time, Chris Smith and his staff and Bernie Aronson were working hard to persuade the Foreign Affairs Committee to hold a hearing on the issue of child abduction, with Sean's case as the centerpiece. Although the committee was controlled by the Democratic majority and Chris was a Republican, he was a senior member of the minority and had worked with his colleagues across the aisle in the past to pass groundbreaking legislation to curb child sex trafficking around the world. Bernie called the chairman of the committee, Howard Berman of California, and the subcommittee chairman, William Delahunt of Massachusetts, an old friend, urging them to schedule a hearing. Chris's chief of staff, Mary Noonan, cajoled and persuaded other staffers on the committee.

Early in October, I received an invitation to testify as the lead witness on October 29, 2009, before Delahunt's Washington Subcommittee on International Organizations, Human Rights, and Oversight on Parental Child Abductions. Bernie Aronson and Tricia Apy were also scheduled to testify. Finally, we were getting somewhere. For weeks I worked on my testimony. This was really going to make a difference, I was sure. Then the bottom fell out from under me. Just days before the hearing was to convene, I was called by one of the subcommittee's staffers. The hearing had to be postponed.

The explanation the staffer gave me was that Chairman Delahunt had to meet another commitment, but later we were told something else. Some Democrats on the committee, including some from New Jersey, seemed increasingly envious of the national attention Chris Smith was receiving in the media for championing my case. We heard rumors that there were fears that this could be damaging politically to other representatives in Congress including my own congressman, Rush Holt, a Democrat, who had been late in providing his support.

For whatever reason, partisan envy and politics, or something else entirely, a forum to bring national attention to the plight of thousands of American children abducted and held in dozens of countries around the world was being scuttled. Didn't these congressmen understand? Did they have a clue as to the heartrending pain gripping thousands of American families who had an empty chair at every dinner, every birthday, Thanksgiving, and Christmas, where a child, grandchild, brother, sister, niece, or nephew used to sit? I had wanted to move my struggle from Tinton Falls to Washington because I was sure our nation's capital was where serious issues such as parental child abduction could be solved. Now I began to wonder if I was right.

The cancellation of this second hearing was a serious setback. If the government of Brazil thought the U.S. Congress no longer viewed our case as a pressing matter, they might stonewall even more, and the kidnappers surely would be emboldened.

CHRIS SMITH WAS also a member of the Tom Lantos Human Rights Commission, named in honor of the late California congressman, the only Holocaust survivor to serve in the U.S. Congress. After the Foreign Affairs hearing was canceled, Chris worked to arrange a hearing by the caucus on the problem of parental child abduction. In November, the hearing was finally scheduled, primarily at the insistence of Congressman Smith. I was now to appear before the Lantos Commission on December 2, 2009, again as the lead witness.

The Lantos commission did not have the same standing as Delahunt's subcommittee, which could propose and vote on legislation, subpoena witnesses, and oversee the workings of the executive branch. The commission could only advise. Still, it was an official entity of the U.S. Congress, an opportunity to tell our story to the world.

The Lantos commission was cochaired by representatives Frank Wolf of Virginia and James McGovern of Massachusetts. Unfortunately, McGovern could not stay for the entire session, but Frank Wolf, Chris Smith, Rush Holt, and Virginia congressman James Moran were there.

We met in Room 1310 of the Longworth House Office Building, a stately complex just south of Capitol Hill. The hearing attracted a large crowd of media, embassy officials from various countries, and other concerned citizens. Extra chairs had to be brought in to accommodate the overflow crowd of spectators and press. I sat at a long table in front of the committee members, along with three other "left-behind" fathers. Behind me sat my mother and father. Wendy, Mark, and dozens of our Web site friends were in the crowd to give me support and solidarity. Their presence helped.

Congressman Smith opened the hearing with a powerful statement. "International child abduction is a huge scandal," he told the committee, "that has been significantly enabled by ignorance, indifference, incompetence, or outright complicity by far too many governments around the world. The present state of affairs is unconscionable and must change."

The congressman then briefly outlined the history of the four dads scheduled to speak. "David Goldman's situation cries out for an immediate and final resolution," he said. "Under the Hague Convention, Sean should have been returned within six weeks. David, however, has been forced by incessant and frivolous appeals in the Brazilian legal system to pursue his case for over five long years—at an astronomical cost in personal heartbreak and financial resources."

Congressman Smith recounted some of the details of my case. Then he shocked me by saying, "I would be remiss if I did not note here that David Goldman has demonstrated remarkable resolve, clarity of purpose, uncommon bravery, and deep and abiding love for his son. David Goldman is an inspiration—a true hero. He has not only made bringing Sean home a near-term probability, but has tangibly helped every left-behind parent and abducted child—especially those who had lost hope. David's tenacious persistence for the return of his son has launched a movement, a noble cause of left-behind parents uniting for justice, their rights as parents, and the return of their kids."

I sat with my hands folded, my head slightly bowed. I was so honored by the congressman's words. I didn't see myself as a hero; I was just a dad who loved his son, just as the other three men sitting at the table loved their children. Congressman Smith also effusively heaped praise upon them before concluding his remarks.

"Most of these cases, as we will hear, have been dragging on for years—years of loving relationships and happy memories that these parents will never get back even if they do see and are reunited with their children someday.

"Abducted children often lose their relationship with their mom or their dad, half of their identity and half of their culture. They are at risk of serious emotional and psychological problems and have been found to experience anxiety, eating problems, nightmares, mood swings, sleep disturbances, aggressive behavior, resentment, guilt, and fearfulness. As adults, they may struggle with identity issues, their own personal relationships, and parenting."

I could tell that Congressman Smith was winding up for a big finish, and he came through powerfully. "Child abduction is a serious crime," he said, "that no legitimate or self-respecting judicial body anywhere on earth should ever countenance, support, or enable. Child abduction is child abuse. We must call it what it is. And we must take action to back up our words."

And then it was my turn. I proceeded to explain to the committee as succinctly as possible the basic details of Sean's abduction and continued retention in Brazil. I told them of the ongoing, contrived legal machinations used to keep Sean in Brazil even after the Brazilian courts had said he should come home. I also told them of the psychological abuse Sean was undergoing, as attested by the Brazilian court-appointed psychologists. I admitted my own discouragement and disappointment that despite statements from President Obama and Secretary of State Clinton, Brazil continued to drag its feet in returning Sean and so far had suffered no consequences for its flagrant violations of its treaty obligations.

"We cannot dwell on or bring back the years we have lost," I said in closing, "but we can hope to look forward to the remaining precious years ahead. My son, Sean, is still a young boy and he can still heal, but he needs to come home now." I paused briefly and looked up at the committee members. "I appeal and plead to all of you at the most basic level of human decency to respect the sanctity of the parent-child relationship. Please take action to make a difference, to bring change, to bring our children home."

Next, Commander Paul Toland, who had served our country for more than twenty years in the U.S. Navy, shared his heartrending story in full-dress uniform. In 2003 his daughter, Erika, had been abducted by his former wife, Etsuko, from their home on the U.S. naval base in Yokohama, Japan. Suffering from depression, Etsuko committed suicide in 2007. Though devastated by his former wife's death, Commander Toland was certain he would be immediately reunited with his daughter. But Erika now lived with her maternal grandmother, and the Japanese government, which refused even to sign the Hague Convention, would not lift a finger to return his daughter. Like me, Commander Toland had incurred staggering legal fees. "Japan," Commander Toland stated, was a "haven" and a "black hole for abduction, from which no child ever returns." Indeed, he informed the commission, his late wife's family had refused him any contact with his daughter.

In gripping testimony, Commander Toland described how he had flown to Japan and stood on a street corner waiting for his daughter to get out of school, simply so he could give her some birthday presents. "I knew that if I tried to take Erika to the embassy and get a passport, I would likely meet the same fate as Christopher Savoie met when he tried to retrieve his children from Japan." Savoie's former wife violated a Tennessee court order and absconded with their two children, taking them back to her Japanese homeland. Savoie followed, tracked her down, and attempted to retrieve his children after his ex-wife dropped them off at school. When he showed up at the U.S. embassy, the police were waiting for him, and charged him with child abduction. Savoie was still in a Japanese jail even as we sat in the hearing room. Commander Toland risked receiving the same sort of treatment. He was able to deliver the presents to his daughter, but it was a very brief visit.

"I never dreamed," Commander Toland testified, "that serving my country overseas in one of our allied nations would result in the loss of my only child." He then asked the question that was on the minds of nearly everyone in the room: "How can a nation we call an ally be guilty of such despicable human rights violations and get away with it?" When he was done, there wasn't a sound in the chamber. His unanswered question hung in the air.

Patrick Braden of Los Angeles also testified. The last time he saw his daughter, Melissa, was in 2006. She, too, was abducted to Japan. Tom Sylvester's daughter, Carina, was a mere thirteen months old when she was abducted and whisked off to Austria. As Tom spoke of her before the committee, Carina was now fifteen years old. "For the past fourteen years I have lived in a world where right is wrong and wrong is right," Sylvester concluded. I knew exactly what he was talking about. That was the world I had lived in every waking hour since Sean was stolen from me.

By the time the four of us fathers finished, Congressman Wolf was connecting the financial dots to the lack of compliance. "Wait a minute," he addressed Tom Sylvester. "Your daughter is in Austria? Wasn't Austria rebuilt with American dollars under the Marshall Plan? And your daughter, sir"—he looked in Commander Toland's direction—"is in Japan. Wasn't Japan rebuilt with American dollars?" The congressman's point was clear: the countries the United States had helped so dramatically in the past had done absolutely nothing to help return illegally abducted American children to their parents.

The hearing continued with testimony from Patricia Apy and Judge Peter Messitte, both highly regarded experts on the Hague Convention; also testifying was the president of the National Center for Missing and Exploited Children, Ernie Allen, as well as Bernie Aronson.

Bernie made a powerful presentation from the start. Looking at the members of Congress, he declared, "If twenty-eight hundred American children were abducted tomorrow by Somali pirates, or a transnational kidnapping ring, or a group of terrorists, the president of the United States would summon congressional leaders to the White House, convene an emergency meeting of the National Security

Council in the Situation Room, dispatch Delta Forces and aircraft carriers to where the children were being held, send his United Nations ambassador to convene an emergency meeting of the Security Council, and go before the nation in prime time to report on what the U.S. government would do to secure the return of these abducted children.

"As you know, two thousand eight hundred American children *have* been abducted," Bernie emphasized, "and are being held illegally in other nations—not in one dramatic action, but in ones and twos, month after month, year after year. But there is no emergency meeting in the White House or the State Department, and no sense of crisis."

Bernie then used a clever rhetorical device to make a dramatic point with the commission. He quoted strong statements about international child abduction made by the chairman of the House International Relations Committee, two members of that committee, the chairman of the Senate Foreign Relations Committee, and a ranking member of that committee. Then Bernie sprung the trap.

"Every one of us would agree with these sentiments," he testified, "but here is the problem in quoting them. The quote from the chairman of the International Relations Committee dates from a hearing, 'A Parent's Worst Nightmare: The Heartbreak of International Child Abductions,' which was held June 22, 2004—more than five years ago—and the chairman is the late Henry Hyde."

That was a mere six days after my own son was abducted, I thought.

Bernie continued: "The quotes from the two members of the same committee were from an earlier hearing on abducted children held more than ten years ago [October 14, 1999] . . . The statement I cited from the chairman of the Senate Foreign Relations Committee is from a hearing eleven years ago on the U.S. response to international Parental Abduction [October 1, 1998], and the chairman quoted is the late Jesse Helms. The second senator quoted from the same hearing was then ranking member, now vice president, Joseph Biden . . . But let's be honest with each other: all of the statements

I quoted from your colleagues a decade ago could have been made at this hearing and are just as relevant today. And that is the central problem . . . the time for speeches about the plight of America's abducted children is over; the time to do something about it is now."

Bernie then went on to offer tangible suggestions to the committee about what essential steps should be taken.

I sat in awe as I listened and silently breathed a prayer of thanks that Bernie Aronson, like Chris Smith, had become a champion of this cause.

I had barely exited the hearing room when CNN grabbed me for an interview, asking me what good I thought might result from the hearing. The following morning, I appeared again on the *Today* show, expressing hope that the hearing might prompt some action in Brazil regarding Sean's return, as well as the return of the sixty-six other abducted children in that country.

On December 8, 2009, six members of the Tom Lantos Human Rights Commission sent a letter to President Obama asking him to meet with us regarding the issue of international parental child abduction. Although a meeting never took place, the issue was once again squarely in front of the president.

Congressman Smith and Bernie Aronson also encouraged me to meet again with New Jersey senator Frank Lautenberg, which I was happy to do. Bernie had been introduced to the senator when he was first elected to the Senate in 1982, and Lautenberg had asked him to serve as his administrative assistant. Though Bernie could not take the job, they stayed in touch over the years. In another one of those moments of serendipity, they ran into each other in December at the Kennedy Center Honors in Washington. Bernie took the opportunity to talk to the senator about my case. He told Lautenberg about the anti-Semitism the Ribeiros and Lins e Silvas had been fomenting against me in Brazil. On one of my recent visits, Paolo Lins e Silva had participated in a demonstration against me outside my hotel, where marchers called me a "dirty Jew." Later, as I maneuvered through the airport crowd on my way home, hecklers called out, "Go home, Jew." Lautenberg, who was Jewish himself and active in Jewish causes, listened carefully. He told Bernie he had been very moved in his meeting with me and wanted to help in any way. Bernie said he believed that unless Brazil and other countries that refused to return abducted American children faced real consequences, they were unlikely to meet their treaty obligations, because public opinion and nationalism worked in favor of the abducting parent. Bernie suggested that suspension of trade privileges would get Brazil's attention.

In the halls of Congress, I saw real statesmanship and caring, and Senator Lautenberg was a prime example of this. But I also saw childish partisan behavior between people who ostensibly wanted to help me. I realized that if people truly want to help, they will do so on the basis of what is good for *you*, not necessarily on the basis of what is best for them. If they get offended because you don't want to do things their way, that's probably a good indication of misguided motives. That's one of the reasons I appreciated Congressman Chris Smith so much. From the very beginning, he said, "I'll do whatever you want me to do to help. You are the quarterback." And he was true to his word. At his own expense and with no notice, he had hopped on a plane with me to Brazil. It made a difference. The embassy paid attention to a visiting congressman, and the media hung on his every word.

THROUGHOUT NOVEMBER AND early December 2009, Bernie and Bob Gelbard called the State Department and the White House on a regular basis, encouraging them to keep the heat on Brazil. In November, President Obama traveled to Europe to attend another meeting that Brazil's president Lula also attended. With a crucial decision looming before the Brazilian Supreme Court, Bernie urged that Obama mention the case again to President Lula. Later, a former State Department colleague hinted that it had happened, but we never knew for sure.

Renewal of the annual Generalized System of Preferences bill granting most favored nation trade status was before Congress, too. Senator Lautenberg came through with flying colors. He threatened to put a senatorial "hold" on the legislation, saying he would lift the hold only when Sean Goldman was permitted to return home. It was a legislative atomic bomb. GSP privileges allow countries to avoid paying import excise taxes on certain items, a privilege almost every developing country has with the United States. Its renewal was vital, not only for Brazil, but for 111 other nations. The State Department got the message—and so, I believe, did Brazil. Congressman Smith supported Senator Lautenberg's decision to keep the pressure on Brazil until our case was resolved. The senator promised to do his best for as long as he could. That was not easy to do. In fact, the senator was threatening the global trading system and eventually would have to yield. But this was a potential game changer, and I was overwhelmed with gratitude. At great political risk, Senator Lautenberg was willing to stall a trade bill that affected three quarters of the countries of the world simply to help get Sean home.

As the clock ticked toward another year's end, pressure was mounting on the Brazilian government from Congress, the State Department, the White House, and, increasingly, public opinion in Brazil, which to the great credit of the Brazilian people had started to swing to our side. Something had to break soon. And on December 15, 2009, it did.

19

=== ■ ■ ■ ===

The Decision

L ATE ON THE EVENING OF DECEMBER 15, TRICIA APY GOT WORD from Ricardo that the Brazilian Federal Regional Tribunal, a three-judge appellate court, was about to make a decision regarding the appeals to Judge Pinto's June 1 decision ordering Sean's return to me. We were not exactly sure when the court might act, or whether the Lins e Silvas and Ribeiros might find another way to obfuscate the proceedings, but my lawyers and I agreed that if a ruling came down, I should go back to Rio. As bleak as my last trips to Brazil had been, I didn't want to miss any chance to bring Sean home.

Sure enough, the following day, on Wednesday, December 16, the court issued a unanimous ruling upholding Judge Pinto's return order of seven months earlier, demanding that the Lins e Silvas and Ribeiros return Sean to me at the U.S. consulate in Rio de Janeiro by Friday, December 18.

Almost immediately, reporters showed up on the front yard outside my home. They posed all the usual questions: What do you expect? Do you think this is it? Will you be bringing Sean home?

I replied with an answer that became almost a mantra for me. "I'm hopeful," I said. "I can't be optimistic because I've gone down there so many times, always under the guise that the rule of law will be followed and I will be reunited with my son and able to bring him home. The judges upheld the first return order, so hopefully this time Sean and I will come home together."

I quickly put some clothes in a suitcase and was ready to head to the airport. I also packed a number of Christmas presents, hoping to give them to Sean.

When I contacted Congressman Smith to tell him the news, he was ecstatic. It wasn't even a question for him—he offered to go back to Brazil with me, but only if I wanted him to and if he could be helpful. He never imposed; indeed, he left the final decision up to Tricia Apy, Ricardo, and me. We unanimously agreed that his presence would be invaluable.

Although it was a mere nine days before Christmas, Congressman Smith immediately committed to traveling with me to Rio for the third time in less than a year. He knew only too well the legal gamesmanship that might be employed, even at this late point. He and his wife, Marie, were willing for him to travel as a private citizen, at his own expense if necessary, so he could be there with me. Fortunately, as it turned out, he was able to travel with House approval, which not only covered his travel expenses but also gave him added strength with Brazilian officials and our own State Department and consulate.

Moreover, Congressman Smith told me that he was determined to stay as long as necessary to bring Sean home. For the congressman and his wife, it was not about money or politics; it was about family. Marie Smith had met with me and was as emotionally invested in seeing Sean come home as anyone. Still, it touched me deeply that she and Chris would be willing to make such a sacrifice—for the congressman to be apart from their children and grandchildren at this special season—especially when we had no guarantee of the results.

BECAUSE NEWARK'S AIRPORT was being staked out by the media, and possibly by an insider for Lins e Silva, I decided to fly out of John F.

Kennedy Airport in New York at 9:45 PM on Wednesday evening. Just before I left for the airport, I received an e-mail from Bob D'Amico informing me that Secretary of State Hillary Clinton had issued a statement expressing her pleasure at the appellate court's decision and her hope that the long legal process was complete.

I greatly appreciated Secretary Clinton's remarks and her expression of support. She continued to be a true soldier in this battle. And as much as I shared her hope that the long nightmare was nearly over, those of us close to the front lines of the fracas knew all too well that the Lins e Silva and Ribeiro families would file appeals to the Supreme Court.

I boarded the plane, leaned back in my seat, and closed my eyes for another late-night flight from New York to Rio. Sleep eluded me; my thoughts raced. Although I had hopes that I'd soon be flying home with Sean sitting next to me, there were still a lot of loose ends. We now had the return order, but at any moment we knew that the Lins e Silvas might try to secure another stay order holding Sean in Brazil. We also worried that even with a return order, if we were stalled at the airport, waiting for a commercial flight back to the States, we would still be vulnerable to the whims of the Brazilian legal system should the Lins e Silvas persuade a Supreme Court Justice to stay Sean's return. Of more concern was the possibility that the Ribeiros or the Lins e Silvas would spirit Sean away, rather than comply with a valid order of the court. These people had seemingly unlimited resources, and to my knowledge the Ribeiros also held Italian passports. Although my attorneys had been assured that the Italian authorities would work closely with us in the event someone tried to secretly remove Sean from Brazil, we were certainly concerned.

Bernie Aronson, Mark DeAngelis, and I had discussed renting a private plane to have standing by at Galeão airport in Rio, ready to whisk us away, but rentals were extremely expensive, especially considering that we didn't know when or even if we'd be able to take off. Bernie's former executive assistant at the State Department, Bill Brownfield, now an ambassador to Colombia, offered to meet Sean and me in Bogotá should we choose to fly to that country, a relatively short plane flight that could be done without a high-powered jet air-craft. From there we could make our way back to the United States on a commercial flight. That, too, however, seemed a complicated and risky venture.

As I looked out the airplane window to once again see Rio's giant statue of Jesus rising in the distance, I still had no definitive exit plan. It was Thursday, December 17, 2009, what would have been Bruna's and my tenth wedding anniversary.

EVEN WITH THE three-judge panel ordering the kidnappers to turn over my son, I had no illusions about the whole nightmare being over. From the time Judge Pinto issued his initial return order in June, the Lins e Silvas and Ribeiros had filed more than forty appeals in their incessant attempts to delay Sean's return to me. I had no reason to expect any better of them now. I had too much experience with these people; my hopes had been dashed too many times. I could no longer allow myself to get excited; nor did I try to anticipate the next strata-gem of Sean's abductors. Instead, I attempted to remain on an even emotional keel, hoping for the best yet realizing that the powerful people we confronted, well-connected members of the Brazilian elite, were used to having their way. I knew they would manipulate the system to produce a judicial finding, however ridiculous its merits, if they thought they could keep Sean in Brazil. They had already pulled more legal rabbits out of more hats than I could fathom, and I was convinced they would try to do so again.

I landed in Rio around 1:30 PM, headed toward the baggage claim, and retrieved my suitcase. The moment I exited the immigration, cus-toms, and security areas, I was greeted by a cacophony of catcalls, some of which were obscene, mixed in with encouraging words from other onlookers. I was instantly surrounded by a throng of photog-raphers, reporters, and television cameras, with people pushing and pulling in every direction. "The boy belongs here!" I heard someone holler. "You just want money!" someone else yelled out, echoing the

Lins e Silva smear campaign. Others shouted, "He's your son. The boy belongs with you." I remained silent and looked straight ahead, trying not to make eye contact with anyone. I wanted to get out of there as quickly as possible. Airport security personnel and military police surrounded me as I made my way toward the exit. I ignored the scrum and pressed through the crowd and toward the street, where I paused long enough to respond to questions.

When reporters asked me what I thought our chances were of bringing Sean home, I again answered, "I'm hopeful. I've been on the roller-coaster ride too many times. I've made a dozen trips to Brazil, ready to bring Sean home each time, and I've returned empty-handed and feeling as though I was kicked in the teeth again. So I'm hopeful."

My heart was pounding as I pulled my luggage toward the car that would take me to my hotel. The press crush followed me, and the crowd picked up more people and became more animated as I went along. Police cars with sirens blaring had to surround the car just to get me out of the airport grounds.

Congressman Smith had flown on a different flight, but he arrived in Brazil about the same time I did. Immediately upon landing, he issued a strong statement. "For the sake of Sean's emotional and psychological health, he should be on a plane back to his home in the United States on Friday," he stated emphatically. "The courts in Brazil have once again determined that Sean Goldman must be returned to his father in the United States, vindicating the right of a father to be with his son, and a son to be with his father."

Then Congressman Smith inserted a subtle reminder that Sean's return was Brazil's moral duty and had been so since I first applied for help under the Hague Convention. "The decision upholds Brazil's commitment under the Hague Convention to return abducted children." Revealing a bit of the bulldog side to his personality, Congressman Smith spoke bluntly. "Further frivolous and delaying motions and appeals by the [Lins e] Silva family must stop."

Congressman Smith said what we were all feeling. "It is long past time for Sean to come home. Sean was four when he was abducted, and now he is nine. For five years, the wheels of justice in Brazil have been torturously slow. David Goldman has been robbed of a large part of his son's childhood. But David is a father who has never given up in his fight to bring his son home. He will not surrender his right to raise his child— rights of which he was wrongly deprived in the 2004 abduction."

Then, in case there was any doubt about the U.S. position and the potential damage to U.S.-Brazil relations, Congressman Smith added, "The U.S. Congress is strongly behind him." In his inimitable manner, the congressman spoke frankly and firmly about the consequences to Brazil if they refused to do the right thing. "I hope there are no more delays," he said. "The world would remain left with the impression that Brazil will not enforce the treaties it signs, and cruelly leaves children like Sean Goldman trapped for years in an endless judicial maze.

"All the world is still watching and waiting to learn if Brazil is a nation of the rule of law, a nation that lives up to its international commitments."

As we arrived at the J. W. Marriott hotel on Avenida Atlantica, across from Copacabana Beach, the early morning skies were blue and the sun was already shining brightly. I took that as a good sign. I checked into my room under the name "Richard Spain," as instructed by an intermediary from the U.S. embassy, who had helped arrange my lodging. The Marriott graciously gave me the government rate of $200 a day—still a hefty sum for me—instead of the usual winter holiday daily rate of $550. I hoped that I would not be staying long.

ALMOST IMMEDIATELY, THE ground shifted below our feet. On Thursday, December 17, before I barely had time to settle in at the hotel, I received news that the Brazilian Supreme Court justice Marco Aurelio de Mello—the same justice who had stymied Sean's coming home in June—issued another stay order on Sean's return, retaining him in Brazil. The Supreme Court was scheduled to go on recess the next day until February 2010! Justice Aurelio de Mello's rationalization of the stay was that it would permit time to review a writ of habeas corpus filed by Silvana Ribeiro, who was a party to the Hague case. Even more perplexing, Aurelio de Mello told the media that the case should be reviewed in accordance with the UN Convention on the Rights of the Child, rather than on the basis of the Hague Convention. Singlehandedly, Aurelio de Mello shunted aside his government's commitment to cooperate according to the Hague Convention. How could it be that one man could effectively repudiate Brazil's international agreement?

Silvana Ribeiro was now insisting that Sean himself take the witness stand to testify in court regarding his wishes, stating whether he wanted to stay in Brazil or return to the United States. Sergio Tostes displayed a poster that he claimed Sean had drawn, depicting a sad boy saying, "I want to stay in Brazil forever."

I vehemently opposed putting my son on the witness stand. Both the Brazilian Central Authority, on behalf of the Brazilian government, and Ricardo filed immediately to lift the stay with the Brazilian Supreme Court in Brasília, seeking to exclude the most recent injunction issued by Justice Aurelio de Mello. Congressman Smith also responded vigorously by speaking boldly on the Friday, December 18, edition of the *Today* show, on which we appeared together, sitting side by side.

"David's legal team will file, and will aggressively push that an egregious harm is in the process of being done," the congressman told Meredith Vieira. "Three psychologists have found that David's son, Sean, is being hurt psychologically every day that he is away from his real father—parental alienation." The Brazilian court-appointed psychologists who had examined Sean warned that the abductors inflicted more psychological damage upon him every day he remained in their captivity. Congressman Smith wasn't going to let either the Brazilian or the American public forget that.

Meredith then asked me, "If the court rules that Sean may testify—and that's the reason for this injunction right now—and if he does testify and says that he wants to stay in Brazil, as his Brazilian relatives have said he will say, then what recourse will you have?"

"First of all, the judge has not put Sean in the position to testify," I explained. "He already has testified. He's been heard loud and clear by three Brazilian court-appointed psychologists. This family did not like the results: that they are abusing him and that Sean was fine with coming home. They read the report, they saw us together, and they could not stand it." I could feel the color rising in my face as I spoke passionately. "They took him upstairs and have been using him as a hostage, brainwashing him, torturing him, while the father of the man who is holding my son lectures throughout this country about how he can turn the child as an attack missile against the parent . . . and how a clever lawyer can keep a child in Brazil indefinitely by filing endless motions and appeals."

Congressman Smith added, "If the precedent is set, that nine- and eight- and seven-year-olds can be put in front of a video camera and coerced or coached into saying, 'I want to stay in Brazil or Japan,' that precedent will lead to the kidnappers' having incredibly more power over the abducted child, because they have to go home that night."

In another interview, when asked for my reaction, I spoke tersely but honestly. "I'm very frustrated," I said, "that my son is still held here, in this environment, and I cannot do a thing to get him out of there. I'm not giving up; he's coming home. It's not over."

Back in Washington, on Friday, when New Jersey senator Frank Lautenberg heard the news about the most recent stay order in Brazil, as he had threatened to do, he slapped a hold on the GSP trade bill in the U.S. Senate. The bill had provided $2.75 billion in benefits to Brazil the year before, and the nation stood to receive a similar concession or more in 2010. According to the senator's office, Brazil was the fifth largest recipient of these privileges. For the first time since Bruna had ignored the court orders and the Hague Convention requirements to return Sean in 2004, the stakes for Brazil had suddenly gotten higher. Brazil now faced serious economic punishment for its recalcitrance. Moreover, Senator Lautenberg's hold not only affected Brazil; it also stalled similar concessions to more than one hundred other countries.

"You can't hold a child that belongs to an American citizen with any excuse," Senator Lautenberg told reporters. "Just bring that boy back."

Whether it was directly connected to Lautenberg's actions—I had no idea—but that same day in Brazil, Luis Inácio Adams, the Brazilian advocate general, a position similar to that of the attorney general in the United States, filed a "writ of mandamus" in Brazil's Supreme Court against Supreme Court justice Marco Aurelio de Mello for granting the stay order. The writ of mandamus ("we command" in Latin) essentially stood in rebuke of Aurelio de Mello, mandating that he perform his duties correctly. The advocate general asked that the stay order by Justice Aurelio de Mello be annulled. Ricardo and our legal team filed a similar writ. We could only hope that the chief justice of Brazil's Supreme Court would decide in our favor.

Ricardo also attempted to inform the Ribeiros that I was in town and that I wanted to see Sean. According to court orders, upon giving them seventy-two hours' advance notice, I was supposed to be able to see my son, but the Ribeiros never responded to Ricardo's request. It may have been just as well. As much as I wanted to see Sean, I knew the Ribeiros would pressure him to show no affection toward me and then punish him if he did. I didn't want to put him through any more "supervised" visits. I just wanted to take him home.

In one of the sickest moments of what Congressman Smith had come to refer to as "the theater of the absurd," Tostes, the Ribeiros' attorney, appeared to hold out an olive branch to me, extending an invitation from the Ribeiros to have Christmas dinner with them and Sean. Silvana or Ray didn't call and say, "David, would you please come over for dinner and gather with us as we used to do?" No, quite the contrary; the "invitation" was delivered much the same way as a subpoena. Tostes then read the invitation during a taped interview on ABC's *Nightline*. "We want a truce. We want to bring the family together for a family reunion," he said.

I could just imagine that scene. I pictured Tostes as a vicious cartoon caricature holding out an invitation to Christmas dinner with one hand while grasping a hatchet behind his back in the other. There was no way I was going to trust that guy.

While sequestered in the hotel room, I happened upon the ABC television interview featuring Tostes. Jeffrey Kofman, a highly professional and respectful reporter with whom I had done several brief interviews, asked Tostes, "If the courts say that Sean should be home with his father, what will you do then?"

"We have more proof," Tostes lied, "that the man is an unfit father."

"Oh, you have proof?"

"Of course we do!" replied the bombastic attorney. I just rolled my eyes as I listened to his lies. The man had no integrity. Apparently, to him, a statement devoid of fact could be considered true if it could be used to his advantage. I shook my head and changed the channel. Trying to respond to Tostes's absurdities would be expending energy I did not have. Nor would I stoop to his level in this fight.

THE THRONG OF television cameras, journalists, and protesters clamoring for information outside the hotel was getting increasingly boisterous. The hotel manager was concerned for the safety of the other guests, and asked me to address the crowd. "Please go down there and make some sort of statement," he asked. "No one can even get in or out of the building."

Ricardo cautioned me to be careful about what I said, and to watch out for any traps—questions planted by the opposition to make me look foolish or untrustworthy. I understood Ricardo's concerns, but told him I had nothing to hide and I would speak only the truth. Congressman Smith and I walked outside the Marriott's front entrance and were immediately surrounded by a mob of reporters and cameras. I was casually dressed in a golf shirt, but I looked tired and strained. It was obvious I was not on vacation. Once I got away from the Marriott's front door and out onto a walkway, I stopped and addressed the crowd.

I began by thanking them for coming. "I thank all of the Brazilian citizens who see the right of a parent and a child," I said. "It's not a difficult thing to imagine. Sean is my family. Sean is my son. I'm his dad. Not 'He's Brazilian,' not 'He's American,' not 'He's from anywhere.' He's my son.

"I'm just a dad who wants to be with his son. My son has been here; we've been separated for five years. He tragically lost his mom. He should have never been taken; we should never have been torn apart. And all of you can understand that. They're trying to paint this picture of 'Brazil versus America,' and it is not. In a case like this, a parent could be from Istanbul or from Greece. It's not about that.

"It's about a parent's right to be with his child, and a child's right to know and be with his or her parent. And people anywhere in the world in all walks of life can understand that."

As I was speaking, I noticed that several reporters had lowered their microphones and were simply listening. A few cameramen had done the same. Many of their faces were fraught with emotion. Several of them were crying. It was as if they finally got it. They understood.

One of the older television reporters dropped to his knees in front of me, still holding his microphone stretched out in my direction. I recognized him as one of the most esteemed television journalists in Brazil, sort of the Walter Cronkite of that country. And there he was on his knees at my feet, tears welling in his eyes.

I looked at him and spoke passionately. "You're on your knees, as I'm on my knees, begging for my son to come home, begging for justice, begging. Why is it so hard? I don't understand why . . . and it's wrong and it's cruel and it's sad, and my son is suffering and is losing his innocence as a child."

One of the reporters brought up that Sean had drawn a picture and had written that he wanted to stay in Brazil.

"How do I know that he wrote it?" I held up a postmarked but unopened card from November 16 that had been returned to me after I had sent it to Sean. "They won't even let him receive letters," I said, showing the unopened card.

Someone asked what I hoped to gain from all this. I responded passionately, "I'm hoping to leave with my son and bring him home to his family, to enjoy Christmas, and to go play in the yard, and build a model and do the things we had once done as a father and son, and just go to a movie, and eat popcorn, and do like anyone. Anyone in Brazil, in America, in Istanbul, knows the right of a parent and a child."

People on the street began calling out, "He's your son. He belongs with you!" Several seemed deeply moved as they called out, "Forgive us, Mr. Goldman. Forgive our country."

The interview ran on local television and all over the country on O Globo. It was a turning point in the Brazilian people's understanding of my case. Prior to that time, because of the media cap on the case, the Brazilian public had been kept in the dark about why I refused to relent in my quest to be reunited with my son. The little information that was leaked to the public purposely led people to believe that the case was a legal imbroglio between Brazil and the United States, with the northern "bully" attempting to coerce Brazil to give up one of its own. Once the media cap was lifted, Brazilians were mostly influenced by the smear campaign perpetuated by the Lins e Silvas. Many people in the country received misinformation about the case, and especially about me.

Now, for the first time, Brazilians saw the human side of the story. They could identify with a father's love for his son, and they were repulsed and embarrassed by the sort of selfish manipulation and influence that wealthy, well-connected Brazilian families had exerted in their country for so long at the expense of ordinary citizens. More than a few were convinced that justice existed only for the rich and powerful in their country, and they now identified Sean and me as one more set of victims of Brazil's ruling elite.

In one article written subsequent to my impromptu press conference, an O Globo Web site commentator known as André Thomaz Filho said, "It's impressive how the Lins e Silva family achieved an almost unheard-of feat in this country: it united the great majority of the Brazilian population in favor of an American! Who would have thought?"

20

•••

Tension Rising

Sunday morning, December 20, dawned a gorgeous day—and it got better, although, to me, the beauty of that day had nothing to do with the tropical weather. Late that day, an announcement was made by Brazil's Supreme Court that Chief Justice Gilmar Mendes would issue a ruling on Monday deciding on the appeals made by the advocate general and me. If Mendes decided in our favor, the ruling would lift the stay on the December 16 decision that Sean should be returned to me. That was great news! It meant we would not have to wait until February, when the full membership of the Brazilian Supreme Court was back in session, before getting a decision.

Upon hearing the news, Sergio Tostes temporarily took a more conciliatory tone, saying that he would like to see a negotiated settlement, piously stating that he "wanted to end the damage being done to Sean and to U.S.-Brazil relations."

"We're raising the white flag," Tostes told other reporters, "and saying, 'Let's get together; let's talk. We're the adults; we have responsibilities, so let's start to have a constructive conversation.'" In almost the same breath, he then suggested that he preferred to negotiate with Bernard Aronson because of his diplomatic experience, as though Tostes were Bernie's Brazilian counterpart. It was just another diversion; Bernie and I rejected the idea out of hand.

Though I remained calm publicly, the Ribeiro attorney's audacious propensity for twisting the truth irritated me. There was nothing to negotiate. When a reporter asked me about the Tostes proposal, I answered straightforwardly, "This isn't about shared custody. I'm Sean's dad; I'm his only father and his only parent. This isn't a custody case—it's an abduction case."

Another reporter asked me whether the Brazilian family would be able to visit the boy if Sean and I were reunited. It was a seminal moment, but I had already answered that question in my heart. "I will not do to them what they have done to Sean and me."

MONDAY, DECEMBER 21, was one of the longest days of my life. Outside, people were in a festive mood as they prepared for Christmas week in Brazil. Inside the Marriott, I stayed holed up in my room, hopeful that Judge Gilmar Mendes would issue a decision in my favor—lifting the stay and releasing Sean to go back to the United States with me.

Earlier that morning, Ricardo and one of his partners, Marcos Ortiz, had come to Rio from their office in São Paulo, while their third partner, Paulo Roberto Andrade, stayed in Brasília keeping watch at the Supreme Court, where Chief Justice Mendes was said to be readying a decision.

Sometimes when I thought about how young and inexperienced Ricardo and his team were, and that Sean's fate and mine were in their hands, I shuddered. At one point, in 2008, when the case had stalled and nothing was happening, Ricardo and I agreed to seek out more influential attorneys. We checked with six major law firms in Rio. One legal team could not take the case because it claimed prior knowledge through another party. All five of the other law firms refused to go up against the Lins e Silva family. So Ricardo had handled the case thus far all on his own, with Tricia Apy's help in New Jersey.

Representing the Ribeiros was Sergio Tostes, whose partner was the former president of the Tribunal of Justice. Their firm employed sixty-five lawyers and represented some of Brazil's biggest names. The Lins e Silvas themselves boasted that they had fought more than one thousand family law cases.

Often, when Ricardo put on his black legal robe before entering a courtroom, he looked so young and timid compared with the seasoned players against whom he was preparing to do battle. Nevertheless, despite their youth, Ricardo and his partners were as bold as they were brilliant. They had brought us a long way.

By midafternoon on Monday, however, nothing had happened; no ruling had come down. Though Ricardo and Marcos tried to maintain hope, I could see the tension in their faces. Even Congressman Smith seemed concerned. From one of his many calls back to his chief of staff, Mary Noonan, he had learned that Senator Frank Lautenberg's Democratic colleagues were demanding that the senator withdraw his hold on the GSP money by the time the Senate was to go out of session, which was likely December 23 or 24, whether Sean was released or not.

On the phone with Senator Lautenberg, Congressman Smith discussed separating the bill, releasing the GSP provisions for all countries *except* Brazil. While Senator Lautenberg was mulling that over, Congressman Smith handed me the phone. The senator asked me how I was holding up, and then briefed me on what was happening regarding the GSP.

"Thank you so much, sir," I began respectfully.

He cut me off. "Sir? I'm Frank," he said amiably. "Look, I have this hold that is affecting over one hundred countries, and even my staff is telling me that this is political suicide to do this. I told them, 'Suicide? I'm eighty years old. What suicide?' But the truth is, David, I can't keep the hold on forever, but I will keep it on as long as possible. When will a decision be made?"

"We're hoping no more than two days at the latest," I replied.

"Okay, let me know as soon as possible."

"Yes, sir . . . er, yes, Frank, I will. Thank you so much."

"Hang in there, David. I won't go away, and I'll do whatever I can to help get your son home. But keep me updated."

As HOUR AFTER hour dragged by, the tension increased commensurately. I stayed in the hotel room, ready and waiting should there be a decision. I kept telling myself, *There's a reason why the judge is taking so long. He wants to make a really sound decision, and hopefully that will work to our advantage.*

Waiting . . . waiting . . . and more waiting. I couldn't go out anywhere without causing a public spectacle. I suppose there was also some measure of danger. Because of the visibility of the case, I no longer considered threats to my life as likely. Still, crazier things had happened. My attorneys advised me to stay inside as much as possible, just to be safe.

During those tense days in December, Mark DeAngelis and I kept in touch by e-mail, and Bob D'Amico wrote daily updates for our Web site, trying to keep people apprised of the surreal situation in which we were immersed in Brazil. Bernie Aronson called several times from Wales, where he was spending the holiday season with his daughter, and offered great encouragement and sound advice. Bob Gelbard continued to provide information to the administration and to both U.S. and foreign diplomats with whom he had connections to keep them informed of the developments.

Larry King e-mailed me, "As the father of two children, my heart is with you."

John Walsh, the host of television's *America's Most Wanted*, also called to encourage me and offered to help. "Anything I can do, anything you need," he said.

I've always respected John and the tremendous work he has done helping families find justice. On some level I understood the pain he has suffered with the loss of his beloved son, Adam. For every child John helps, with every criminal he tracks down and brings to justice, he is answering a calling of honor and truth and justice that he didn't receive. John knows he can't bring his son back, but he refuses to stand by idly when he can do something to help others avoid the same emotional scars with which he lives every day.

There was some concern that the Ribeiros or Lins e Silvas would take Sean and hide somewhere. John assured me that if that happened, he would use every resource at his disposal to help track them down and bring Sean home. I thanked him for his commitment and his calm words of assurance. I was very grateful for John's kind offer and his encouraging words.

LOOKING OUT THE window of my oceanfront hotel room, I watched families with young children Sean's age frolicking on Copacabana Beach. Ordinarily, I would have enjoyed a room like this. Earlier in my life, I associated hotel rooms with happy times, with vacations to exotic places and new experiences. Now I was beginning to think that I might never want to see another hotel room. Besides, this was more like a war room than a hotel room. It had television and Internet access, so we could keep up with what was happening regarding our case. Congressman Smith worked with his computer and cell phone. I spent long hours on my computer and cell phone, as well. From morning to night, the room was constantly filled with people, so the atmosphere was a perpetual frenzy. Ricardo or Marcos darted in and out, giving instructions or opinions and taking phone calls. Orna Blum, the U.S. embassy press officer, nearly got calluses on her thumbs from working with her BlackBerry communicating with both the embassy in Brasília and the people in the State Department back home.

Benita Noel, the NBC producer, and her assistant stopped in regularly, coordinating coverage with the NBC staff in Rio and setting up coverage with the network. Since our first meeting following my initial appearance on the *Today* show, Benita had been the consummate media professional, but I knew her heart was with Sean and me.

Now here she was giving up her pre-Christmas festivities to be with us in Brazil. She was a real trouper. This was her fourth trip to Brazil to cover the story, and each trip provided her less advance warning and less certainty about the outcome. She had literally gotten the call for this trip while trimming a Christmas tree with her six-year-old daughter. She was hoping to get home in time to finish the decorations before the holiday.

Karen Gustafson de Andrade worked quietly in the corner of the room. She was the U.S. State Department's resource person for all matters pertaining to the Hague Convention. Karen had been with me during the first "supervised" visits with Sean, and had seen firsthand the abuse to which he was subjected. This was no longer just a "case" for her; it was personal.

U.S. consulate officials, lawyers, journalists, and television reporters constantly came and went. Each morning, Congressman Smith and I were interviewed by Meredith Vieira as we sat in front of the window, with Copacabana Beach in the distant background.

Instinctively, I knew that I dared not get caught up in the chaos, that somehow I had to "ice my emotions," to remain calm, clearheaded, and focused. So while the room often turned into a madhouse, I sat stretched out on the bed, wearing casual shorts and a T-shirt, working puzzles in a book that Wendy had given to me. I refused to let my emotions be batted back and forth like a Ping-Pong ball by the latest pronouncements from the opposition or all the legal machinations swirling all around me. Though the outward signs looked promising, I had seen this movie before. Glimpses of progress, an expected ruling, my hopes soaring and then dashed to the ground again. I could not take that anymore.

Throughout the ordeal, Congressman Smith remained steady; he was a tremendous encourager, keeping all of us focused on one issue: "Let's bring Sean home." He stayed close to me the entire time. He sat with me during the intensely stressful moments. He prayed with me. We watched the news reports and ate our meals together. He went with me for every interview, often interjecting things that I could not say without putting myself in legal jeopardy. He was like a big brother to me, providing a strong shoulder for me to lean on. Whenever Congressman Smith had to take a sensitive call from Washington, speaking with other congressmen and senators, he slipped into the hotel room's bathroom or went out in the hallway. Other than that, as long as we were awake, he stayed by my side, shoulder to shoulder, just as he had promised when we first met.

At one point, with the pressure in the room rising because of the opposition's manipulations, against my lawyers' cautions, Congressman Smith and I made a quiet exit, went down the elevator, and slipped out the side door of the hotel. We hastily walked down the street to a nearby church and stepped inside. It felt good to be out of the hotel room, and even better to be in a house of worship. The sanctuary was small and quiet, with people moving about reverently. Congressman Smith and I were immersed in our own silent thoughts and prayers when a man walked over to me. He stared at me for a few seconds and then asked, "Are you the one?"

I didn't say anything, but simply gave him a friendly nod and made it clear from my body language that I wanted to pray. It was a weird moment, and I wasn't sure how to interpret it. The man didn't say anything else; he simply sat down in one of the church pews. Maybe he was praying for me; I sure hoped so.

The NBC crew members covering the story discovered that we were missing and followed the congressman and me to the church, although they were very respectful of our privacy. They allowed us to have our moments of meditation undisturbed by prying cameras.

The constant competition between television networks was interesting to observe, and might have been downright humorous at times, had it not centered around Sean and me. Understandably, NBC felt protective of the story, since they had aired the initial *Today* show interview and the subsequent *Dateline NBC* piece that drew so much attention to my plight. I was glad they wanted to cover the story, but I was unwilling to give anyone exclusivity, and, in fact, I was thankful for any and every news agency that could bring light to the insanity with which we were dealing and help keep the pressure on the Brazilian government to do the right thing.

"Look, I'm not signed with anyone, and I don't want to be. I am not obligated to do anything," I told the various network representatives. "I know you have been kind to me, and I appreciate it. I understand that this is a business for you, but I'm here to get my son. That's all that matters to me. I'm not here to meet your demands and expectations, or to get in the middle of your media fight with other networks. I have to worry about my son and getting us back together."

At no point did I receive any money from any media source for our story, and I personally took no money from anyone associated with our story. We received some donations to the Bring Sean Home Web site, and that money was specifically given to help defray the costs of my attorneys. Other funds were used to help raise public awareness about other abduction cases.

I felt confident that the folks at NBC were truly trying to help me. Plus, I had forged a strong relationship with Meredith Vieira and Benita Noel, who had been covering the story in earnest for nearly a year. For the most part, NBC's attitude seemed to be "We have the resources; we can help this guy, so let's do it." At the same time, ABC was now aggressively pursuing the story as well, with reporters on the scene in Rio. CBS also was covering the story from Brazil, but because the network had brought Silvana, Lins e Silva, and Tostes to the United States to do an interview with Harry Smith and allowed the abductors to blatantly lie and slander me on national television while they held my son illegally, I was skeptical of their intentions. Nevertheless, the network's coverage helped keep the heat on Brazil, so I was grateful for it. CNN and Fox jumped in anytime it seemed something significant might happen in the case.

By six o'clock Monday evening, we were all on tenterhooks, waiting for a call from Brasília that would bring news of Chief Justice Mendes's ruling. His decision, no doubt, would not be as long as

Judge Pinto's eighty-two-page explanation of why Sean should be returned to me—unless Mendes was explaining the opposite. So every moment the process dragged on without a ruling intensified our concern. Marcos had kept his telephone line open so Paulo Roberto Andrade could get through to us immediately if anything happened at the Supreme Court. Suddenly his phone rang, and the flurry of activity in my hotel room instantly stopped. All eyes turned toward Marcos. He pressed the phone to his ear, then quickly shook his head. It was nothing.

By six-thirty, I was resigned to the fact that Sean and I would not be reunited that day. Worse yet, Ricardo's partner had called again from Brasília with news that the Lins e Silvas and Ribeiros had reopened a previous case—one dating back prior to Bruna's death—at the Superior Tribunal of Justice. Ricardo was furious. I was numb, but inside I moaned, *No, no, no! This cannot be happening!* We had a case before the Supreme Court of the land. How could they possibly be allowed to circumvent that by opening a case in a lower court?

Around eight o'clock, Paulo Roberto Andrade called once more from Brasília. "The decision on the writs of mandamus has been postponed until tomorrow."

I was devastated, but Ricardo remained hopeful. "Gilmar Mendes could simply have said there was no rush and that he would wait for the end of the judicial recess," he said. "To do so, he would need to write no more than five lines. He wouldn't need to take as many hours as he is."

With no decision forthcoming that evening, one by one, the crowd of people began to slip from my room. The lawyers and embassy officials were camped out in Ricardo's room. Benita went back to her own hotel room. Orna Blum went to her room, and Karen went home to her family. One of the last to leave was Congressman Smith.

The congressman is a kind man and a good man, a bulwark of integrity and composure, but with the legal shenanigans being played out in the Brazilian courts, and the subsequent emotional distress inflicted upon all of us, especially me, his patience was wearing thin.

That night, after we learned that the decision had been postponed and another legal case reopened, he told NBC reporter Jeff Rossen, "We need to take the gloves off." The congressman again suggested U.S. sanctions against Brazil until they allowed me to take Sean home.

Alone, back in my room, I turned down the volume on the television. The sudden silence and loneliness enveloped me, and I felt as though it would squeeze the breath right out of me.

It had not been a good day. I prayed that perhaps tomorrow would be better. But I had been mouthing that silent prayer since the day I first learned Sean had been abducted. Now, nearly six years later, alone in a hotel room in Brazil, a country whose legal system I could not understand, a nation whose language I did not speak, all I could do was pray one more time. "Dear God, please let my son come home."

21

■ ■ ■

The Christmas Miracle

Unfortunately, Tuesday started out much like Monday, with nothing but silence coming from the Supreme Court in Brasília. Justice Mendes arrived at his office around 11:00 AM, but seemed in no hurry to issue his decision. Paulo Roberto Andrade called us, however, with a bit of encouraging news. When a staff adviser to Gilmar Mendes learned of the Brazilian family's latest appeal to the Superior Tribunal of Justice, the adviser muttered, "This is devious. What do these guys think they are doing?" In my hotel room in Rio, Marcos considered the adviser's comment to be indicative of his boss's attitude. I hoped he was right.

In the meantime, Tricia had been working with law enforcement officials regarding Sean's safe return to the United States. Even if air marshals were on a commercial flight, they might not be able to provide protection for Sean and me. We were concerned about the abductors booking the same flight on a commercial airline and making a scene, or reporters subjecting Sean to further intense media scrutiny.

Benita Noel called to let me know that NBC had sent a private jet, a Gulfstream G-4, to get her crew home for the holidays. She said that she had room on the plane for Sean and me, if and when we were free to leave. Congressman Smith would have to fly commercially, since House ethics rules prohibit members of Congress from accepting travel from corporations. Although Benita hadn't said so directly, I understood that the plane was going to leave before Christmas, with or without Sean and me.

Some of the NBC crew had flown to Rio on the same flight as I had. Others flew in from Texas, or were pulled from assignments elsewhere to meet up in Brazil. Most of the crew, however, lived in New York's metropolitan area, so they would be flying back to New York, close to our home. I knew that if I accepted the ride on the NBC plane, they would be getting exclusive coverage. I was okay with that; after all, I felt personally beholden to NBC for their coverage, and they had always handled our interviews with the utmost respect, compassion, and professionalism. But the most important concern was how to safely transport Sean, without exposing him to any physical or psychological dangers. I accepted their offer; it removed a great burden from my shoulders. While I was ready to fight through what surely would be a media frenzy at Brazil's Galeão Airport, and fly into Newark or JFK if we had to, I really didn't want to put Sean through even more chaos. The NBC arrangement would allow us to get out of Brazil and back home to the United States with the least amount of stress on Sean and in the shortest amount of time. But first, we had to get Sean.

TUESDAY MORNING, SILVANA Ribeiro, perhaps sensing that public opinion was turning against her family, issued an "open letter" through the press to President Lula. In Brazil, she wrote, when there is a death of the mother in the family, the grandmother cares for the child. "That's how it's done in Brazil," she said, "from north to south, regardless of race, religion, or social class. It's natural that foreigners, with a different foundation, would not understand these authentically Brazilian feelings." For someone who had aided and abetted in the abduction of Sean, this was really a stretch, trying to elicit nationalistic sentiments from the public—and from one person in particular, Justice Mendes.

When asked about Silvana's plea, I reminded people that Sean had another set of grandparents, Barry and Ellie Goldman, and other relatives who had not seen or talked with him in more than five years. Few people thought Silvana's ploy would be effective, but we didn't know.

SHORTLY BEFORE NOON, Chief Justice Mendes received a visitor at his Supreme Court office, Marcio Bastos, a former justice minister under President Lula. When Ricardo and his team learned about the visit, they were intrigued. Why would such a powerful man be dropping in on the chief justice a few days before Christmas? I could only hope that some of the political pressure applied to the Lula administration was finally making an impact, but there was no way to be sure.

Each tick of the clock on Tuesday seemed to reverberate through my brain. Why was it taking so long? This was a clear-cut, black-and-white case. Why wouldn't the Supreme Court Justice say it and be done with it?

By three in the afternoon, we still had heard nothing from Brasília. Then Andrade called Ricardo. The news was not good. The Ribeiros and Lins e Silvas had filed a second provisional custody appeal with the Superior Tribunal of Justice. There was nothing we could do but helplessly sit and wait, hoping that the lower court appeals would not influence the Supreme Court chief justice's decision.

By the end of the day, Mendes had issued no ruling. Our nerves were frayed, conversations terse. Several of our team watched the evening national news together, hoping we might get a hint about the decision, but the reports were more of the same. "We're expecting a decision at any minute."

Benita wanted to have a camera crew in my hotel room when the decision finally came down, but I really didn't want that. She took the crew to Ricardo's room instead, where he and Marcos and Orna Blum waited impatiently. Even Ricardo's stalwart attitude was shaken. "Actually, yesterday morning I was confident about the Supreme Court's decision," he said. "But I'm not anymore. It's taking too long."

Around 9:00 PM, Orna Blum received a call from an Associated Press reporter. She couldn't be certain whether the reporter was merely fishing for information, but she repeated his words aloud to Marcos and Ricardo: "AP is reporting a message on Twitter from the Supreme Court. Mendes is coming out in support of the Goldman side!"

Marcos starting whooping and hollering so loudly Ricardo could barely make out Orna's words as she continued to pass along the information from the AP reporter, but he heard all he needed to know: "Annul the injunction and return the boy to his father." When he calmed down, Marcos called Paulo Roberto Andrade in Brasília, and the lawyer confirmed the report.

Ricardo called me in my hotel room. "We won, man. He annulled the injunction. I don't know the details of the ruling yet."

My heart nearly leaped out of my chest. *Could it really be true? Are Sean and I really going to be reunited this time? Will we be able to go home?* For a minute or so, I couldn't hear anything else Ricardo was saying. Finally, the thumping in my heart calmed down to the point where I heard him still talking, reminding me not to start celebrating yet, to be cautious. "First I need to read the text of the ruling. This has happened before and we haven't been able to enforce the ruling. We've been through this before and we haven't managed to carry it out. So let's read the whole thing calmly and see where to begin. Get some rest, and we will talk as soon as I have everything in my hands."

When the full text of Chief Justice Mendes's ruling appeared on the Web site Consultor Juridico, Ricardo was ecstatic. Within a few minutes the news was out: Chief Justice Mendes, in a thirty-page written decision, ruled that Sean must be returned to me immediately. Certainly, as in so many of the rulings, the potential for appeal was there, but it seemed unlikely that the court would entertain further appeals. In fact, Mendes seemed to be closing the door on any further appeals by saying, "Registering the legal ruling on the premises of fact, there are no more ways to challenge them, whether ordinarily or extraordinarily." Justice Mendes's ruling was emphatic: It is over.

Congressman Smith was sitting a few feet away from me when I received the call from Ricardo. He saw the expression of relief and elation cross my face as I broke into a huge smile, and he could interpret the message without my saying a word. I quickly sobered up. "I'm not going to let my guard down until it's wheels up," I said, repeating my often-stated commitment.

Benita knocked on my door and entered, followed by her camera crew wanting to get my reaction on tape. I'm sure they were hoping for some dramatic response on my part, but when Benita asked me how I felt, I could think of only one answer: "When are we leaving? When will this really end?"

Following Ronald Reagan's adage of "trust but verify," Congressman Smith encouraged the embassy representatives to notify local and national law enforcement, and the international police agency, Interpol, lest Sean's Brazilian family try to spirit him out of the country before a transfer could be facilitated. Congressman Smith then spoke with reporters late Tuesday night and told them that the authorities had been notified, just in case the Lins e Silva and Ribeiro camp got any bright ideas. He hinted that such a foolish move would discredit their reputations even more. "Our hope," he said, "is that given the prominence of this family in legal circles, that's less likely to happen."

Back in Washington, Senator Lautenberg lifted his hold on the GSP legislation, releasing the more than $2.75 billion in benefits to Brazil. The Senate quickly passed the bill.

I received a phone call from my dad that night. He and my mom had heard the good news, although I could still sense the anxiety in his voice. "Keep your fingers crossed," I told him, "and keep up those prayers and hopes."

The following morning, Ricardo and Marcos went to work hammering out the details of the handover of Sean to me, having to fight with Sergio Tostes, who was now willing to meet face-to-face with my attorneys, over every tiny aspect of the transfer. Even before Chief Justice Mendes had rendered his decision, Tostes and the lawyers for the Lins e Silvas and Ribeiros had wanted to discuss the "terms" under which they would "agree" to peacefully relinquish Sean. *Peacefully? Peacefully relinquish Sean? What does that mean?* As part of those conditions, Silvana wanted to fly back to the United States on the same plane with Sean.

"No. No, no, no!" I reacted when Ricardo informed me of Silvana's conditions. "This is not an *agreement*. Sean's coming home because he is being returned by the courts. Six years is far too late to be considering an agreement under which these people would be exonerated of all their wrongdoing. I'm sticking with the law. I've worked with the law, waiting patiently for the law to work for me, and this is not a negotiated agreement. These people have been unlawfully holding my son, and I am not going to sign any agreement that does not hold these people responsible for the torture they have put my son through. No, she is not coming on the plane." I also consulted with Tricia Apy, who repeated in no uncertain terms that Silvana could not fly to the United States with us.

I could see the fatigue in Ricardo's face. He had given this case his best effort, and we were so very near to closure. He encouraged me to make a deal. "David, if that is what it takes to get Sean home, do it. Who knows what these people might do? They might try to take your son, flee the country, and hide." He pressed further, "Look, if you want to get this done, let her on the plane."

"No, Ricardo. I am not going to do it."

Then Tostes added, "And I want to come along on that plane, too. And my wife."

It was clear that the opposition was simply tossing up one obstacle after another in an attempt to see if we would be willing to compromise. Ricardo realized this and recoiled.

"No!" he practically screamed at Tostes in the negotiating room. "No, no, no! I cannot let the grandmother travel."

The opposition presented all sorts of other subterfuges. For instance, Silvana wanted to meet with me in their home the day before any exchange of Sean was made, ostensibly to discuss his eating habits and his dietary needs. I agreed to meet with her briefly at the American consulate in Rio.

The kidnappers still demanded to put their own stamp on how they returned Sean. They refused to accept the U.S. consulate's offer to bring Sean into the building through the private, secure garage entrance, which would have made it easy to avoid the media and any potential distress and trauma to Sean out in the streets. Instead, they actually contacted the media and announced that they would park two blocks away and *walk* Sean—dressed in the colors of the Brazilian flag—down the street to the consulate.

ACCORDING TO THE Supreme Court's orders, the abductors were supposed to deliver Sean to me at the U.S. Consulate no later than 9:00 AM on December 24. The morning of the exchange, I awakened early, feeling extremely nervous. I was hoping for the best, but I knew that anything could happen. The abductors might bring Sean all the way to the consulate and then something could blow up in our faces. I was glad to know that Interpol had been notified in case the Ribeiros or Lins e Silvas, in a desperate last-minute move, attempted to sabotage the handover and flee the country with Sean. We had learned the hard way that these people could not be trusted. We had a court order that Sean was to be returned, and the police stood by on alert. If Sean's grandparents and the Lins e Silva family did not turn him over, the authorities were instructed to go to the home and retrieve Sean.

Benita Noel rose early, left the Marriott unnoticed in a rented van, and headed straight to Galeão Airport, to make sure everything was ready with the plane, and to wait for Sean's and my arrival.

By 7:20 AM, I was ready to go. I didn't have much choice; my room had been bustling with people since 7:00, as our team members gathered, including the NBC camera crew. I could see the excitement and optimism on the faces of the NBC crew. They really believed this was the day; it was over, and Sean and I would be reunited. I wouldn't allow myself to share in that feeling—not until the wheels were up. I gave everyone a thumbs-up as I left my hotel room, hopefully for the last time, and was ushered downstairs and out a back door of the hotel to where a black embassy car was waiting.

Congressman Smith and I traveled from the Marriott to the consulate in the embassy SUV and entered the building through the secure garage entrance. My heart was pounding as I went upstairs to the second floor, where I was to meet Sean. Was this really happening? This was the day I had waited for, prayed for, hoped for, and now we were actually here. Ricardo remained downstairs at the entryway, in case there were any last-second attempts to pull more legal shenanigans. Upstairs, a room had been prepared where I could meet Sean privately. We had agreed to allow his grandmother to accompany him that far, no more.

A NOISY CROWD of people had gathered early outside the U.S. consulate. It was hard to tell whether they were in support of Sean's return or opposed to it. Most of the throng was composed of reporters armed with microphones and television cameras. Relatively few "ordinary citizens" were in the crowd. It was as though the Ribeiro and Lins e Silva families were hoping to use Sean's return to elicit sympathy for themselves, or to incite feelings of nationalism and anti-Americanism—How can we give up one of our own?—and perhaps, at the last moment, something could yet stir the country to keep Sean in Brazil.

I stood in the second-floor hallway of the consulate, peering out the large-pane window, hoping for any glimpse of Sean. I heard the commotion before I saw the car in which his abductors were transporting him. They were a half hour early. A throng of reporters and television cameras surrounded the car as the occupants got out, Silvana dramatically playing to them with each motion and expression.

Then I saw him. My nine-year-old son, Sean, was dressed in a bright Brazilian soccer shirt and was being dragged through the crowd. Accompanying him were Silvana and Ray. Holding Sean firmly was Lins e Silva, the second kidnapper, with his hand on Sean's head, as though protecting him from the media's cameras; alongside them, Tostes kept putting his hand on Sean's neck. Slowly they pushed their way through the crowd and paraded Sean down the street. People were screaming, car horns were blaring, and helicopters circled overhead. Next to Tostes was a uniformed officer, a security guard of some sort, I guessed, although he was doing little to disperse the crowd. Sean was being jostled back and forth and from side to side, bouncing off one part of the crowd to the next, always collared by Lins e Silva or Tostes as they surged slowly forward with the crowd.

"Get away! Move back!" Tostes shouted at the members of the media as he plowed deeper into the crowd.

"Why did you call us, then?" a cameraman shouted back at the vicious leaders of the parade. "Why didn't you use the entrance in the back?"

It seemed that the abductors were trying to incite a riot, laying out trails of bloody bait, but nobody bit. John Walsh later called this incident "the perp walk," the perpetrators making one last stand.

As they dragged Sean through the streets, it was obvious to even casual observers that this was inhumane and unmitigated cruelty on the part of his abductors. Their actions and attitudes were obscene.

Standing by myself, looking out the window, I couldn't believe that the abductors were doing this to Sean. My son looked terrified, his cheeks flushed red and puffy as he clung to Tostes and Lins e Silva. It was so painful to watch. Finally, I couldn't take it anymore, and I wailed against the window, "Why? Why! How can you be so cruel to my child? Why, God? Why would you allow this to happen to any child?"

Then a thought flashed through my mind: *But this is the end of their hurting him. This is the end of the pain he must endure at the hands of these monsters.*

Congressman Smith came upstairs to check on me. When the elevator doors opened, he saw me with my hands raised over my head, my face pressed against the windowpane. "Look what they're doing to my son!" I cried. I paced back and forth in front of the window.

Congressman Smith rushed to me and threw his arm around my shoulder, attempting to calm me. "David, in a few minutes it will be over," he said. "You will be with your son, and you will be with him for the rest of your life." He then hurried downstairs to make sure all went smoothly there.

At the entryway, the abductors and their cohorts came inside the building. Immediately Silvana made a big scene over the fact that she wanted to see me before letting go of Sean. She had apparently attempted to foist upon Sean the insane notion that since Bruna's death, *she* was now his mother.

Silvana was not the only one making a ruckus. Tostes also demanded bombastically, "I want to talk to David! He must come here to talk to me." Consul General Marie Damour was recounting these ongoing demands back to Tricia in New Jersey, who made it clear that under no circumstances was I to be subjected to any conditions not contained in the order.

One of my lawyers reminded him that "Lawyers talk to lawyers," not to the opposing clients. They also reminded him that I had agreed to allow only Silvana to come upstairs to the second-floor room where I was waiting for Sean. Silvana, and Silvana only.

Tostes continued his bluster. "He has to be man enough to come here to talk to me. If he doesn't, he is not a man." When my attorney reiterated our position, Tostes turned his verbal shots toward Congressman Smith, cussing him out in Portuguese, his eyes bulging out with hatred, dropping F-bombs in English and accusing him of provoking the entire affair. A deeply devout Christian, but also a strong, athletic man, Congressman Smith saw red and momentarily turned toward Tostes with a "bring it on" attitude, then turned away and, with great self-control, restrained himself from reacting to Tostes's insults. Like a child cajoling another, Tostes continued taunting the congressman: "And I hope you lose the next election!"

To the very end, Tostes attempted to stoke anti-American sentiment. When Orna Blum asked him why they had chosen not to accept the consulate's offer to bring Sean in through the private entrance, Tostes alluded to our refusal to grant him and Silvana a free ride to the United States. He railed first in Portuguese: "This is a protest, because the boy is traveling alone." Then in English, he added, "We are in Brazil. This is our country. This is a protest."

From my location on the second floor, I couldn't hear the rabble below. I sent word to Ricardo. "Okay, let's get this thing over."

The plan was for me to wait in the room prepared for our meeting, but I decided to walk out to the hallway and meet Sean at the elevator. The doors opened, and there was my boy, so grown-up now, nearly ten years old, and looking quite confident, considering that, according to all he'd been told, he was going to meet the enemy, me.

I hugged him immediately, and we embraced tightly. Silvana hovered nearby. I got a chair for Sean to sit down. "I'm very hot," he said.

I knelt down next to his chair, held his hand, and smoothed his hair. "I love you so much, Sean." He exhibited no resistance to me, nor did he say anything like "I don't want to go with you" or "I want to stay here." He just seemed to be drained from the traumatic events of the morning.

After he calmed down, he seemed to relax. He looked up at me, wide-eyed. "I'm going to need some snow boots," he said. "Do we have a lot of snow? I'll need to get some ski pants."

I didn't know whether to laugh or cry. "Don't worry, buddy," I said. "We'll get you some." I looked up at Silvana and got to my feet to face her.

"Oh, David," she said, "so many things have changed."

I wasn't interested in discussing anything with her. I had only one question. "Why?" I asked. "Why didn't you drive into the embassy? Why did you—you dragged him down the street."

Silvana stared back at me, her eyes dark, cold, and devoid of emotion. "Will you allow me to see him?"

I answered her as I had the reporters who asked me that same question. "I will not do to you what you have done to me."

She recoiled. Apparently, all she heard me say was, "I will not."

"You . . . you will not?"

"I will," I said. "In time, we'll arrange that." She had been my bitter adversary for more than five and a half years, but she was still my son's grandmother, and I respected that. So Sean would know that this was not about animosity toward his grandmother, I made a point of hugging her, too. But as I hugged her, I whispered loudly into her ear, "You need to tell him that you remember how good a father I was." She looked back at me blankly. "Say it, Silvana. He needs to hear it. Tell him that I was and am a good father. For his sake."

Silvana spoke to Sean in Portuguese, supposedly saying, "Your father is a good man. He will take good care of you."

Silvana and I then talked briefly about what Sean liked to eat. "He's allergic to shellfish," she said. That was news to me; he'd never been allergic to anything while living in New Jersey, but I nodded and thanked her for the information. Then it was time for her to go. She gave Sean one last tearful hug and said good-bye.

Sean and I talked for a few minutes, and then Congressman Smith came into the room. "The cars are ready to go," he said.

We went downstairs and piled into the vehicles that would take us to the airport. Sean, his three sacks of clothing, Karen Gustafson de Andrade, a security guard, and I rode in the first dark gray van. A second vehicle carried Congressman Smith, Ricardo, Marcos, Orna, and a security guard. Several police cars led the way and others followed behind us. The caravan quickly pulled away from the consulate. We were on our way. I looked at Sean and smiled, but it wasn't time to celebrate yet. We were still in Brazil, and the powerful opposition forces were capable of anything.

The short ride to Galeão seemed to take forever. I couldn't wait for us to get on the plane and be in the air. We arrived at the private aircraft waiting room, and everyone hustled inside and began saying good-bye. I thanked everyone for their marvelous work, especially Ricardo, but I never let Sean out of my sight.

We waited only briefly. Sean was hungry, so we quickly ate a couple of hamburgers. The consulate had prepared a new passport for Sean's departure, so after going through minimal security checks, we stepped outside onto the tarmac and started walking toward the plane. The engines on the NBC jet were already revved and roaring. The door on the side of the jet was open and waiting to receive us.

The dilemma of who goes up the stairs first suddenly dawned on me as we approached the plane. I didn't want to have Sean go up ahead of me, as if I were forcing him to leave. I knew someone would take a photo of such an arrangement, which no doubt would bear the caption "Boy forced on plane against his will." I wanted it to be obvious to all that he was leaving of his own free will. Yet, as his dad, I was concerned that he might slip, stumble, or fall on the portable staircase, or even collapse from the trauma he'd experienced. I wanted to be behind him to catch him if he fell, as I had done so many times when he was just a toddler. I looked up to the sky and prayed a silent prayer. "God, I'm going to walk up those stairs. Please, God, when I turn around, let Sean be behind me." I went up the stairs first, and each step was a step of faith, hoping and praying all the while that Sean was still following behind me, knowing that at any moment he could bolt, or the Ribeiros or the Lins e Silvas could yet make a final desperate attempt to delay or derail our plans to depart. What if he threw a tantrum or refused to board the plane? With the engines running, I couldn't hear whether he was behind me; I simply had to believe. As I got to the top of the stairs, I turned around. Sean was right there with me, looking up at me with a big smile on his face and an expression that said, "Why are you stopping? Let's go." We both waved, and smiled at the people standing below on the tarmac, watching us from outside the waiting room.

Congressman Smith waited on the tarmac along with Karen, several of the embassy officials, and a pediatric nurse whom we had asked to accompany us—just in case. I waved to Congressman Smith from atop the stairs and gave him a thumbs-up before Sean and I stepped inside the plane. I couldn't see the congressman's eyes clearly from the distance, but I knew they were filled with tears. In fact, looking around, I didn't see a dry eye within two hundred feet of us. The congressman remained with the rest of the people on the tarmac, waving good-bye until we taxied out onto the runway. He then went back inside for one final encounter with the Brazilian press.

During those horrible minutes that Sean had been paraded down the street toward the consulate, Marie Smith had called her husband from New Jersey. She had been watching the television coverage of Sean's abductors marching him down the street, attempting to give the impression that Sean was being returned against his will. Marie realized the potential damage those images could cause. "Chris, you have to get a picture of David and Sean as quickly as you can when they calm down, to counter what is going out around the world." The congressman took several cell phone pictures and sent them to Mary Noonan to get to the networks, but nothing was of good enough quality.

Before we got on the plane, Congressman Smith had a word with Benita Noel. "You have to get a picture of those two when there is a brighter moment, and get it out to the world." Benita agreed, and once Sean and I were settled in our seats, she took what was to become a memorable shot, with Sean wearing his blue sunglasses, smiling from ear to ear, sitting next to me, both of us with elated expressions on our faces. To their credit, *O Globo* posted both pictures—the one of Sean horrifically being dragged down the street, and the one of us happy together aboard the jet—side by side on their Web site later that day.

SITTING BACK IN my seat, next to Sean, with our seat belts fastened and the jet engines whirring outside our window, I dared not let down my guard. We were still on the ground in Brazil. After what seemed like a dozen or more cross-checks, the captain finally headed the plane down the runway. We were in the air! It was 11:53 AM on Christmas Eve.

I turned to Sean and said, "Give me a high five! Wheels up, buddy!" I threw my arms up into the air. We were on our way home!

I sent a text message to Tricia: "Wheels up. Wheels up! Wheels UP!" As soon as possible, I sent a similar message to Wendy, Mark, Bob, and others close to us.

The jet whisked us higher and higher, flying six thousand feet higher than commercial flights, closer to heaven than either Sean or I had ever been before, as we left the moldering mess behind us in Brazil. I hugged Sean, then leaned back for a moment and closed my eyes. It was Christmas Eve. Obviously something—or Somebody— much bigger than us was involved in Sean's release.

On board the plane, everybody was teary-eyed but relieved. I could see that Sean was relieved, too. He was reserved at first, talking cautiously, trying to ascertain not just the new surroundings but also his new relationship with me. It seemed to me that he was trying to reconcile what he had been told about me with his new reality. In his mind, no doubt, he was coming home to "the enemy." He had been told such horrible things about me—that I had abandoned him as a child, that our home was the kind of dilapidated shack that should be condemned, that New Jersey was an awful place. I knew that I couldn't convince him with words; I had to let time, love, and consistency show him who I was.

I sat next to Sean on the copilot's side of the plane for takeoff. Then, once the jet reached cruising altitude, we moved to two across-the-aisle seats that stretched out into beds. I knelt down next to him, patted his head, and held his hand. "I love you so much, Sean. We're going to have some fun. And you're going to see your grandma and grandpa."

Sean smiled and lay back in his plush leather seat. I knew he must be exhausted. I could imagine that his abductors had kept him up late the night before. So I wasn't surprised when he closed his eyes and, within a few minutes, fell fast asleep.

I couldn't take my eyes off him. He was here, right next to me; we were together, and we were on our way home. I was physically and emotionally drained, but there was no way I could sleep. The adrenaline was still pumping through my body. While Sean slept, I couldn't resist reaching over every so often and placing my hand on his head or shoulder.

A tinge of sadness flitted through my mind as I thought of all that Sean had endured so needlessly. It never had to be like this. He'd suffered so much. My poor boy. I couldn't protect him. His innocence was gone. More than five years lost. Why? My mind momentarily flooded with questions that could not be answered, memories of actions that could not be explained, words that could never be taken back. I didn't dwell there long.

We have now, I thought. *We have our future.* Sean has *his* future, and I will make certain that the remaining years of his youth are filled with love, understanding, and guidance; that one day he will look back at his childhood with more fondness than sadness. That when he is a man, he will be a good man, an honest man, a man who knows what it means to be a father, not because I've told him so, but because he's been able to see in me a father's love.

ABOUT TWO THIRDS of the way through the nine-hour flight, Sean woke up, so the flight attendant offered us some food. Afterward, he and I had a bubble-gum-blowing contest, and of course Sean won. One of the network's lead reporters on the story, Jeff Rossen, was on the plane, and before I knew what was happening, he and Sean were engaged in a food fight at forty thousand feet! We all were pretty lighthearted, and we did clean up the mess.

It was a long flight but it seemed to go by pretty quickly, mainly because I spent most of it gazing at Sean, my thoughts bouncing back and forth between heartfelt gratitude and near-disbelief that we were actually here, on our way home. At some point someone informed me that the plane's captain, Mike Funiciello, had piloted a similar mission once before. He had been the pilot on the private plane that flew six-year-old Elián González back to Cuba in 2000, after his mother had died attempting to flee to the United States. Elián's relatives in Florida wanted to keep him there, but the U.S. government insisted on returning him to his father in Cuba. Now Mike was flying another boy home to begin a new life with his father.

The jet landed in Orlando at 6:14 PM and taxied all the way into a private hangar. Once we were on the ground, I let Sean use my cell phone to call Silvana. She didn't answer, so he left a brief voice mail message for her. "Hi, Nona. I'm here already. I'm very happy. Kisses. Bye."

Before the day was out, the message was aired on Brazilian television.

Bernie Aronson had talked with me from Wales several times during those last couple of days, offering advice and encouragement. I sent him an e-mail: "Wheels down. God bless. We did it."

We deplaned inside the hangar, to avoid the crush of media waiting outside the executive airport. A contingent of Florida state police greeted us, lined up and standing at attention as sort of an honor guard on our behalf. It was truly a touching gesture.

The state police were concerned that we might need an escort to get through the swarm of reporters and television cameras. The officers manned several black SUVs and headed the caravan out in one direction, with a phalanx of media in hot pursuit on the ground and several helicopters in the air. A few minutes later, Sean and I and a couple of NBC representatives inconspicuously climbed into a vehicle that looked like a rather ordinary airport shuttle van. We rode across town unimpeded and were guided inside a back entrance to Universal Studios.

With my full consent, NBC had arranged a fantastic Christmas welcome for us at the network-owned theme park. I felt that it would be much better to gather our family and share our first holiday together away from the media flurry that was sure to follow us when we arrived back in New Jersey. As much as I appreciated the media's role in Sean's release, the last thing he needed right now were ubiquitous cameras following his every move. I wanted him to have the opportunity simply to be a boy, and to share these first days with his loved ones, who had also suffered every day he'd been gone.

Sean and I went to our room, stepped inside, and did a double take. We were staying in the presidential suite, a palatial composite of rooms the square footage of which was probably bigger than my entire house. Mom and Dad were on their way, as were my sister, Leslie, and her family, and Wendy and her children. We'd probably take up every room in the suite. But for right now, it was just Sean and me, our first night, and all I could think about was getting my son tucked into bed.

I ran a bath for him, and we ordered room service. Sean got chicken nuggets—just like those he used to enjoy when he was a four-year-old. We sat down and watched cartoons for a while, and before long, he grew tired. He pulled out a big stuffed dog from one of his three plain sacks of clothing and we went into the bedroom, where I tucked him in and told him I loved him—about a million times! I was overwhelmed with joy. I knelt next to his bed and stroked his hair as he drifted off to sleep. I don't know how long I stayed there; I didn't want to move. A short while later, the clock struck twelve. It really was a Christmas miracle.

22

Home at Last

B Y THE TIME MOM AND DAD ARRIVED AT THE HOTEL LATE ON Christmas Eve, Sean was already sound asleep, but we couldn't resist looking in on him in his bed. All of our faces were beaming and streaming with tears of joy. "Can you believe he's in there?" I said to Mom over and over. "I can't believe he's in there. I keep going in and looking at him."

That night, the first night Sean and I had spent together in more than five and a half years, myriad thoughts and emotions surged through me. I felt compelled to get out a word of thanks to the people on our Web site and on the other child abduction sites who had so faithfully supported us. I knew in my heart that for the rest of our lives Sean and I would always want to be there for them the way they had been there for us. The night before the handover, I had written a note for Congressman Smith to read to the press on my behalf, after Sean and I were in the air and out of Brazilian airspace. I passed along that same message in an open letter to all the groups who had helped us:

Please accept my most sincere and humblest gratitude for getting the truth to Brazilian and American citizens alike, and for your help to make our reunion possible.

I am grateful for the so many truly amazing and wonderful people who have put forth an extraordinary and tremendous effort to reunite our family with our beautiful Sean.

Please know that my love and the rest of Sean's family's love for him knows no boundaries and we will go to the ends of the earth to protect him and shower him with every ounce of love that we have.

It is now time for our new beginning, the rebirth of our family at such a special time of the year. I hope the momentum keeps growing, and the attention does not fade, because there are more fathers and mothers and children to reunite.

God bless you all,
David

After we awakened on Christmas Day, and my mom and dad got to greet their grandson, we all had breakfast together. Then, before things got too hectic, I gave Sean my cell phone and told him, "Call your grandmother and grandfather in Brazil. Wish them a Merry Christmas." Sean did, and I think the Brazilian grandparents were surprised. Even if their actions and responses were not reciprocal, I wanted ours to demonstrate kindness.

My sister, Leslie; her husband, Chris; and their two children arrived at Universal that morning, and despite not having seen one another since Sean was four, the cousins were instant pals again. Sean seemed to especially enjoy being around other kids, and just being a boy. Before long, the kids had commandeered the entire hotel suite, running through the rooms, shooting toy guns, and using Dad's arms as a basketball hoop to play basketball.

Dad loved it! He and Sean had already reestablished their former names. "I'm 'Pop-Pop,'" said Dad, "and Sean is 'Little Buddy.'"

Congressman Smith and Marie called to wish us Merry Christmas and Happy Hanukkah. After he got back around 8:00 AM on Christmas morning, the congressman and his family had held hands around the tree and prayed for Sean and me and our family, that the transition would go well, that Sean would quickly adapt, and that any emotional damage that had occurred would be undone.

Wendy and her kids got there a short while later, and we all had a ball enjoying the park's attractions. Along with the other kids, Sean hopped right on the park's many rides, some that might have scared a less resilient child. He played pinball in the park arcade, ate ice cream, and shot some hoops with me.

The day after Christmas, Meredith Vieira visited, and she and I did some on-camera interviews. In return for their kindness to us, I had happily agreed to give NBC exclusive access for those first interviews. We did not, however, film or interview Sean directly. Benita's assistant Justin—someone whom Sean would not find intimidating because he had flown with us from Brazil—took inconspicuous shots with a mini Flip video camera and captured Sean playing with his cousins and family members, laughing and having fun.

The entire family stayed at Universal for three days. We went on all the rides, swam in the luxurious pools, saw great shows, and generally had a blast. We felt no pressure, only peace. The hotel staff even wheeled in extra beds so all the kids could have a "sleepover" in one room. They watched movies, ate junk food, and had lots of fun just being kids. Perfect.

When it was time to leave, we drove from Orlando to Jacksonville to avoid the media frenzy; flew from Jacksonville to Philly; then traveled to our house by car with a driver arranged by NBC. It was a long, tiring trip, and along the way, as we sat together in the backseat of the SUV, Sean looked at me and asked, "Where's our home? When are we going to be home?"

Home. *When are we going to be home?* Coming from his mouth, the words thrilled my heart. I had been waiting for so long to bring him home, and I had wondered if I should even use the words "Welcome home, Sean," but now, before I even had had a chance to say them, he was already acknowledging my house as his home. I didn't want Sean to have to be overly sensitive about his responses to his new life, so I choked back my emotions and attempted to maintain my composure. But my heart was pounding with joy.

IT WAS EVENING by the time we pulled into our neighborhood, and the December sky was dark, with bright stars twinkling like diamonds against black velvet. It was as though nature itself were celebrating Sean's return. I noticed only a few media trucks in front of our house, since most of the media didn't know when we were scheduled to arrive. The inside of the house looked mostly dark, but there were large candy canes, decorations, and Christmas lights all around the outside. Some of my close friends and neighbors had decorated the house to welcome us home.

As we turned into our driveway, somebody inside the house opened the door to our basement-level garage so we could drive right inside. We came upstairs, and the first thing Sean saw was the Christmas tree with all the lights and presents. Our local fire department had provided the tree, and friends had filled the area around it with brightly wrapped gifts. Sean and I both dove for the floor and started pulling out Christmas presents, many of them from people Sean did not know but who had wanted to express their love for him. Sean's eyes were sparkling like the stars outside as he ripped the paper and bows off the packages.

Tuey, our cat, came out and rolled over in front of Sean as if to say, "Welcome home." Sean began petting her as though they were old friends, which, in fact, they were. On the fireplace mantel hung a Christmas stocking for Tuey, right next to the one for Sean.

I watched in awe as I realized this was our new beginning. It was beautiful to me, almost like a dream. I didn't have to pinch myself to know that it was real, but it felt so fantastic to see my son playing with his cat in our own home. I struggled to keep my emotions under control, because as much as possible, I wanted everything to feel "normal" to Sean—because it was! He just hadn't experienced a truly normal life in nearly six years.

Adam followed us around the house with his Flip video camera as I reintroduced Sean to our home. I took him into the guest room that had also served as his playroom and was once my office. I showed Sean the toys he had played with as a four-year-old, and some of the pictures of him as a baby.

Upstairs, he found the marks on the banister he had made with his teeth as a little boy. I had left them just as they were, along with the safety gate at the top of the steps. He got a kick out of both. Then we went into his room, the room that I had kept exactly as it had been the day he was taken to Brazil. His eyes lit up as he recognized his clothes, his bed, and the decorations on the wall. Then he noticed the one thing about the room that had changed: that the aquarium was empty of fish. They had died during a power outage when I had been away from home.

"We need to get some fish," he observed.

"Don't worry, buddy," I said as I put my arm around his shoulder and we both peered through the glass. "We'll get some."

The following day, I did a brief press conference from Patricia Apy's office conference room. With the cameras and microphones everywhere, the first question was, "How's Sean?"

"He's fine," I said. "He's home." What wonderful words!

The more time Sean and I were together, the more I realized what a gentle and loving little boy he'd remained. Despite the horrific things he had experienced, he smiled quickly, laughed easily, and spoke articulately for a nine-year-old, especially considering that his English was a bit rusty due to lack of use. He was mischievous and playful, but wonderfully polite, well mannered, and thoughtful. Sometimes, because of the swirl of public attention with which we had lived, it was easy for some people to forget that he was still just a child. I never did. He was and is a beautiful little boy.

I had agreed to do an update interview with NBC, and they chose to do it on the *Today* show, where my relationship with them had begun. The network later took a lot of heat for supplying the "get-away plane" in exchange for the first interview. Other networks and media watchdogs accused NBC of engaging in "checkbook journalism." This simply was untrue. We never had an agreement to that effect. I did, however, feel more obligated to NBC than to anyone else. Nobody else had seriously offered to fly Sean and me out of Brazil, or had a plane sitting on the tarmac ready and waiting to lift off as soon as we could get there—not any other network, not the U.S. State Department. And I certainly couldn't have afforded to hire the services of a private jet.

Had it been necessary to take Sean through the commercial airport, purchase him a ticket, and wade through what would surely have been a media circus, I would have been willing and prepared to do that. But I definitely didn't want to. So when NBC offered the plane, at no small expense to itself, I was totally grateful.

In one of my first interviews after Sean's return, on *Dateline NBC*, I talked about the "Christmas Miracle." Bernie Aronson, who is Jewish, later kidded me, "You sold us out, David. It was a Hanukkah miracle!" Regardless, there was enough happiness in the moment for all faiths to enjoy.

WE SPENT OUR first few days back home simply allowing Sean to acclimate to me and his surroundings. We talked easily, and I told him, "I'm sure a lot of things have happened, and we've both been hurt a great deal. Now our job is to be father and son, and for you to be a child again, so you can learn and play and go to school and have fun." I didn't try to make every moment a "teaching" moment, but I wanted him to know that he had my complete support and my unconditional love.

We shopped for some winter clothes, went fishing, and enrolled in a public school close by our home. The kids at school received Sean with open arms. Some of them were aware of the story and welcomed him back. For the most part, the kids treated him just like any other ten-year-old, and for that I was grateful. Friends and family members stopped by our house often, and we had more than a few sumptuous meals at Mom and Dad's. Dad especially noticed the new buoyancy in my step. In an early interview after Sean's return, he said, "David got his son back, and I got my son back, too."

I was always surprised when Sean recognized someone from his past. My good friend Gene Quigley, the first friend I contacted following Bruna's fateful phone call, visited shortly after Sean came home. As soon as Gene walked into the house, Sean went right over to him, smiling, put his hand in the air, and gave him a high five. "Hey, Quigley," Sean greeted him. Gene and I just looked at each other, amazed that Sean remembered him, but also surprised at Sean's unabashed familiarity.

I HAD TWO concerns during those first few days after Sean's return. First, he never cried or had any emotional outbursts. He showed no regret at being removed from his family in Brazil. Of course, I was elated that he felt so comfortable and happy with me, but I knew better. It was psychologically impossible to be ripped from a familiar environment, culture, language, and lifestyle and be dropped into a totally different set of circumstances without some sort of emotional turmoil. Add to the mix his mother's death and the traumatic details of his departure from Brazil, and he could easily have been an emotional basket case. But he wasn't—at least not externally. I worried that perhaps he had not yet fully processed all that had happened to him, or that he had developed some sort of defense mechanism that allowed him to remain outwardly calm yet inwardly in pain.

I longed for him to open his heart and mind to me, but I remained patient. In good time we would deal with Sean's emotions. Right now we'd take our first baby steps on what would be a long journey toward healing.

The second matter of concern was that Sean hadn't called me Dad since our being reunited. As he had done during the second day of our visit in Rio, he artfully avoided having to address me at all. He'd say, "Please can I do this?" or, "Come on and play with me." But he shied away from calling me Dad. I knew that his former captors had inculcated in him how he was supposed to regard me. Sean told me that he wasn't allowed to call me Dad after our first visit in Brazil. Certainly, it hurt, but at least he was home. I called Sean "son" and "buddy" right from the start. I figured if he didn't call me Dad for a period of time, I could live with that, because he was home.

Then, on our third day home, he was out in the backyard, down by the river, when he needed my help. "Hey, Dad!" he called. "Come here and help me."

The words were like a tonic to my soul. I pretended that I hadn't heard what he said, so I asked, "What do you need?"

He said it again. "Dad, come here." I hurried to help him.

It was as though he had turned on a switch in his heart and mind that now allowed him to call me Dad. From then on, it was "Dad this" and "Dad that," and every time I heard him say the word, my heart overflowed. It is still indescribably sweet music to my ears.

Within a few days of Sean's return, we began meeting every week with Dr. Charles Diament, a professional counselor in Red Bank. In addition to his outstanding credentials, Dr. Diament had family in Brazil and we thought that he would be culturally sensitive to any issues of Sean's adjustment and Brazilian identity. The counseling was expensive, but Tricia and I felt it was important. The benefit of that investment was incalculable. In addition to enabling Sean to adapt to his new life, and providing wonderful, compassionate support, Dr. Diament's insights proved invaluable when a few days after we were home, the Ribieros' lawyer began to advance their conditions for their contact with Sean.

One of the issues with which Sean and I had to deal was his lack of self-esteem. With such a whirlwind of activity swirling around him and extending to two continents, it might have been easy for him to think that he was king of the world, that everything revolved around him. Quite the contrary; in Brazil, his self-worth was based solely on what he meant to his abductors, the value they placed upon him. As the Brazilian court-appointed psychologists wrote in their extensive report, when Sean found out that Bruna was involved with Lins e Silva, he was extremely upset. He was still very sad and confused about being separated from me. But he was told that his mother could do what she wanted, and she wanted to be with this other man because he made her happy.

During the handover at the U.S. Consulate, Silvana had told me that Sean suffered from "headaches and other illnesses." He was also a bit overweight and out of shape from his sedentary lifestyle in Brazil. He had been enrolled in a school that began in the afternoon, so he stayed up late at night and slept late in the mornings. Once home, Sean lost weight and began to feel better about himself. With an improved diet, consistent rest, a more robust and active lifestyle, and a stronger self-image, many of the "illnesses" that followed him home disappeared.

MOST OF THE people Sean and I meet nowadays express their joy that he is home and have no idea that the ordeal is not over. The Ribeiros and the Lins e Silvas are still contending for Sean's return to Brazil and have asserted their own terms of access in the United States regarding visitation privileges. In April 2010, the Ribeiros came to the United States and filed an emergency application seeking that an immediate order be entered by the New Jersey court, compelling their visitation with Sean. With unabashed audacity, the Lins e Silvas even sued me in the Brazilian courts for money. Outrageous, isn't it? They kidnap my son, then sue me for financial compensation. But no amount of money could ever satisfy them or placate their sense of entitlement. They waged a war against a "gringo," a regular guy, an ordinary dad who loves his son, and they didn't get the results they expected, so their pride and arrogance compels them to press the fight further.

Even when they returned him to me, Sean's grandparents attempted to sabotage our relationship. They set up secret e-mail accounts in the name of "Sean Bianchi" for Sean to use to communicate with them without my knowledge. They gave him two international cell phones, one that I knew about and another that was supposed to be kept hidden from me. They created code words for Sean to use when he spoke to them on the telephone, especially if I was anywhere nearby.

I often think, *Why can't they just be normal grandparents? Why don't they stop this litigation and quit trying to get Sean back to Brazil?* Having Lins e Silva make the claim for my son was their legal strategy, although most people close to the case knew who was—and still is—driving the train.

They have never expressed remorse for kidnapping Sean, nor have they ever apologized to Sean or me for their actions and attitudes. They were international child abductors who willfully, flagrantly, and repeatedly violated court orders in both the United States and Brazil. They lied about Sean and me on national television, and attempted to disparage and denigrate everything about me before the entire world. That causes me to be cautious.

As for João Lins e Silva, to date as I write this memoir, he has not called once or sent a single letter or card to Sean since he returned home. Apparently, shortly after Bruna's passing, Lins e Silva became involved with another woman. Sean was aware of this, and was deeply hurt and disappointed by this transfer of affections to another woman, not to mention the lack of interest Lins e Silva showed toward him.

Once Sean returned home, we attempted to live a normal life. Despite repeated media requests, we remained out of the public eye. When the Ribeiros' case was filed, Tricia was contacted by the Associated Press. The Ribeiros and their lawyer had given extensive interviews to Brazilian media indicating that they were still seeking the return of Sean and diplomatic assistance for access to Sean on their terms. In an AP interview, Tricia confirmed that a case had been filed in New Jersey by the Ribeiros, and once again stated our position: We were willing to give the Ribeiros access to Sean *in time*, but we want his mental health professional involved in that process. Speaking of the Ribeiros, Tricia said, "We requested from Silvana and her husband in January that there be a process to deal with the ongoing family relationship, which is complex because David is getting to know Sean. This was not a process that they were willing to be involved in."

During our postreturn press conference in Tricia's office, a Brazilian journalist asked how much this fight had cost me. "In excess of five hundred thousand dollars," Tricia stated. The bills for the legal fees, translation costs, travel expenses, and a raft of other fees still coming in for both the U.S. and Brazilian litigations is astronomical. The costs have increased another $200,000 because of the kidnappers' ongoing litigations. I was not a wealthy guy to begin with—a point about which the Ribeiros were always quick to remind me— so things have been tight around our home. My family and I have shelled out a fortune, and I still owe more.

Thankfully, Tricia and Ricardo have been very gracious about accepting whatever I can pay, whenever I can pay it. They well understand the people with whom I am dealing, which perhaps gives them more patience regarding my inability to quickly eliminate the enormous financial burden. As Tricia says, "It is an ungodly amount of money," and with the continuing litigation, the amount is still growing. Looks like I'll be on the boat for many years to come. To show my appreciation, I occasionally stop by and bring Tricia and her paralegal, Amy, both of whom now seem like family members to me, the catch of the day. Fortunately for me, they love fresh fish.

DESPITE THE LEGAL saber rattling from Brazil even since Sean has been home, I refuse to denigrate the character of his mother, grandparents, or the Lins e Silva family or speak evil of them to him. As he grows older, no doubt, he will discover the truth for himself. For now, I'll often remind him when we are out someplace, "Oh, we used to go here with your mom," or "Your mom always loved that restaurant." I bring things up with Sean only if they are good memories of his mom. There's no reason to remind him of the sadness we endured because of her. In fact, we had only good memories when we all lived together as a family, a point that Sean remembers well.

I did find it almost humorous that, after the Ribeiros went to such extreme measures to make sure that Sean was dressed in a Brazilian soccer shirt when we left Brazil, my son had no real desire to play the game once we were home.

Bernie Aronson called one day shortly after we were back in New Jersey. "How's Sean doing?" Bernie asked. "How's he acclimating? Do they have a soccer team at his school?"

"Bernie, you're not going to believe this," I said. "Sean really doesn't like to play soccer."

Bernie cracked up laughing. For Bernie, it was the ultimate irony.

SEAN AND I established three foundational principles for how we conducted business in our home, how we would deal with every situation: we were committed to being honest, kind, and humble.

One time when I was reiterating these principles to Sean, he said, "Wow, Dad, that's completely opposite to how I have been living these past few years."

I smiled, but held my tongue. I refused to allow myself to slip into any negative comments about his grandparents, his mother, or the family of Bruna's Brazilian husband.

DURING THE SUMMER of 2010, Sean expressed a desire to learn how to ride a bicycle. Most of his friends got around the neighborhood on bikes, but Sean had to walk. He came home from Brazil saying that he could ride a bicycle, but when he was at his friends' houses and they were all riding their bikes or scooters, I'd get a call from a parent saying that Sean had a headache or wasn't feeling well.

I'd rush over to pick him up only to discover that he wasn't sick. He was simply humiliated that he was nearly ten years old and had never learned how to ride a bike.

When we got home, we had a talk. "Son, I want you to be honest with me and tell me what you can do, what you can't do, and what you want to do. I'm here to help you to do those things that are appropriate for you. I'm here for you. You're a ten-year-old boy, and if you want to ride a bike, I'll help you."

Pop-Pop bought Sean a bike for his tenth birthday, so throughout the summer, once a week or so, we had practice sessions out in the front yard. Sean wouldn't go anywhere else, because he was too self-conscious about his inability to ride. Our driveway, however, is a half-moon and doesn't lend itself to good bicycle practice. There's not enough of a straight area to travel before the wheel has to turn to the right or the left.

In August, the week before school was to start up, we worked on the bike out front again, but Sean wasn't doing so well. "Okay, let's take a different approach," I said. "Let's go over to the school grounds, where there is a long, straight, flat field to ride on."

"No, Dad, I don't want to go over there. The other kids will see me."

"It's the week before school, and the last place most kids will be is at school. Let's go. We're going to get out in that field and we're going to ride this bike."

It was a really hot late summer day, so we tossed a case of bottled water into my Jeep and carefully lifted Sean's new bike into the back. We drove over to the school yard.

The grassy fields at the school were perfect. The ground was solid but had a nice layer of soft, low grass, in case Sean fell. For about two hours, I held on to the seat and handlebars and ran with him as he pedaled. "Feel how you lean," I encouraged him. "Okay, get ready. I'm going to let you go on your own."

"No, Dad. Don't let go. No, I can't."

"Yes, you can. You're doing great. Okay, here you go." I was certain by this time that he would be able to ride a short distance before falling, and it was important that he knew he could do it. I let go of the seat and handlebars, and Sean rolled forward about five or ten yards before losing his balance and toppling over. He looked like a little fawn taking his first steps before slipping and falling.

"Are you okay?" I asked.

"Yes, I'm fine," he responded.

"Great, let's try it again." We did the same routine, with me pushing him while he pedaled. "Here you go," I called. I let loose of him, and he rolled a little farther before losing his balance. "You're almost there," I encouraged him. We kept doing this until we had gone through about the entire case of water, and by the end of the day, Sean was able to ride his bike home from the school, with me following a short distance behind him in the Jeep.

When we pulled into our driveway, Sean was glowing with a huge sense of accomplishment. It was a good lesson for both of us. For him, it taught him that if he didn't give up, he could accomplish what he wanted to do. For me, it was a parable of our entire life together, with me pushing him a bit, helping him do what he wanted to do, and then letting go and enjoying the ride as he navigated on his own.

At first Sean attempted to downplay his happiness at being able to ride. "I shouldn't be so excited. It's no big deal," he said. "I should have learned a long time ago."

"No, Sean, you can be proud of that," I told him. "You need to be taught things, and I'm glad to help you. You didn't know how to ride a bike, but now you do."

Now when somebody comes over to the house, Sean will casually say, "I think I'm going to ride my bike later." I smile with satisfaction.

"Let's ride our bikes over to your friend Jake's house," I suggested one day. We rode through the neighborhood, about eight houses down to where Jake lives. After that, when Sean came home from school, he'd often ask, "Hey, Dad. Can I ride my bike down to Jake's house to see what he's up to?"

"Absolutely."

It is a shame that Sean wasn't taught to ride a bike while living in Brazil, but in some ways I was glad, as it was one of the father-son milestones that I had looked forward to and that they weren't able to steal from us. I'm grateful that I had a chance to teach my son how to ride a bike, just as I had dreamed I might when I first saw him in the hospital a few hours after he was born. Thinking of him taking those first tenuous rides is still a very emotional experience for me.

ON WEDNESDAY, SEPTEMBER, 1, 2010, Sean and I launched out into the Atlantic Ocean, heading to one of my "secret spots," looking for just the right location to fish for bluefin tuna. It was a dream-come-true day for a couple of fishermen, as we saw every sort of marine life imaginable. We saw whole families of whales around us the entire trip. We also watched enormous feasting basking sharks, some of which were thirty feet long, swimming back and forth under our boat. We saw porpoise dolphins near our boat, too, swimming so close that Sean and I could reach out and touch them. There were sea turtles and tuna and more. It was almost as though we were in a giant aquarium.

Sean flipped out his lure, let a line out, and caught his first bluefin tuna, all by himself. We pulled the fish aboard, and Sean was beaming from ear to ear as he stood next to the huge fish while we took his picture. I was so proud of him, and happy for him, but even more than that, I was excited for him for the great sense of accomplishment it afforded him. On the way back to shore, Sean was exhausted after fighting with the fish. He sat down on one of the marine beanbag seats on my boat, and within a few minutes, he was curled up like a bug in a rug, fast asleep. We snapped some photos and later posted them along with the one of Sean and his fish on the Shore Catch Web site daily fishing report page. Sean was thrilled to see that he had "made the page."

I realized that so many of the experiences that had been stolen from us during the time Sean was abducted we were now getting to enjoy together after all. It was almost as though God were restoring to us double what we had lost.

In October 2010, we took a family trip to New Orleans to attend the wedding of my cousin George. George had traveled to Brazil twice along with me, hoping to reunite Sean and our family. New Orleans was still struggling to recover after Hurricane Katrina and the BP oil spill. But the people had done a great job, and the waters looked clean as we headed out to sea to do some fishing early one morning. This was the first time the two cousins, Sean and Coltrane, who is less than a year older than Sean, and Grandpa Goldman had ever had the opportunity to do something like this together. As I watched the three of them interact, I recalled afresh that not only had I been robbed of Sean and Sean robbed of me for six years, but his cousins had been cheated, too, and my dad had been robbed of his grandson for that long. Dad was now nearly seventy-eight, and those six lost years seemed exponentially important.

Dad was always excited to be with the boys. During the summer of 2010, Sean and I took a trip to go tubing down the Delaware River. Joining us were Dad, Leslie and her family, and Wendy's youngest son, Jesse, who was a year older than Sean. Once we arrived at the river's edge, the kids couldn't wait to jump in and start floating down the river in their inner tubes, so Dad jumped right in with them. I knew that it was physically taxing for him, but he wasn't about to miss this experience with his grandsons.

Afterward, Dad looked exhausted but happy. "So what did you think of it?" I asked him, nodding toward the tubes.

"I got another one off my bucket list," he said with a hint of a smile. He recognized the fleeting quality of life on earth, and he didn't want to miss living a day.

His own mother, Phyllis Goldman, Sean's paternal great-grand-mother, had passed away while Sean was still in Brazil. She had lived in a condo on the beach, and Sean and I had gone to visit her a few days before the abduction. We had just recently seen *The Lion King* at Disney World in Orlando, and Sean was really fascinated with the "circle of life." That day while we were at Grandma's, Sean took a stick and drew a large circle in the sand. "Look, Dad, the circle of life." He drew little stick figures inside the circle to represent the elephants and the giraffes and the other animals. I could never have imagined that in a few short days, he'd be gone, his normal life inter-rupted for nearly six years.

Grandma Goldman was as sharp as a tack until the day she died. She had looked forward to being reunited with her great-grandson, but she took her last breath without ever learning the results of our quest to bring Sean home. While we were happy to jump-start life again, there are some losses that can never be reclaimed. But the circle of life goes on, and now it is Sean's and my turn to grow into men of integrity, men who will continue to embrace and express a father's love.

THE TRANSITION HASN'T been totally smooth, but it has been marvelously without major incidents. When Sean and I first returned home together, I wanted to give to him and do for him whatever he wanted. But I knew that wouldn't be good for either one of us. I tried to evaluate, without obsessing over every little point, what in his behavior was a typical ten-year-old trying to get away with this or that, and what in his behavior was a direct result of his abduction, caused by the influence of his captors. I realized that I needed to assert an "authority with love" approach.

During the first weeks, I was waiting for him to say he missed Brazil or wanted to go back and I gave him every opportunity to do so, but he never did. I was emotionally prepared not to discount his feelings and to embrace him no matter what. I sometimes brought up subjects that may have made him feel uncomfortable, but I never pressed any one issue. I didn't want him to close down and box up his feelings. He hadn't been allowed to talk about me in Brazil, and I didn't want him to feel that sort of repression here. I let him know that it was okay to talk about his mom, his half-sister, or his grandparents in Brazil, or even João Lins e Silva. "Sean, you can love whomever you want," I told him. "Don't feel that you have to keep your thoughts and feelings inside. Express them. My feelings won't be hurt. I will always love you and do what I can to bring joy to your life."

The first issue where we experienced conflict was homework. We did (and still do) a lot of that together and we discovered that I'd probably do pretty well on *Are You Smarter Than a 5th Grader?* When Sean and I worked on homework, I took the approach that my dad had taken with my sister and me. Homework isn't just filling in the blanks or answering questions; it's understanding what the answers mean. At times Sean got very frustrated and angry, telling me that I was making him do more work than he should. "It's only homework, and it's okay to get it wrong," he'd say. He got unusually combative, and in some ways I wished that he'd say something more than just about homework, that he would open up. But he was merely angry that I was creating more work for him. He spoke to me disrespectfully, and I told him to go up to his room and cool off, and that he shouldn't talk to me or anyone in "that tone," which I described as one of degrading arrogance. I knew instantly where it had come from. It wasn't the usual way a ten-year-old would argue. When Sean calmed down, we talked again about our three main operating principles: to be honest, kind, and humble.

He had a tendency to say things or to behave in a superior manner. That, too, I realized, was a learned behavior we'd have to work on improving. I also saw the sweet little boy who was at times very uncomfortable in his own skin. "There is no need to act a certain way to impress people, Sean," I would say. "You don't have to brag or build yourself up. Just be a kid. If you say you're great at something, eventually you will have to show your skills, and people will see the truth. So just be yourself and always tell the truth."

Even when I have had to correct or reprimand Sean, he has never once said, "This is awful. I hate you! I want to go back to Brazil." He has responded remarkably well.

I do my best to arrange my work schedule so I can be there every day when Sean gets home from school. We do everything together; he accompanies me everywhere I go, except for date nights with Wendy—although it is not unusual to see Wendy and me with her boys and Sean, enjoying everyday life together. Sean knows that I love him, and that he is home, right where he is supposed to be.

23

======= ... =======

Giving Back

I'M LOOKING FORWARD TO HELPING OTHER HURTING PARENTS. BE-hind the scenes, I'm already doing what I can. I'm in communication with other left-behind parents, offering them guidance and hope, but right now my top priority is raising Sean. Nevertheless, everywhere I go, I try to share the surprisingly simple lessons I learned through my ordeal: No matter what situation a parent goes through with a child, you have to believe; you have to remain focused and stay the course. As you do whatever you have to do because of the love for your child, you draw energy and stamina from deep within. All of heaven and earth is on your side, though you may encounter many obstacles along the way. Stay with the truth and maintain your dignity and integrity, and you will be amazed at who will come forward to help. You can't give up, because you are motivated by the love of your child. This is the message that resonated in my heart for five and a half years, and it is the message I share with hurting parents everywhere I go these days.

Sean and I are enjoying life together. We've been reunited; we are healing; we are loving; we are father and son. Sean has a great group of friends, is doing well in school, and continues to adapt well to his new life in America and to the home he once enjoyed so much, where he received so much love prior to his abduction. People who meet him for the first time might notice a slightly different inflection in his speech, in the pronunciation of certain words. Apart from that, they would assume he is a typical ten-year-old boy—because he is! Most folks could never imagine what my son has experienced already in his young life.

Sean and I both know that we can never repay all the people who had a part in reuniting us. But because of what we endured, and what we learned, we hope to help other families who have been victimized by parental abductions. Nearly three thousand American children remain in international abduction situations at this writing, and that number grows annually. Those parents and family members are struggling to hold on, to endure, to make it through another day. It is with great pain that I see so many other parents and children living the perpetual nightmare of being separated, with seemingly no end in sight. They desperately need a team of champions as I was so privileged to have. I want to do all that I can to help them.

I realize that had Bruna not died, it is highly unlikely that our story would have surfaced the way it did, in the media and in diplomatic circles. I was just one of many left-behind parents appealing for help. In an ironic and tragic twist, Bruna's death gave me back the son she had attempted to tear away from me.

I am concerned for others who have been victimized by parental child abductions. What can be done to help them? Up to now, apart from Sean, no other unlawfully abducted American child has ever been returned to the United States by Brazil under the Hague Convention. And consider what it took to get Sean home: the death of my son's mother; the airing of the story on national television that just happened to catch the attention of Congressman Smith and Bernie Aronson, two men willing to sacrifice their time and influence to help get Sean home. How often is that going to happen for other left-behind parents?

Then consider the unanimous resolutions in both the House and the Senate, the personal statements by the president of the United States and the U.S. secretary of state, the hearing by the congressional Human Rights Commission, Senator Lautenberg's holding back nearly $3 billion of aid to Brazil, and the multiple trips to Brazil by Congressman Smith. I am forever grateful for all of these, but let's be honest. How often will such things happen for the parents of other abducted children?

Not often. Maybe never.

Thousands of American families whose children have been abducted by a parent can't mobilize this kind of pressure, and they shouldn't have to.

Yet during Sean's abduction, we knew of at least sixty-five other American children who had been abducted to Brazil. That number may be higher today. Similarly, Japan has never even signed the Hague Convention agreement, so is it any wonder that at least ninety-nine American children remain abducted in that country? There may be many more. A large number of the abducted children in Japan are sons and daughters of American servicemen or -women who wore their country's colors proudly, married Japanese men or women, had kids, and then were utterly abandoned. As Bernie Aronson has said, the system to bring back abducted children is broken and needs to be fixed.

The game plan for most abductors is fairly simple. Keep filing legal actions until the left-behind parent gives up due to financial, physical, or emotional exhaustion. The abductors play the clock out until they break down the left-behind parent. Sadly, that is what usually happens.

That's why Congressman Chris Smith proposed leveling the playing field through the legislation he introduced in June 2009 making the battle for abducted children a government-to-government issue, rather than a government-to-individual or -family issue. Most individuals or families lack the resources to fight against a foreign legal system for any prolonged period of time. Currently, there's no real mechanism for parents in the United States to fight for their kids—no system that works with the help of the government, that is. That's why, along with Congressman Smith, Bernard Aronson, and the Bring Sean Home Foundation, I have been calling for reforms.

From Sean's and my experience in dealing with an international abduction, and of course, through my many conversations with Bernie Aronson and Congressman Chris Smith, I've settled on two main steps that could help prevent international parental abductions and provide for immediate assistance when such abductions happen.

First, we need a high-level advocate in the State Department, a special ambassador, so to speak, empowered to deal directly with abduction issues. This person should report to the U.S. Congress about every abducted child. Think of it. I went more than four years before anyone in the government really took action to help bring my son home. Just knowing that such a high-level position existed, that a parent could not expect to abscond with a child without the full weight of the U.S. government being brought to bear in opposition, could deter many parental abductions. In Congressman Smith's bill, HR 3240, the International Child Abduction Prevention Act, he advocates for an "ambassador-at-large" to work on these issues with a single-minded focus. A similar position in human trafficking legislation proved very effective.

Second, our government should impose a range of sanctions and other punitive measures on countries that refuse to comply with the Hague Convention guidelines for dealing with international parental child abduction.

HR 3240 lists eighteen specific punitive measures our country would take against countries that harbored or facilitated the abduction of children by their parents. We have established these kinds of stipulations to combat the horrendous crime of human trafficking, through legislation also written by Congressman Smith, and the same sort of penalties can be imposed on those who engage in or foster international parental child abduction. These punitive measures would be clearly spelled out in advance. No surprises, but no compromise either.

Thanks in part to the worldwide attention this issue received because of Sean's abduction, in 2010, Secretary of State Hillary Clinton called for a special ambassador to deal with the issue of abducted children. That's progress, and it is a good first step, but not enough. We all know that rules without consequences are meaningless. If a parent reprimands a child for misbehaving, and the child promises to behave but doesn't, if there are no consequences, nothing will change. The same can be said of nations that flagrantly abuse abduction. As long as we keep saying, "We're really upset. We're really upset," but do nothing to motivate compliance, nothing will happen. Or, as Bernie puts it, "A diplomatic request for which there are no consequences for refusal is just a sophisticated version of begging." If nations harboring or facilitating abductors don't pay a price, nothing will change. Until other countries learn that the United States is willing to put some teeth into these measures, we will continue to be regarded as a paper tiger. And children will continue to disappear.

Senator Frank Lautenberg saw the relationship between punitive measures and Sean's return. "It didn't happen because we were being nice. It happened because we decided to get tough," he said. "We put a hold on a bill that would give Brazil $2.75 billion worth of trade opportunity, and then they decided to listen to their courts, who said return the boy to his father. I put a hold on the bill with a promise that if the boy was returned, I would take it off, and I responded quickly, because the mission was not to punish Brazil; the mission was to get the boy back to his natural father."

PEOPLE SOMETIMES ASK me, "Were there any good guys? Were there any white hats in your story?"

I reply, "Yes, lots of them." I'll be forever grateful to every person who helped Sean get home, from Mom and Dad and our extended family, Mark DeAngelis, and Congressman Smith to the little lady three thousand miles away who said a prayer for us in her church. Every prayer was needed, every positive thought and letter was important, because, as it was, we got out of there by the skin of our teeth. When I stop to think how many heroes showed up in Sean's and my life, I am overwhelmed. Honestly, there are too many to list, but I am truly thankful for each one.

The Brazilian legal system, though often a source of great consternation to me, eventually worked in Sean's and my favor. It took far too long, but they did the right thing. Bernie offered me valuable insight into the attitudes in Brazil that influenced our case. "In fairness to the Brazilians, it was sort of a war between the old Brazil and the new Brazil—the old Brazil represented by the Lins e Silvas and their cronyism, and the modern Brazil that is trying to become a player on the international scene and a nation ruled by law." The new Brazil was exemplified by the courageous and articulate Patricia Lomego, who, once the Brazilian Central Authority unreservedly supported the case, was a tireless advocate for the application of the Hague Convention. There were and remain good people in the judiciary and the Supreme Court of Brazil who wanted to do the right thing.

Ricardo and his young lawyers fared well in facing up to one of the most powerful and influential families in the country. Tricia Apy served well, too, especially in advancing my Hague petition in a timely manner, a key point that gave me a firm foundation from which to operate. Had Tricia and Ricardo not been so meticulous with every court filing and response, surely Sean's abductors would have found some legal loophole, however small it might have been.

To me, the Brazilian people who rallied to my side were heroes. Some Brazilian journalists changed their tune, and were more honest and almost sympathetic in their coverage of the story.

The court-ordered psychiatrists who brought the report describing the parental alienation to which Sean was being subjected were also heroes. It took enormous courage on their part to go against what the Lins e Silvas expected.

Secretary Clinton and President Obama should also receive some credit. Nobody would have criticized them had they not raised the issue of Sean's abduction, especially when there were so many other important, pressing matters that begged for their attention. Moreover, it is likely that neither of them, nor Tom Shannon and Dan Restrepo, who went above and beyond the call of duty in mobilizing the U.S. government behind my case, would have done so without the quiet persistence of Robert Gelbard.

And of course, Bernard Aronson was a hero. Bernie spent a year of his life working on Sean's case. Without Bernie's willingness to use his knowledge and influence in positive ways, it is highly unlikely that our case would have risen to such high political levels. Moreover, Bernie's savvy in evoking media interest and coverage was a marvelous gift to us. A few months after Sean was home, Bernie invited us to attend a baseball game with him in Washington, D.C. Bernie arranged for us to go down onto the field to watch batting practice and get autographs from the players. Sean loved it, and so did I!

Later that summer we went to another game, and at the end of the game, the Nationals allowed the kids attending to run the bases. Sean and one of Wendy's boys went down onto the field with me to run the bases.

Watching from the stands, Bernie said, "This is just perfect. A normal day: a father and his son at the ballpark. This is what the fight was all about."

During that trip, we also got to visit the television studio of *America's Most Wanted*, located at the National Museum of Crime and Punishment. Wendy's boys and Sean even got to listen in on the tipsters' calls during a segment of the show in which a bad guy was profiled. Avery Mann, John Walsh's assistant, showed us around and gave us practical tips on how to help and encourage families of abducted children. Like John Walsh, Avery shares our passion for helping bring home abducted children, and we hope to work together closely in the future.

Certainly, Congressman Chris Smith; his wife, Marie; and his chief of staff, Mary Noonan, are true heroes to whom Sean and I will remain forever grateful. It is impossible to express how much respect and admiration I have for them, and how deeply thankful I am for their self-effacing, indefatigable efforts to bring Sean home. Similarly, Mark DeAngelis and Bob D'Amico, who first set up the Web site and formed the foundation Bring Sean Home, worked as though Sean were their own son. Today, they continue to lead the organization as we attempt to bring attention to other parental child abduction cases. The organization itself, Bring Sean Home, and the power of the Internet became major factors in our case. At one point, while I was holed up in my hotel room during the last trip to Brazil, I watched a thread on our Web site log more than fifty thousand hits in twenty minutes. Supporters were constantly on the site, posting news, providing updates, and organizing vigils. Interestingly, many of the supporters were from Brazil. They are all heroes to Sean and me.

I don't know how I can ever give back to the many people who helped me bring Sean home, but I will be forever grateful. Right now, the best way I can give back to them is to pay it forward. My commitment is to be the best father possible, and to help other parents be reunited with their children.

The long-lasting effects of Sean's and my story will hopefully be manifested on a much more personal level, too. For instance, our friend Dan Langdon is a tough federal law enforcement officer. He has seen and heard it all, but somehow Sean's abduction and subsequent return after six years touched Dan at a deep emotional level. "I want to be a better father," he said. "I want to be there for my son."

FOR SEAN AND me, the transition from nightmare to normalcy continues, and we are healing more each day. We work together, play together, and laugh together. We talk openly about everything that touches our lives. Although it is probably not the best time, we've found that right before bed is often our best opportunity to talk about serious things. That seems to be the time when Sean starts thinking about things that might bother or upset him. I remind him of the old proverb "Never take your problems to bed with you because they make poor bedfellows," and we talk things through.

One evening after Sean had been home for more than ten months, I stepped into his room to tuck him in—he had already crawled under the covers, along with Scooter, our new Yorkie puppy that Wendy had bought for him—when I thought I heard him gently crying, not really sobbing, but sort of whimpering.

I went over and lay down next to him, and he slid over and put his head on my shoulder. "Hey, buddy, what's wrong?" I asked. "Are you feeling okay?"

He rose up slightly on his elbow. I could see the tears in his eyes. "Oh, I just miss Mom," he said sadly.

I nodded in understanding. I always encourage Sean to express his true feelings, and I never discount them. No matter how old a person is, he or she still can feel the emotional pain of loss, and I realized that this was some of what Sean was experiencing.

"What kind of thoughts are you having? What are you missing about your mom?"

"I don't know. The fun things that we did. The fun times. She was my mom. No one can know how I feel," he said. "No one can know."

"Well, actually there are a lot of people who know how you feel, Sean. There are children who never see their parents, and there are some parents whose children have been abducted and never returned. You and I have a lot to be grateful for." I shared with him a few of the instances in which families had been torn apart because a child had been abducted. "You've been through a lot, more than most ten-year-olds and many adults. But there are other children your age and younger who have suffered through similar experiences and have come out on the other side stronger, wiser, and able to turn that pain around to become good, productive, positive, people; more loving, more caring, thoughtful, and kind." We had talked about these kinds of things before, so it wasn't new information for him. He nodded in understanding.

"You're not alone, and I know that doesn't make it any better for you at this moment. But it's the parent's job to help the child be happy. And your mom would be happy knowing that you are happy." I hugged him a little tighter and tried to comfort him.

"Sean, your mom would be so proud of you now. The way you are so well adjusted, and doing so well in school. You have a great group of friends and you are sleeping well, and you are eating healthy foods, and you have lost weight and look great. More than that, she'd be proud of you because you are growing up to be a good person on the inside, Sean. So she'd be happy knowing that you are happy. Think of that and strive to be happy for her, strive to be happy for me, and most of all strive to be happy for yourself."

Sean looked up at me and said, "I know, Dad. But I still feel sad and I still miss her."

"And that is natural, buddy. You'll always miss your mom, but as time passes, your pain should lessen and your heart will heal. I'm here and I'm always going to support you. Anytime you want to talk about it, you have my shoulder. And you have my heart."

We talked a little more and I tucked Sean in snugly. Just as I was about to leave his room and turn out the light, he looked over at me, his eyes still watery, sniffled a bit, and said, "Hey, Dad?"

"Yes, Sean?"

"Dad, I'm so glad you never gave up on me."

Hearing those words and knowing what was behind them made it all worthwhile.

I swallowed hard and tried to answer, but all I could say was, "I love you, Sean. I'm glad you're home."

Afterword

Even after I returned with Sean from Brazil, the Ribeiro family continued to harass us in the courts, not only in Brazil, seeking an overturn of the Hague Convention decision there, but also in the New Jersey courts, demanding virtually unlimited visitation rights. So the pressure remained as did the constant drain of my financial resources attempting to defend against these lawsuits. It was an enormous relief to me when, on February 17, 2011, in the Superior Court of New Jersey, the Honorable Judge Michael A. Guadagno dismissed the Ribeiros' case. In his strongly worded forty-four-page opinion, which was based on the law in considering Sean's best interests, the judge dismissed the Ribeiros' claims and demands and upheld what I had been saying for the previous six years about the illegality of Sean's original abduction and the damage that had been inflicted on Sean emotionally in Brazil by his abductors.

Judge Guadagno agreed with Brazilian judge Pinto that "even under Brazilian law, Sean's rightful domicile after the death of his mother was with David . . . Judge Pinto found that the 'illicit detention' and refusal to return Sean to David after Bruna's death violated the Hague Convention. He flatly rejected the defendant's contention that "David abandoned Sean" (p. 14).

Judge Guadagno continued, "More importantly, for this court's analysis, Judge Pinto found that there was an 'urgent need to order the immediate return of the child to the United States' because the court-appointed experts had 'clearly and convincingly' demonstrated that 'Sean has been subjected to a pernicious process of parental alienation.' He found that Sean had suffered 'psychological damage' that was related to 'his stay here in Brazil' and that a return to the United States was necessary to limit that damage to Sean which would continue if he remained in 'the possession and custody of the defendant . . . [and] the other maternal relatives'" (pp. 17–18).

Judge Guadagno concurred, "Nor, can there be any question that these contemptible actions caused harm to Sean, who had enjoyed a secure, stable, and intimate relationship with his father for the first four years of his life only to have that bond severed, all contact cut off, and his young and impressionable mind filled with complete fabrications and misrepresentations as to why his father was no longer in his life. It is difficult to conceive of a more dramatic example of emotional abuse of a young child" (p. 30).

The judge emphasized, "The bond molded by the Ribeiros with their grandson is tainted by a similar infirmity, as it was achieved as a result of Bruna's wrongful retention of Sean and their continued illicit efforts after her death. To allow the Ribeiros to rely on a bond that was formed through their flagrant contempt of the laws of this state and the orders of this court is contrary to every concept of sound and rational jurisprudence. As Judge Pinto found, to accept the Ribeiros' position would permit them 'to benefit from an illicit act' and 'signify . . . that illicit acts entail rights, which, as it is very well known, is inconceivable'" (p. 32).

Throughout his opinion, the judge noted that I had "agreed to allow visitation under certain conditions, but the grandparents have rejected these conditions and seek to compel visitation . . . Rather than accept David's conditions and begin visitation immediately with their grandson, the Ribeiros chose to initiate this litigation and continue their relentless and quixotic court battles in Brazil in an attempt to overturn the decision that reunited Sean with his father. Given the documented harm that the Ribeiros have caused Sean in the past, David's visitation conditions were eminently reasonable. The Ribeiros' penchant for incessant litigation seems to have eclipsed their professed desire to see their grandson" (pp. 2 and 36).

Judge Guadagno also noted, "The Ribeiros continue to pursue several different actions in the Brazilian courts against David. Currently, they are seeking reversal of the Brazilian Supreme Court's decision to return Sean to the United States in accordance with international law. Lins e Silva also continues to file applications seeking the reversal of the decision and the return of Sean. The continuing litigation combined with the Ribeiros' statements to Sean reasserting their efforts to return him to Brazil, reaffirm the reasonableness of David's position that dismissal of all litigation in Brazil is a non-negotiable condition before any visitation will be permitted" (p. 38).

Judge Gaudagno poignantly concluded: "While the complaint of the grandparents will be dismissed, they continue to hold the keys to the portal of visitation with their grandson. Compliance with the fair and reasonable conditions established by David will allow them to again enjoy the special relationship recognized by the legislature" (pp. 39–40). With this definitive opinion, I hoped the litigation against Sean and me by the Ribeiros would finally come to an end.

(I encourage you to read Judge Michael A. Guadagno's complete opinion. It can be found at http://www.judiciary.state.nj.us/decisions/DavidGoldman_110218.pdf.)

Acknowledgments

I would like to thank my family members, friends, and loved ones, including my new friends, U.S. Congressman Chris Smith and his entire staff, Bernie Aronson, Bob Gelbard, Bob Barnett, Ken Abraham, U.S. Senator Frank Lautenberg, Secretary of State Hillary Clinton, members of the U.S. State Department in Washington, D.C., and the U.S. embassy and consulates in Brazil, who assisted me; the community of Tinton Falls, New Jersey; the New Jersey State Senate; the many people involved from NBC's *Today* and *Dateline,* and other television news broadcasters from CNN, Fox News, ABC, and my local CBS affiliate; *America's Most Wanted*; Clare Ferraro, the president of Viking, and my editor there, Paul Slovak; attorneys Ricardo Zamariola, Tricia Apy, their partners and staff; and a special thanks to Judge Rafael Pinto of the 16th Federal Court of Rio de Janeiro for his courageous decision and to Bill Handleman of the *Asbury Park Press*, who passed away recently but whose tireless efforts to cover my story will never be forgotten. I'm also deeply grateful to the FBI agents in Red Bank, New Jersey, as well as those in Washington, D.C., and Brazil for their involvement in our story. And finally, I would be remiss not to mention the overwhelming support from people all over the world who prayed, blogged, attended vigils and rallies, sent letters and e-mails, made phone calls, or just sent a positive thought my way. I am forever grateful for every single ounce of help and effort from so many that enabled Sean and me to finally be reunited. I thank God.

We did it once, but there are more children and parents to be reunited and I will continue to work toward bringing abducted children home to their parents. The work of the Bring Sean Home Foundation is just beginning, and there is much work to be done to put an end to this tragic separation between abducted children and their left-behind parents.

A portion of my proceeds from *A Father's Love* will be donated to the Bring Sean Home Foundation. For more information about how you can help, contact: bringseanhome.org.

Notes

Chapter 12 ▪ To See My Son

118 *by João Paulo Lins e Silva's own admission:* This material is from an open letter by João Paulo Lins e Silva, addressed to the National Council for the Rights of Children and Adolescents, dated March 5, 2009. The letter can be found in its entirety at www.bringseanhome.org.

122 *"The truth about that agreement":* Ricardo Zamariola, Esq., in a letter to the National Council for the Rights of Children and Adolescents, March 16, 2009. Ricardo wrote this letter in response to João Paulo Lins e Silva's letter to the same organization. Both letters can be found in their entirety at www.bringseanhome.org.

Chapter 13 ▪ Date with Destiny

133 *Brazilian president Luiz Inácio Lula da Silva:* President Luiz Inácio Lula da Silva's name is usually shortened to President Lula in most American media.

Chapter 16 ▪ Family Lies

167 *As frustrating as the King interview was: Larry King Live,* CNN, aired March 4, 2009, 21:00 ET; transcript available at www.archives.cnn.com/TRANSCRIPTS/0909/04/lk1.01.html.

Chapter 17 ■ Good News, Bad News

173 *"Sean's birth, making him a Brazilian citizen"*: João Paulo Lins e Silva, to the National Council for the Rights of Children and Adolescents, March 5, 2009.

176 *suspend Brazil's portion of the Generalized System of Preferences*: Congressman Chris Smith introduced this bill, HR 2702. Unfortunately, efforts by some members of Congress to tie up the bill in minutiae led to its ignominious death.

180 *"Sean wants to stay in Brazil"*: The Early Show, CBS-TV, June 23, 2009.

Chapter 18 ■ Pressure Points

189 *"Child abduction is child abuse"*: Statement by Congressman Christopher Smith to the Tom Lantos Human Rights Commission on Child Abduction/Parental Access, December 2, 2009, Longworth House Office Building, Washington, D.C.

190 *"Japan" . . . a "haven," and a "black hole for abduction"*: Written testimony submitted by Commander Paul Toland, U.S. Navy, to the Tom Lantos Human Rights Commission on Child Abduction/Parental Access. December 2, 2009.

192 *"no emergency meeting in the White House"*: Statement of The Honorable Bernard Aronson, Assistant Secretary of State for Inter-American Affairs (1989–1993), to the Tom Lantos Human Rights Commission, December 2, 2009.

Chapter 19 ■ The Decision

207 *"unheard-of feat"*: Seth Kugel, "Brazil: More Sympathy for David Goldman?" *Global Post,* December 18, 2009, http://www.globalpost.com/dispatch/brazil/091218/sean-goldman-custody-battle.

Chapter 20: Tension Rising

210 *fought more than one thousand family law cases*: Veja magazine, July 2009.

Chapter 21 ■ The Christmas Miracle

229 *"He's allergic to shellfish"*: I thought Silvana might supply medical records to me or to my attorneys during the "handoff." But to this day, neither the Ribeiros nor the Lins e Silvas have sent me any of Sean's medical records. Five years of medical history, and I have none of it.

Chapter 22 ■ Home at Last

245–46 *"a process to deal with the ongoing family"*: Geoff Mulvihill, "New Dispute Over Boy Brought to NJ from Brazil," Associated Press, April 5, 2010.

Chapter 23 ■ Giving Back

258 *"a sophisticated version of begging"*: Statement of The Honorable Bernard Aronson, Assistant Secretary of State for Inter-American Affairs (1989–1993), to the Tom Lantos Human Rights Commission, December 2, 2009.

258 *"mission was not to punish Brazil"*: Senator Frank Lautenberg, news interview, December 30, 2009, FoxNews.com/v/3957430/political-hammer.

Index